T0305390

Global City Makers

NEW HORIZONS IN REGIONAL SCIENCE

Series Editor: Philip McCann, *Professor of Urban and Regional Economics, University of Sheffield, UK*

Regional science analyses important issues surrounding the growth and development of urban and regional systems and is emerging as a major social science discipline. This series provides an invaluable forum for the publication of high quality scholarly work on urban and regional studies, industrial location economics, transport systems, economic geography and networks.

New Horizons in Regional Science aims to publish the best work by economists, geographers, urban and regional planners and other researchers from throughout the world. It is intended to serve a wide readership including academics, students and policymakers.

Titles in the series include:

Global City Makers

Economic Actors and Practices in the World City Network

Edited by

Michael Hoyler

Geography and Environment, School of Social Sciences, Loughborough University, UK

Christof Parnreiter

Institute of Geography, Hamburg University, Germany

Allan Watson

Geography and Environment, School of Social Sciences, Loughborough University, UK

Edward Elgar
PUBLISHING

Cheltenham, UK • Northampton, MA, USA

Published by
Edward Elgar Publishing Limited
The Lypiatts
15 Lansdown Road
Cheltenham
Glos GL50 2JA
UK

Edward Elgar Publishing, Inc.
William Pratt House
9 Dewey Court
Northampton
Massachusetts 01060
USA

A catalogue record for this book
is available from the British Library

Library of Congress Control Number: 2018944031

This book is available electronically in the **Elgar**online
Economics subject collection
DOI 10.4337/9781785368950

ISBN 978 1 78536 894 3 (cased)
ISBN 978 1 78536 895 0 (eBook)

Typeset by Servis Filmsetting Ltd, Stockport, Cheshire
Printed and bound in Great Britain by TJ International Ltd, Padstow

Contents

Figures

Tables

Contributors

David Bassens is Associate Professor of Economic Geography in the Geography Department of Vrije Universiteit Brussel where he acts as co-director of Cosmopolis: Centre for Urban Research. He doubles as Associate Director of Financialization of the Globalization and World Cities (GaWC) research network and is Executive Committee member and Treasurer of FINGEO, the Global Financial Geography network. His current research focuses on understanding processes of world city formation under conditions of financialized globalization, with an empirical focus on continental Europe and emerging markets. His work has been published in leading journals in the field of human geography.

Niels Beerepoot is Associate Professor in Economic Geography at the Amsterdam Institute for Social Science Research of the University of Amsterdam. His research interests include globalization and regional development, service outsourcing and offshoring, online freelancing/microwork and impact sourcing. He is co-editor of *The Local Impact of Globalization in South and Southeast Asia* (Routledge, 2016) and *Globalisation and Services-driven Economic Growth: Perspectives from the Global North and South* (Routledge, 2017).

Sarah Hall is Professor of Economic Geography at the University of Nottingham. Her work focuses on advancing cultural economy approaches to understandings of markets, power and elites under conditions of finance-led capitalism. She is the author of *Global Finance* (Sage, 2017) and has been an editor of the journal *Geoforum* since 2013.

Markus Hesse is Professor of Urban Studies at the University of Luxembourg, Faculty of Humanities. He has an academic background in geography and spatial planning, which are also his teaching domains. His research focuses on urban and regional development; mobilities, logistics and global flows; metropolitan policy and governance; and spatial discourses and identities. He is an elected member of the Academy for Spatial Research and Planning (ARL) in Germany and sits on various advisory boards and scientific councils. He is co-editor of *Cities, Regions and Flows* (Routledge, 2013).

Michael Hoyler is Reader in Human Geography at Loughborough University and Associate Director of the Globalization and World Cities (GaWC) research network. He is an urban geographer interested in the transformation of cities and metropolitan regions in contemporary globalization. His recent publications have focused on (world) city and city-regional network formation. He is also co-editor of *Global Urban Analysis* (Earthscan, 2011), the *International Handbook of Globalization and World Cities* (Edward Elgar, 2012), *Megaregions: Globalization's New Urban Form?* (Edward Elgar, 2015) and *Doing Global Urban Research* (Sage, 2018).

Wouter Jacobs is Senior Research Fellow at the Erasmus Centre for Urban, Port and Transport Economics, Erasmus University Rotterdam. His research focuses on the role of port cities in global networks and on the economic geography of maritime business services and commodity trading. As contract researcher, Wouter has been involved in strategic advisory work for the City of Rotterdam, Port of Rotterdam Authority, Port of Amsterdam Authority and the City of Antwerp. He currently leads the development of an executive masters in Leadership in Commodity Trade & Supply at the Erasmus University Rotterdam.

Jana Kleibert is Junior Research Group Leader at the Leibniz Institute for Research on Society and Space (IRS) and at the Department of Geography at Humboldt University of Berlin. Her research interests are economic and urban geography, global production networks, global cities and transnational spaces of production. She is co-editor of *Globalisation and Services-driven Economic Growth: Perspectives from the Global North and South* (Routledge, 2017).

Bart Lambregts lectures in urban planning at the Faculty of Architecture of Kasetsart University in Bangkok. His research concentrates on the interplay between processes of globalization, economic transformation and urban development, with special attention to the role of services industries. A second key interest concerns urban development practices, their spatial outcomes, and the implications for sustainable development and urban resilience. Bart is co-editor of *The Local Impact of Globalization in South and Southeast Asia* (Routledge, 2016) and *Globalisation and Services-driven Economic Growth: Perspectives from the Global North and South* (Routledge, 2017).

Colin Lizieri is Grosvenor Professor of Real Estate Finance at the University of Cambridge where he heads the Department of Land Economy and the Cambridge Real Estate Research Centre. Colin's research spans urban economics, geography and finance, and focuses on global real estate investment flows, real estate risk and return, and the dynamics of office markets in major global cities – research which has led to advisory work with government departments, international organizations, regulators, city governors and major private investors and consultants. He is the author of *Towers of Capital* (Wiley Blackwell, 2009).

Daniel Mekic is an Associate Principal at Results International, a boutique investment bank that has advised on real estate sales for a number of pharmaceutical majors. Prior to this role, Daniel was a member of the Department of Land Economy at the University of Cambridge, with research interests in social housing and the financialization of real estate. He is a Chartered Financial Analyst (CFA) charterholder and has active research interests in corporate finance and healthcare.

Christof Parnreiter is Professor of Economic Geography at the University of Hamburg and an Associate Director of the Globalization and World Cities (GaWC) research network. He is an economic and urban geographer interested in the role specific cities, particularly those in the Global South, play in the management and governance of the world economy. His recent publications have focused on Mexico City and Hamburg as nodes in global commodity chains, and on the urban restructuring that accompanies a city's transformation into a global city.

Saskia Sassen is the Robert S. Lynd Professor of Sociology and Member of the Committee on Global Thought at Columbia University. Her research and writing focuses on globalization, immigration, global cities, the new technologies, and changes within the liberal state that result from current transnational conditions. Her books include *The Global City: New York, London, Tokyo* (Princeton University Press, 2nd edition 2001), *Territory, Authority, Rights: From Medieval to Global Assemblages* (Princeton University Press, 2006), *Expulsions: Brutality and Complexity in the Global Economy* (Harvard University Press, 2014) and *Cities in a World Economy* (Sage, 5th edition 2018).

David Scofield is Associate Professor at the Ted Rogers School of Management at Ryerson University. His research interests include the microfoundations of markets, and exploring the effects of organizations, networks and institutions on real estate investment practices around the world. David's research has been funded by the Economic and Social Research Council (UK), the Investment Property Forum (London) and the University of Sheffield. He has studied in Canada, Korea and England and has worked in all three world regions (Americas, EMEA, Asia Pacific).

Michiel van Meeteren is Lecturer in Human Geography at Loughborough University. He holds a research masters in the social sciences from the

University of Amsterdam and a PhD in geography from Ghent University and previously worked at Cosmopolis, Vrije Universiteit Brussel. His work covers a broad scope, engaging with urban, economic, financial and political issues. The overarching themes in this work are a focus on methodological rigour, bridging different theoretical traditions, and a strong historical-disciplinary awareness. This results in the ambition to generate a better understanding of our accelerating, globalizing world.

Allan Watson is Lecturer in Human Geography and member of the Centre for Research in Communication and Culture (CRCC) at Loughborough University, and an Associate Director of the Globalization and World Cities (GaWC) research network. Allan's research investigates urban cultural and creative economies, with a particular focus on the global music, film and media industries. Allan is author of *Cultural Production in and Beyond the Recording Studio* (Routledge, 2014) and co-editor of *Rethinking Creative Cities Policy: Invisible Agents and Hidden Protagonists* (Routledge, 2015).

Sakura Yamamura is Postdoctoral Fellow at the Max Planck Institute for the Study of Religious and Ethnic Diversity in Göttingen. Her research focuses on transnational migration in the global cities network and the transformation of urban space in this context. Sakura's fieldwork for her doctoral project at the University of Hamburg was conducted in Tokyo. She has a background in migration policies, having worked for the Organisation for Economic Co-operation and Development (OECD) International Migration Division as well as for the German Federal Office for Migration and Refugees (BAMF).

Prologue   The global city: enabling economic intermediation and bearing its costs*

Saskia Sassen

One key hypothesis I arrived at early on in my research was that interme-diation was an increasingly strategic and systemically necessary function for the global economy that took off in the 1980s (Sassen, 1991/2001, 2012; Sassen-Koob, 1982). This in turn led me to generate the hypothesis about a need for specific types of spaces: spaces for the making of intermediate instruments and capabilities. One such strategic space concerned the instruments needed for outsourcing jobs, something I examined in my first book. But what began to emerge in the 1980s was on a completely different scale of complexity and diversity of economic sectors: It brought with it the making of a new type of city formation. I called it the global city – an extreme space for the production and/or implementation of very diverse and very complex intermediate capabilities. This did not refer to the whole city. I posited that the global city was a production function inserted in complex existing cities, albeit a function with a vast shadow effect over a city's larger space.

In that earlier period of the 1980s, the most famous cases illustrating the ascendance of intermediate functions were the big mergers and acquisitions. What stood out to the careful observer was how rarely the intermediaries lost. The financiers, lawyers, accountants, credit rating agencies, and more, made their money even when the new mega-firm they helped make eventually failed. Finance became the mother of all interme-diate sectors, with firms such as Goldman Sachs and JP Morgan making enormous profits, followed at a distance by the specialized lawyers and accountants. From the early phase dominated by mergers and acquisitions, intermediation has spread to a growing number of sectors. This also

*   This prologue is an extract from Sassen, S. (2016), 'The global city: Enabling eco-nomic intermediation and bearing its costs', *City & Community*, **15** (2), 97–108; American Sociological Association, with permission of John Wiley & Sons Ltd via the Copyright Clearance Center's RightsLink service.

included modest or straightforward sectors: For instance, most flower sellers or coffee shops are now parts of chains, they only do the selling of the flowers or the coffee, and it is headquarters that do the accounting, lawyering, acquisition of basic inputs, etc. Once, those smaller shops took care of the whole range of items; they were a modest knowledge space. Intermediation can now be thought of as a variable that at one end facilitates the globalizing of firms and markets and at the other end brings into its envelope very modest consumer oriented firms. It also contributes to explaining the expansion in the number of global cities and their enormous diversity in terms of specialized knowledges.

Elsewhere I have conceptualized intermediation as a logic of extraction. For instance, unlike traditional banking, finance can be thought of as an extractive sector and I say this only partly as provocation (Sassen, 2014). It has developed instruments that allow it to extract 'value' even out of low-grade assets or mere debt.

A major concern for me was to capture the fact that intermediate functions needed to be produced, developed, refined, mixed with other types of instruments, and so on. In its narrowest sense, then, I conceived of the global city function as a space of production; a silicon valley for advanced services, notably finance. Finance could not have become as complex and innovative (to put it kindly) if it had not had a network of global cities. Eventually, I expanded the category to incorporate a diversity of meanings, including the instruments needed by counter-systemic actors to operate in complex global settings from environmental to human rights activists. And eventually I began to include conventional actors such as museums engaging in international exchanges often for the first time because now they had access to a range of complex legal, accounting, and insurance instruments. It also enabled a massive scale up of irregular actors, from traffickers in drugs and people to an irregular market for armaments.

As a space of production, the global city generates extreme needs. These include state of the art infrastructures that almost inevitably go well beyond the standards for the larger home cities; thus, for instance, the financial centres in New York and London in the 1990s had to develop types of digital infrastructure that were on a completely different level from most of the rest of the city. Further, the global city generates a sharp rise in the demand for both high-level talent and masses of low-wage workers. What it needs least are the traditional modest middle classes so central to the era when mass consumption was the dominant logic; larger cities with more routinized economies do continue to need them. Finally, as the global economy globalized, this global city function spread to more and more cities: It was a sort of frontier space enabling global corporate actors to enter national economies.

What started as a hypothesis and then became a researched fact is that such instruments for intermediation are a marking feature of the type of global economy that emerged in the 1980s and had developed its global reach by the late 1990s. This, then, also explains the rapid increase in the number of global cities during the 1990s and onwards. Today, we can identify about 100 plus global cities, no matter how diverse their power to shape major global trends and their capacities to develop/invent new instruments; one, mostly overlooked, fact is that even minor global cities have invented new instruments and built new markets, often based on a single commodity.

The global city function is *made*, and that process of making is complex and multifaceted: It needs to factor in laws, accounting practices, logistics, and a broad range of other components, such as the existence of diverse cultures of investment depending on the country and the sector. This process of making could not take place simply in a firm or a laboratory situation. It had to be centred at the intersection of different types of emergent global economic circuits with distinct contents, all of which varied across economic sectors. It needed a space where professionals and executives coming from diverse countries and knowledge cultures wound up picking up knowledge bits from each other even if they did not intend to do so. I saw in this process the making of a distinctive 'urban knowledge capital', a kind of capital that could only be made via a mix of conditions among which was the city itself with its diverse knowledge and experiential vectors. I saw this both in its broad sense (all the knowledge-making institutions, individuals, experimental moves), and in the narrower sense of the global city function (highly specialized and dedicated knowledge systems).

Finally, and critical to the whole project, was what I refer to as the infrastructure to ensure maximum performance by high-income talent – the broad range of conditions enabling their work-lives. Prominently included in my analysis was a range of lowly rewarded tasks, ranging from low-level office to low-wage household work. I argued that in many regards the homes of top level staff are an extension of the corporate platform. The actual tasks were only part of the story. To get it out of the language of 'low-wage jobs', I described these tasks as the work of 'maintaining a strategic infrastructure', one that included the households of top-level workers as these had to function like clockwork, with no room for little crises.

REFERENCES

Sassen, S. (1991), *The Global City: New York, London, Tokyo*, Princeton, NJ: Princeton University Press.

Sassen, S. (2001), *The Global City: New York, London, Tokyo* (2nd edition), Princeton, NJ: Princeton University Press.

Sassen, S. (2012), *Cities in a World Economy* (4th edition), London: Sage.

Sassen, S. (2014), *Expulsions: Brutality and Complexity in the Global Economy*, Cambridge, MA: Harvard University Press/Belknap Books.

Sassen-Koob, S. (1982), 'Recomposition and peripheralization at the core', *Contemporary Marxism*, **5**, 88–100.

1 Agency and practice in the making of global cities: towards a renewed research agenda

Michael Hoyler, Christof Parnreiter and Allan Watson

1.1 INTRODUCTION

Since Saskia Sassen's (1991) seminal book *The Global City*, a heterogeneous body of literature has developed under the umbrella of 'global' or 'world' city research. Broadly, one might draw a distinction between economic approaches and urban studies approaches to understanding the global city. With regards to the former, one major strand of global cities research has been constituted by quantitative assessments of global urban networks, for example in research on the 'world city network' using an 'interlocking network model' for estimating the connectivities of cities (Taylor, 2004). From an urban studies perspective, a significant body of work has developed which seeks to understand the relations between global city formation or globalization processes more broadly and urban phenomena, such as the restructuring of labour and real estate markets, income polarization, and immigration (Derudder et al., 2012).

While these two threads of the global city literature have deepened our knowledge of urban economic, spatial and social dynamics under the impact of globalization, and of the cross-border connections of world cities and their individual trajectories, many of these studies have bypassed the theoretical core of the global city paradigm, namely a city's function in the management and governance of the world economy. Relatively few studies have examined how intermediaries, identified by Sassen (2018) as the key actors of global city formation, operate to articulate and control economic activities at various scales (e.g. Rossi et al., 2007; Hanssens et al., 2012; Jacobs, 2014; Parnreiter, 2010, 2015; Boussebaa, 2015). As Bassens and van Meeteren (2015, p. 753) point out, the 'overall consensus is that capitalist command and control is exercised from a limited set of cities which function as nodes for transnational flows of capital, goods, people, and information, from which actors operating from these places draw their power'. Indeed, as Sassen suggests (2001, p. 347–348, emphasis added), 'A key purpose of the model is to conceive of economic globalization not just as capital flows, but as the *work* of coordinating, managing and servicing these flows. . . . The global city network is the operational scaffolding of . . . the global economy'.

For us, the global city concept as proposed by Friedmann (1986) and Sassen (1991) consists of four interrelated claims (Parnreiter, 2014): (i) global cities are clusters for advanced producer services (APS) (producing localized externalities); (ii) global cities operate in a worldwide network constituted through the cross-border organizational structures of APS firms (producing network externalities); (iii) global cities are centres for the management of the world economy; and (iv) global cities are centres for the governance of the world economy. Inter-firm relations (between APS firms and their clients) are thus critical in this conceptualization.

What implications arise from such a perspective on global cities? If the key functional linkages in global city formation are those between APS and their client firms, then the main agents in the formation of global cities and their networks are APS. While this is, of course, a widely accepted premise of Sassen's (1991) thesis, such an economic geography reading of the global city concept is nevertheless by no means a majoritarian interpretation. Further, if this premise holds, then the key practices in global city making are the servicing of the clients, and, in particular, the servicing that contributes to the smooth functioning (the management task of global cities) and to the governing (the control task) of global commodity chains (GCCs). In Sassen's words (2001, pp. 359, 361; emphasis added), the 'key indicator of global city status is whether a city contains the capabilities for servicing, managing, and financing the global operations of firms and markets. . . . *The question is whether coordination and specialized servicing of global firms and markets is taking place.*'

There are two important conceptual and methodological implications to this. The first is that global city research necessarily has to adopt a relational approach: the very idea of a world/global city as expressed by Friedmann and Sassen only makes sense if these cities are seen in a relational perspective, tied to each other (Taylor, 2004), but also to all the 'ordinary' cities (Robinson, 2006) where production for the world market is carried out. The second implication is that global city researchers need to adopt, in addition to (rather than instead of) the measurement of external city connections (e.g. Taylor et al., 2011; Hanssens et al., 2011), qualitative research strategies in order to appropriately assess the management and governance relations between APS firms and their clients. Watson and Beaverstock (2014) forcefully argue that the emphasis on analysing the structure of the world city network has gone at the expense of examining and explaining *agency* in global cities. Such pleas to focus on agency are very much in line with Sassen's call for studying 'the *practices* that constitute what we call economic globalization and global control' (2001, p. xxii; original emphasis). As Bassens and van Meeteren (2015, p. 755) argue, 'command and control has been . . . too crude a notion to specify the relation between world cities and the exercise of power'. Instead, 'it is the assemblage of resources and abilities that enables command and control in world cities'. We therefore need to focus on 'the *practices* of financial and business elites . . . that involve modes of power such as manipulation, seduction or inducement other than top-down domination and control' (emphasis added). As Sassen (2018, p. 3; emphasis in original) notes, 'The global city function is *made*, and that process of making is complex and multi-faceted'.

With this in mind, the aim of the book is to begin the task of setting a renewed agenda for world cities research that centres on the economic actors and individual and collective economic practices that lie at the heart of global city and world city network formation. We start from a conceptualization of global cities as places from where the world economy is managed and controlled through the *practices* of advanced producer service firms and, more specifically, the professionals operating within them. We term these actors *global city makers*. An explicit objective is to consider how current approaches within economic geography can enhance our understanding of the role of economic actors in the world city network. Relational thinking in world cities research has developed in parallel to a relational turn in economic geography yet there has been little mutual engagement (Watson and Beaverstock, 2014). In this book, we are interested in how a relational economic geography perspective can contribute to relational understandings of the world city network.

To achieve this goal, this book brings together contributions that engage critically and constructively with current global cities research from an economic geography perspective, and which suggest innovative avenues for its theoretical, methodological and empirical development. The book's chapters examine the role of APS in the management and governance of the world economy, with a focus on financial services, management consultancy, real estate, commodity trading and maritime industries. The contributions draw on a wide range of methods, including interviews, discourse analysis and quantitative data analysis to critically examine the practices through which key economic actors are engaged in making (and un-making) global cities. The studies are located across the world, including major global cities such as Sassen's (1991) original global city triad of New York, London and Tokyo, as well as emerging global cities in the Global South (Mexico and Mumbai) and second-tier European cities (Amsterdam and Hamburg).

1.2   APPROACHES TO RELATIONALITY AND AGENCY

The late 1990s saw the establishment of a relational turn in the study of world cities. This approach argued that cities were not defined by what was contained *within* them, but rather what flowed *through* them; cities were understood as *process*, characterized by flows of people, capital, goods, resources, knowledge and information (Taylor, 1997; Beaverstock et al., 2002). In a pioneering study, Beaverstock et al. (2001) used interviews with key personnel in global financial and business service firms and institutions to examine the changing relations between London and Frankfurt with the introduction of a single European currency and the decision to locate the European Central Bank in Frankfurt. The study challenged the simplistic competition model that dominated public discussion of the London–Frankfurt city dyad and brought economic practices centre stage of research on inter-city relations (see also Pain, 2008).

However, in the early 2000s, research into world city networks took a strong quantitative turn, driven by the specification of an 'interlocking network model' for estimating the connectivities of cities (Taylor, 2001; see also Derudder and Parnreiter, 2014). This not only provided a new approach to measuring external relations of cities in contemporary globalization (Taylor et al., 2010; Taylor and Derudder, 2016), but successfully addressed the paucity of relevant data and associated empirical deficit (Short et al., 1996). However, Watson and Beaverstock (2014, p. 415) have argued that while such quantitative studies are of significant value in mapping the changing patterns of globalization, they have less to offer to 'practice-based discussions which attempt to explain why certain socio-economic processes are located and performed in particular cities' (see also Lai, 2012).

Moreover, Parnreiter (2014) has argued that the interlocking network model carries the danger of losing some critical premises of the global/ world city concept and of diverting the analytical focus from the role of global/world cities in the world economy to a descriptive concern, namely to find the 'best' way to measure inter-city relations. While cities in general are defined by what flows through them – external relations are, as Taylor (2004, p. 2) asserts, 'the second nature of cities' – what is the first nature of global/world cities is that they are the places from where these flows are governed. Yet, although economic power is the subject matter of the global/world city concept, it lacks an adequate theorization (Jones, 2002;

Allen, 2010). We contend that coming to grips with the 'command and control' functions of global/world cities requires an understanding of APS agency, strategies and practices.

Furthermore, Watson and Beaverstock (2014) argue that, despite recent methodological refinements (e.g. Taylor et al., 2014; Lüthi et al., 2018), the interlocking network model is unable to fully account for the complex strategies and the spatial organization of advanced producer service firms. In economic geography, studies of knowledge intensive services have emphasized how knowledge and expertise are embodied in the economic practice and performativity of labour. Professionals such as advertising creatives, consultants, lawyers, accountants or investment bankers are a service firm's main asset to achieve its strategic goals. Such work suggests that the role of APS in global capitalism needs to be understood in more nuanced and subtle terms than 'command' and 'control' (Kleibert, 2017); their business includes such activities as facilitating, switching, advising and circulating knowledge (Bassens and van Meeteren, 2015) and even persuasion, seduction or manipulation, and research needs to be more sensitive to these other modalities (Krijnen et al., 2017). As Sassen (2010, p. 158) argues, the influence of APS firms on clients' strategies is 'embedded' into the services provided. Accordingly, the power of APS is not exercised over clients, but together with them. It is a resource to empower clients vis-à-vis business partners, unions or governments (Parnreiter, 2017).

Jones (2014) identifies how recent work on relational economic geography has been characterized by a growing conceptual concern for *practice* as a 'means better to capture and specify the nature of agency that is caught up in the relations between economic actors' (2014, p. 610). Jones highlights two key developments that are particularly relevant in relation to the aims of this book. First, he notes how relational economic geographers have increasingly been concerned with intra-and inter-firm practices. Here, he suggests, researchers have viewed practices as 'everyday relational processes that constitute economic action and hold communities or firms together within, and in relation to, particular geographic contexts' (2014, p. 611). Second, Jones notes that practice-orientated relational literature has been concerned with how industries and firms are organized through common social practices. These practices, he suggests, are those that 'legitimate, control and coordinate business activities' and which help to 'create the relational proximity (and in some cases trust) needed for firms to act at a distance in a globalized economy' (2014, p. 611).

As Watson and Beaverstock (2014, p. 418) argue, it is surprising, given the relational turn in the study of world cities, that research in this field has remained largely at odds with the shifts happening in economic geography: 'rather than grappling with agency, it is widely criticised for its structuralist underpinnings; rather than attempting micro-scale analysis of networks, it considers networks predominantly at the macro-scale; and rather than focusing on social actors, research focuses almost exclusively on the firm as the main analytical unit'. Insufficient attention has been paid to the actual practices of management and control exercised in global cities and the associated knowledge flows and agencies (Parnreiter, 2014). For van Meeteren and Bassens (2016, p. 64), as APS workers 'socially construct material circuits of value . . ., they collectively produce the WCA [world city archipelago] as a place, a scale, a territory and a network'. Recognizing the centrality of agency is therefore, we argue, key to understanding world city networks. This opens up a number of new lines of theoretical questioning and research, including how the actual practices of management and control are exercised and why certain socio-economic processes are located and performed in particular cities.

As van Meeteren et al. (2016) suggest, global cities research today is characterized by a 'pronounced pluralism', evident through a wide variety of research topics, epistemologies and methodologies (see also Hoyler and Harrison, 2017). They note that, while some authors emphasize model-based approaches, others apply more qualitative research methods and, while some authors emphasize structure, others underline agency. They point for example to those who have built a substantial body of empirical work on how world city formation is linked to the agency of transnational elites through their practices and mobility patterns. Particularly significant in this regard has been the work of scholars such as Jonathan Beaverstock and Sarah Hall on transnational elites and skilled labour markets (Beaverstock, 2002, 2005; Beaverstock and Hall, 2012; Beaverstock et al., 2015; Hall, 2009), and James Faulconbridge on actors and knowledge transfer in the transnational firm (Faulconbridge, 2007, 2008; Faulconbridge et al., 2011). This body of work highlights how these 'elites' (re)produce micro-networks between firms, clients, cities and financial services clusters, spanning nodes in the world city network and constructing knowledge to manage across borders. As van Meeteren et al. (2016, p. 255) note, through such work, the structure of the world city network can be seen as the 'collective product of the agency' of particular actors as global city and world city network *makers*.

1.3 AGENCY AND PRACTICE IN GLOBAL CITY (NETWORK) MAKING (AND UN-MAKING)

This book consists of eight substantive chapters that have been assembled for their shared concern with providing in-depth and rigorous theoretical and empirical studies of the agency of economic actors in the 'making' of global cities. Each chapter contributes not only to our aim of exposing the central role of economic actors and their practices in 'making' global cities, but also to our call for a broadening of the range of methodologies that are employed in global cities research (see also Harrison and Hoyler, 2018).

In Chapter 2, Christof Parnreiter (2018) considers the role of advanced producer service firms as global city makers set in the context of two 'non-prime' global cities, Mexico City and Hamburg. Revisiting the global city concept as originally defined by Sassen (1991), Parnreiter emphasizes how the global city 'model' has been developed as an economic geography concept to comprehend the function and position of specific economic actors in certain cities in the management and in the 'command and control' of the world economy. Parnreiter operationalizes this concept by considering global cities as critical nodes in the organization and governance of global commodity chains (GCCs), highlighting how literature on GCCs has advanced a relational, actor-focused understanding of economic power. Drawing upon a qualitative methodology consisting of semi-structured interviews with professionals in both cities, working in accountancy, advertising, finance and insurance, as well as legal and management firms, Parnreiter shows how APS provide critical support to their clients in conducting global business. Within these firms, professionals assume the role of key actors in the making of the two cities as nodes in GCCs, fulfilling the 'management function' for their clients' global operations and providing commercially sensitive advice to clients designed to provide 'positive business outcomes'. Thus, he asserts that APS are the pre-eminent global city makers, while their servicing of clients is the key practice underlying global city formation.

Engaging further with global commodity chains, but focusing on a different type of economic actor, in Chapter 3 Wouter Jacobs (2018) considers commodity traders as agents of globalization. Jacobs points to three conceptual issues in the study of world city networks that warrant attention: firstly the importance of the *specialization* of the actors that constitute inter-city linkages; second the *physicality* of global networks; and finally the lack of understanding of what agents *do* to make or produce 'global' or 'world' cities. To address these issues, Jacobs undertakes an investigation of the economic geography of commodity trading and the role that traders play in the formation of the world city network. Through a close analysis of business cases from a large commodity trading firm, and drawing conceptually upon the work of James Vance (1970) on the mercantile model of settlement, Jacobs argues that key global cities have evolved from the practices and the physicality of their origins as trading places. He contends that in order for commodity traders to act as global agents, they prefer the agglomeration benefits offered by global cities;

and, further, that traders subject those places involved in the extraction, production and distribution of the commodities traded, to the logic of the 'world city' through their trading practices.

Switching attention from commodities to real estate, in Chapter 4 Colin Lizieri and Daniel Mekic (2018) highlight the importance of commercial real estate as a medium by which major cities are embedded within global capital networks. Office real estate in global cities, they assert, provides the physical infrastructure that allows financial and other business service actors to operate service networks worldwide, while at the same time acting as an important investment vehicle. Drawing upon a close analysis of a proprietary database, Lizieri and Mekic examine the changing patterns of office ownership in the City of London from 1972, uncovering a shift over time in the nature of investors. They argue that global investors have underpinned liquidity that has counterbalanced poor investment performance, and point to the need to assess changes in investor type and shifts in the nationality of ownership in order to understand how invest-ment patterns serve to integrate the City into global financial and urban networks. Further, they highlight how the presence of global brokerage firms provides a key benefit to investors in building global portfolios, and influences the flows of capital across cities. Taken together, these two types of key actors in real estate markets play a critical role in creating the functional form of the global city of London and its dynamic operation.

Continuing on the theme of real estate, in Chapter 5 David Scofield (2018) examines the market practices of APS firms, as both investors and intermediaries, in the commercial real estate markets of New York and London. Scofield focuses on intermediation in the form of brokerage, a key catalyst in the conversion of liquid capital into real estate assets. He specifically explores how local practices of broker intermediation and the individual social networks of highly placed investment managers cor-respond in the commercial real estate investment markets of New York and London. To do so, he employs two complementary methodologies: first, a close analysis of a unique dataset of commercial real estate transactions; and, second, social network analysis of individual (ego-centric) social capi-tal networks of senior investment managers responsible for the acquisition of commercial real estate on behalf of major investment firms based in the US or the UK. Scofield demonstrates how brokers play a central role in the movement of capital into commercial real estate in each city, and thus assume a key role in the making of New York and London as global cities. However, he also exposes how the market behaviours that underlie the definition of these cities as 'global' retain unique differences: double brokerage is more likely to occur in London than New York, which, he sug-gests, offers the London broker a unique *tertius* role in global city making.

Following on from these case studies of London and New York, in Chapter 6 Sakura Yamamura (2018) focuses on the third city of Sassen's (1991) original global city triad, to consider the making of transnational urban space by financial professionals in Tokyo. Yamamura points to the fact that analysis of the role of professionals in global city making has primarily focused on their function and practices within global corporations, and that such a perspective overlooks their impact as *transnational individuals* whose social practices play a key role in the making of global city spaces. She argues that the duality of their role as global city makers derives from these professionals being on the one hand decision-makers and business practitioners in transnational corporations, and on the other hand individuals with social practices that characterize them as transnational migrants. Yamamura adopts a qualitative research strategy consisting of semi-structured interviews with transnational professionals in the finance industry and the drawing of mental maps, to uncover social practices in formal, semi-formal and informal/private settings. Her findings suggest that professionals are directly involved in the creation of transnational 'global city spaces'. Such spaces, Yamamura asserts, are a phenomenon locally anchored in a specific global city, and yet also represent locational choices that are simultaneously embedded in corporate strategies within the global economy. Thus, professionals as economic actors represent the key binding link between the decisions and practices of global corporations and direct impacts on the local economy and on urban spaces in any given city.

In Chapter 7, Bart Lambregts, Jana Kleibert and Niels Beerepoot (2018) consider the role of the offshore services sector in the making of Mumbai as a global city. They highlight the expansion of the financial services industry into many parts of the Global South, driven by the emergence of new markets for services and the industry's desire to reduce costs. Business process outsourcing (services offshoring) has resulted in several million workers in second- and third-tier global cities producing electronically transmittable support services for global financial and other services. Lambregts et al. consider these offshored support services as a clear expression of the global integration of such cities. Drawing on qualitative data obtained from in-depth interviews with current and former senior executives in Mumbai's offshore service industry, as well as with representatives from the public sector and relevant business associations, the authors envisage the industry as a 'backstage global city maker'. They demonstrate that the offshore services industry lends support to the city's onshore finance sector, and thus to the making of Mumbai as a global city, through triggering processes of upgrading in auxiliary services, fostering local demand for financial services, bolstering the city's image and reputation as a financial centre, and crucially contributing to human capital formation. Thus, the authors argue that certain categories of actors who are generally not conceived of as global city makers in the Global North can assume global city making roles in cities of the Global South.

Chapters 8 and 9 perform the important task of problematizing discourses around global city 'making'. Global–local tensions and the role of governance are the central focus of Chapter 8, in which Markus Hesse (2018) considers issues of global city making and localism in Hamburg's maritime network. In opening the chapter, Hesse highlights how port institutions and port-city officials might be viewed as ideal global city makers, in that they target global flows to serve local interests. However, through an analysis of the interplay of a range of public and private economic actors in the making of Hamburg as a global (port) city, Hesse seeks to illustrate the complexities of governance in a city pursuing ambitious planning and development goals. Drawing upon qualitative data from interviews with representatives of maritime firms, port authorities and public officials, as well as document analysis of secondary data material including parliamentary documents, Hesse provides a complex case study of the dynamics of localism and globalization. Global city making, he argues, is not necessarily, and not exclusively, the business of single actors. Rather, global city making requires a particular setting – a community of practice based on shared beliefs among key actors – as well as an ideological framework, which leads to such a project coming into being. He illustrates this argument by considering the relationship between the city and a 'focal' private firm (a major shipping line). In evaluating this relationship, Hesse identifies a 'new localism', which differs from usual globalization discourses and rhetoric, and which he interprets as 'reluctance' to become fully globalized. Thus, through their planning strategies and local decision-making, the agency of local governance and public bodies in actively 'making' or 'not-making' the global city is elucidated.

In Chapter 9, Michiel van Meeteren and David Bassens (2018) study the role of management consultancy in the failure of the Dutch bank ABN AMRO, highlighting the potential for key actors to not only 'make', but also 'un-make' the global city. Specifically, they consider the influence of APS firms on the strategic and tactical management practices of multinational organizations. The authors have assembled an impressive portfolio of primary and secondary data sources, including extensive documentation in the Dutch and English language financial press, annual reports of the bank, and an archive of ABN AMRO employee magazines, in order to undertake a historical reconstruction of key events, decisions and narratives leading up to the failure of the bank. They highlight how APS in general, and management consultancy firms in particular, act as important vectors to tie firms operating from semi-peripheral nodes of the world city network into financial markets centred on core global cities. Yet their account is also highly critical of management consultants as the key actors who linked ABN AMRO from a 'second-tier' global city into an industry field of global highly leveraged banks located in core global cities, and thus played a key part in the bank's demise. Their findings, van Meeteren and Bassens suggest, emphasize the power asymmetries that exist within the APS complex, which play out geographically. Thus the authors provide a 'cautionary tale' for global city makers (in this case, the Amsterdam financial centre growth coalition): buying into the narratives of global consultants for aspirational purposes, they argue, only delayed, but was unable to prevent, the further 'un-making' of Amsterdam as a global city already in decline in the field of international banking.

1.4   A RENEWED CRITICAL AGENDA FOR GLOBAL CITIES RESEARCH

Together, the contributions in this book not only provide sector-specific in-depth accounts of the role of powerful economic actors in the making and un-making of global cities, but encourage us to think critically about the role of agency and practices in a renewed agenda for global cities research. For us, there are at least four key elements in progressing such an agenda, which recognize not only the issues raised within the contributions to this book, but also the many gaps and omissions which are unavoidable in such a project:

1.   *A need to incorporate perspectives on agency and practice from relational economic geography into the conceptualizing and doing of global cities research*   There are a number of ways in which such a project can be taken forward. One, emerging from the contributions in this book, is to undertake more detailed examinations of how different cultures of doing business may lead to a variety of different outcomes in and across different cities. The assumption within current approaches to world city network research that use firm office locations as a sur-rogate for flows is necessarily that practices are homogeneous on a global level, that is to say that one link between offices within a firm (assuming the link exists) has the same purpose, meaning and intensity as every other link. In reality, of course, the situation is much more nuanced; as David Scofield (2018) highlights in his study of real estate, behaviours that underlie the definition of cities as 'global' are not identical, but rather retain unique differences that result in actors in

similar positions operating differently. Further, as Sassen (2018, p. 3) notes, the process of global city making is 'centred at the intersection of different types of emergent global economic circuits with distinct contents', which vary across economic sectors. Sassen sees in this process the making of a 'distinctive "urban knowledge capital", a kind of capital that could only be made via a mix of conditions among which was the city itself with its diverse knowledge and experiential vectors'. We would argue that one cannot understand these vectors without insight into the agency and practices of those carrying, using and transferring these knowledges and experiences.

2. *A need to specify the practices underlying global city making*   Practices are neither unintentional nor value-free. Rather, they serve distinct purposes – in the case of APS firms in global/world cities, these are related to the management and governance of their clients' commodity chains. Relations between APS firms and their clients are embedded into, and serve, the hierarchical relations which APS firms' clients maintain in their production networks (Parnreiter, 2017). In advocating a re-orientation of attention to practices in global city formation, we also encourage doing so in a way that recovers the critical intentions of the early global/world city research (Hoyler and Harrison, 2017) and that explores '*how* cities and the classes within them achieve control over other regions' (Roberts, 1986, p. 459; emphasis added).

3. *A need to recognize the diversity of actors involved in global city making*   While the contributions in this book focus on powerful economic actors across a range of APS, the importance of actors in other sectors must not, indeed cannot, be overlooked. Economic practices and strategic decision-making should not be considered in isolation; they are embedded in wider economic, social and political relations each with their own sets of critical actors (Hall, 2018). One might investigate, for example, key actors in city governance and marketing: Hesse (2018) explores the nature of relations between the city (public) and firm (private) as collective entities but key individual actors such as city mayors can also play an important role in decision making (Ponzini and Rossi, 2010; McNeill, 2014). One could also consider key actors in architecture, urban planning and design (McNeill, 2009; Ren, 2011; Rapoport, 2015; Sklair, 2017), arts and culture (Kong et al., 2015), and in the globalized built environment more generally (McNeill, 2015), to name but a few. It is also important, of course, to critically interrogate the privileging of elite labour in accounts of global city making, and to consider notions of agency as they relate to complex divisions of skilled and unskilled labour. In the prologue to this book, Sassen (2018, p. 3) emphasizes the importance of lowly rewarded tasks as 'maintaining a

strategic infrastructure' that 'ensure[s] maximum performance by high-income talent'. Yet, as Wills et al. (2010) highlight in their examination of new migrant divisions of labour in London, low-paid migrant workers are not only key actors in making global cities work, but are themselves key agents in the *remaking* of the city, through, for example, their impact on global city labour markets.

4. *A need to account for the role of actors and practices not only in the making but also in the* un-making *of global cities*   Conceptualizing global city making as a dynamic and complex process opens up two further important lines of research. First, it requires us to consider the diversity of locations in which these processes occur. As Sassen (2018, p. 1) notes, the term 'global city' was not intended to refer to a whole city, but rather is 'a production function inserted in complex existing cities'. She argues that today one might identify 100 plus global cities, with even minor global cities inventing new instruments and building new markets. In this book, for example, Lambregts et al. (2018) emphasize how services offshoring has resulted in several million workers in second- and third-tier global cities producing electronically transmittable support services for global financial and other services. Particularly relevant to the aims of this book is Krijnen et al.'s (2017) assertion that little of the agency-centred literature on APS professionals has engaged with cities beyond the core of the world city network, or on the 'boundary-spanning' work through which cities beyond the core are incorporated in global accumulation processes.

Second, we consider it crucial to challenge teleological notions and aspirational discourses regarding the immanent 'becoming' of global cities through such processes (Leon, 2017). Processes can also be disruptive and result in the 'un-making' of global cities, as illustrated in this book with the decline of Amsterdam as centre for international banking (van Meeteren and Bassens, 2018; see also Engelen, 2007; Faulconbridge et al., 2007), or as witnessed in the demise of Reykjavik as a banking centre in the wake of the global financial crisis (Derudder et al., 2011). This 'un-making' unfolds through relational networks of practice and dependency resulting in wider systemic impacts. Wójcik (2013a) for example, in his examination of the 'dark side of NY-LON', argues that the commonality, complementarity and connectivity between New York and London as the two leading global financial centres resulted in the formation of a powerful 'axis' in which the global financial crisis of 2007–09 was rooted. Revisiting agency in relation to financial centres, Wójcik points in particular to the role of regulatory bodies and industrial lobbying associations, which not only function in specific places, but which are also 'plugged into key spatial networks' (2013a, p. 2748; see also Wójcik, 2013b). The current debate on Brexit and its implications for London in contrast provides an example of potential un-making through geopolitical and geoeconomic 'separation and disentanglement' (Dörry, 2017, p. 1). With its emphasis on the role of political actors in shaping financial centre relations (Lavery et al., 2018) this debate brings to the fore 'questions of power and politics within the global economy' (Hall, 2018, p. 194) as key aspects of global city making and un-making.

We see the four elements highlighted above as crucial parts of a renewed, critical and potentially more progressive agenda for global cities and world city network research, focused around agency and practice. Our hope is that this book will act as both inspiration and reference point for researchers to progress this agenda, and to address its many conceptual and methodological challenges.

REFERENCES

Allen, J. (2010), 'Powerful city networks: More than connections, less than domination and control', *Urban Studies*, **47** (13), 2895–2911.

Bassens, D. and M. van Meeteren (2015), 'World cities under conditions of financialized globalization: Towards an augmented world city hypothesis', *Progress in Human Geography*, **39** (6), 752–775.

Beaverstock, J.V. (2002), 'Transnational elites in global cities: British expatriates in Singapore's financial district', *Geoforum*, **33** (4), 525–538.

Beaverstock, J.V. (2005), 'Transnational elites in the city: British highly-skilled inter-company transferees in New York City's financial district', *Journal of Ethnic and Migration Studies*, **31** (2), 245–268.

Beaverstock, J.V. and S. Hall (2012), 'Competing for talent: Global mobility, immigration and the City of London's labour market', *Cambridge Journal of Regions, Economy and Society*, **5** (2), 271–288.

Beaverstock, J.V., J.R. Faulconbridge and S.J.E. Hall (2015), *The Globalization of Executive Search: Professional Service Strategy and Dynamics in the Contemporary World*, London: Routledge.

Beaverstock, J.V., M. Hoyler, K. Pain and P.J. Taylor (2001), *Comparing London and Frankfurt as World Cities: A Relational Study of Contemporary Urban Change*, London: Anglo-German Foundation for the Study of Industrial Society.

Beaverstock, J.V., M.A. Doel, P.J. Hubbard and P.J. Taylor (2002), 'Attending to the world: Competition, cooperation and connectivity in the world city network', *Global Networks*, **2** (2), 111–132.

Boussebaa, M. (2015), 'Control in the multinational enterprise: The polycentric case of global professional service firms', *Journal of World Business*, **50**, 696–703.

Derudder, B. and C. Parnreiter (2014), 'Introduction: The interlocking network model for studying urban networks: Outline, potential, critiques, and ways forward', *Tijdschrift voor Economische en Sociale Geografie*, **105** (4), 373–386.

Derudder, B., M. Hoyler and P. Taylor (2011), 'Goodbye Reykjavik: International banking centres and the global financial crisis', *Area*, **43** (2), 173–182.

Derudder, B., M. Hoyler, P.J. Taylor and F. Witlox (eds) (2012), *International Handbook of Globalization and World Cities*, Cheltenham, UK and Northampton, MA, USA: Edward Elgar Publishing.

Dörry, S. (2017), 'The geo-politics of Brexit, the euro and the City of London', *Geoforum*, **85**, 1–4.

Engelen, E. (2007), '"Amsterdamned"? The uncertain future of a financial centre', *Environment and Planning A*, **39** (6), 1306–1324.

Faulconbridge, J.R. (2007), 'London's and New York's advertising and law clusters and their networks of learning: Relational analyses with a politics of scale?', *Urban Studies*, **44** (9), 1635–1656.

Faulconbridge, J.R. (2008), 'Managing the transnational law firm: A relational analysis of professional systems, embedded actors, and time–space-sensitive governance', *Economic Geography*, **84** (2), 185–210.

Faulconbridge, J.R., E. Engelen, M. Hoyler and J.V. Beaverstock (2007), 'Analysing the changing landscape of European financial centres: The role of financial products and the case of Amsterdam', *Growth and Change*, **38** (2), 279–303.

Faulconbridge, J.R., J.V. Beaverstock, C. Nativel and P.J. Taylor (2011), *The Globalization of Advertising: Agencies, Cities and Spaces of Creativity*, London: Routledge.

Friedmann, J. (1986), 'The world city hypothesis', *Development and Change*, **17** (1), 69–83.

Hall, S. (2009), 'Financialised elites and the changing nature of finance capitalism: Investment bankers in London's financial district', *Competition & Change*, **13** (2), 173–189.

Hall, S. (2018), 'Placing politics and power within the making of global cities', in M. Hoyler, C. Parnreiter and A. Watson (eds), *Global City Makers: Economic Actors and Practices in the World City Network*, Cheltenham, UK and Northampton, MA, USA: Edward Elgar Publishing, pp. 192–198.

Hanssens, H., B. Derudder and F. Witlox (2012), 'Managing organizational and geographical complexity: The "positionality" of advanced producer services in the globalizing economies of metropolitan regions', *Erdkunde*, **66** (1), 45–55.

Hanssens, H., B. Derudder, P.J. Taylor, M. Hoyler, P. Ni, J. Huang, X. Yang and F. Witlox (2011), 'The changing geography of globalized service provision, 2000–2008', *The Service Industries Journal*, **31** (14), 2293–2307.

Harrison, J. and M. Hoyler (eds) (2018), *Doing Global Urban Research*, London: Sage.

Hesse, M. (2018), 'Focal firms, grand coalitions or global city makers? Globalization vs. new localism in Hamburg's maritime network', in M. Hoyler, C. Parnreiter and A. Watson (eds), *Global City Makers: Economic Actors and Practices in the World City Network*, Cheltenham, UK and Northampton, MA, USA: Edward Elgar Publishing, pp. 151–169.

Hoyler, M. and J. Harrison (2017), 'Global cities research and urban theory making', *Environment and Planning A*, **49** (12), 2853–2858.

Jacobs, W. (2014), 'Rotterdam and Amsterdam as trading places? In search of the economic-geographical nexus between global commodity chains and world cities', *Tijdschrift voor Economische en Sociale Geografie*, **105** (4), 483–491.

Jacobs, W. (2018), 'Commodity traders as agents of globalization', in M. Hoyler, C. Parnreiter and A. Watson (eds), *Global City Makers: Economic Actors and*

Practices in the World City Network, Cheltenham, UK and Northampton, MA, USA: Edward Elgar Publishing, pp. 41–59.

Jones, A. (2002), 'The "global city" misconceived: The myth of "global management" in transnational service firms', *Geoforum*, **33** (3), 335–350.

Jones, A. (2014), 'Geographies of production I: Relationality revisited and the "practice shift" in economic geography', *Progress in Human Geography*, **38** (4), 605–615.

Kleibert, J. (2017), 'On the global city map, but not in command? Probing Manila's position in the world city network', *Environment and Planning A*, **49** (12), 2897–2915.

Kong, L., C. Chia-ho and C. Tsu-Lung (2015), *Arts, Culture and the Making of Global Cities: Creating New Urban Landscapes in Asia*, Cheltenham, UK and Northampton, MA, USA: Edward Elgar Publishing.

Krijnen, M., D. Bassens and M. van Meeteren (2017), 'Manning circuits of value: Lebanese professionals and expatriate world-city formation in Beirut', *Environment and Planning A*, **49** (12), 2878–2896.

Lai, K. (2012), 'Differentiated markets: Shanghai, Beijing and Hong Kong in China's financial centre network', *Urban Studies*, **49** (6), 1275–1296.

Lambregts, B., J. Kleibert and N. Beerepoot (2018), 'The making of Mumbai as a global city: Investigating the role of the offshore services sector', in M. Hoyler, C. Parnreiter and A. Watson (eds), *Global City Makers: Economic Actors and Practices in the World City Network*, Cheltenham, UK and Northampton, MA, USA: Edward Elgar Publishing, pp. 124–150.

Lavery, S., S. McDaniel and D. Schmid (2018), 'New geographies of European financial competition? Frankfurt, Paris and the political economy of Brexit', *Geoforum*, **94**, 72–81.

Leon, J.K. (2017), 'Global cities at any cost: Resisting municipal mercantilism', *City*, **21** (1), 6–24.

Lizieri, C. and D. Mekic (2018), 'Real estate and global capital networks: Drilling into the City of London', in M. Hoyler, C. Parnreiter and A. Watson (eds), *Global City Makers: Economic Actors and Practices in the World City Network*, Cheltenham, UK and Northampton, MA, USA: Edward Elgar Publishing, pp. 60–82.

Lüthi, S., A. Thierstein and M. Hoyler (2018), 'The world city network: Evaluating top-down versus bottom-up approaches', *Cities*, **72**, 287–294.

McNeill, D. (2009), *The Global Architect: Firms, Fame and Urban Form*, New York: Routledge.

McNeill, D. (2014), 'Mayors and the representation of urban politics', in M. Davidson and D. Martin (eds), *Urban Politics: Critical Approaches?* London: Sage, pp. 100–111.

McNeill, D. (2015), 'Tracking the global urbanists', *Global Networks*, **15** (3), 379–384.

Pain, K. (2008), 'Spaces of practice in advanced business services: Rethinking London-Frankfurt relations', *Environment and Planning D: Society and Space*, **26** (2), 264–279.

Parnreiter, C. (2010), 'Global cities in global commodity chains: Exploring the role of Mexico City in the geography of global economic governance', *Global Networks*, **10** (1), 35–53.

Parnreiter, C. (2014), 'Network or hierarchical relations? A plea for redirecting attention to the control functions of global cities', *Tijdschrift voor Economische en Sociale Geografie*, **105** (4), 398–411.

Parnreiter, C. (2015), 'Managing and governing commodity chains: The role of producer service firms in the secondary global city of Hamburg', *Die Erde*, **146** (1), 1–15.

Parnreiter, C. (2017), 'Global cities and the geographical transfer of value', *Urban Studies*, DOI: 10.1177/0042098017722739.

Parnreiter, C. (2018), 'Producer service firms as global city makers: The cases of Mexico City and Hamburg', in M. Hoyler, C. Parnreiter and A. Watson (eds), *Global City Makers: Economic Actors and Practices in the World City Network*, Cheltenham, UK and Northampton, MA, USA: Edward Elgar Publishing, pp. 23–40.

Ponzini, D. and U. Rossi (2010), 'Becoming a creative city: The entrepreneurial mayor, network politics and the promise of an urban renaissance', *Urban Studies*, **47** (5), 1037–1057.

Rapoport, E. (2015), 'Globalising sustainable urbanism: The role of international masterplanners', *Area*, **47** (2), 110–115.

Ren, X. (2011), *Building Globalization: Transnational Architecture Production in Urban China*, Chicago: The University of Chicago Press.

Roberts, B. (1986), 'Review of Timberlake, M., Urbanization in the World-Economy', *International Journal of Urban and Regional Research*, **10** (3), 458–459.

Robinson, J. (2006), *Ordinary Cities: Between Modernity and Development*, London: Routledge.

Rossi, E.C., J.V. Beaverstock and P.J. Taylor (2007), 'Transaction links through cities: "Decision cities" and "service cities" in outsourcing by leading Brazilian firms', *Geoforum*, **38** (4), 628–642.

Sassen, S. (1991), *The Global City: New York, London, Tokyo*, Princeton, NJ: Princeton University Press.

Sassen, S. (2001), *The Global City: New York, London, Tokyo* (2nd edition), Princeton, NJ: Princeton University Press.

Sassen, S. (2010), 'Global inter-city networks and commodity chains: Any intersections?', *Global Networks*, **10** (1), 150–163.

Sassen, S. (2018), 'The global city: Enabling economic intermediation and bearing its costs', in M. Hoyler, C. Parnreiter and A. Watson (eds), *Global City Makers: Economic Actors and Practices in the World City Network*, Cheltenham, UK and Northampton, MA, USA: Edward Elgar Publishing, pp. 1–4.

Scofield, D. (2018), 'Global cities, local practices: Intermediation in the commercial real estate markets of New York City and London', in M. Hoyler, C. Parnreiter and A. Watson (eds), *Global City Makers: Economic Actors and Practices in the World City Network*, Cheltenham, UK and Northampton, MA, USA: Edward Elgar Publishing, pp. 83–105.

Short, J.R., Y. Kim, M. Kuus and H. Wells (1996), 'The dirty little secret of world cities research: Data problems in comparative analysis', *International Journal of Urban and Regional Research*, **20** (4), 697–717.

Sklair, L. (2017), *The Icon Project: Architecture, Cities, and Capitalist Globalization*, New York: Oxford University Press.

Taylor, P.J. (1997), 'Hierarchical tendencies amongst world cities: A global research proposal', *Cities*, **14** (6), 323–332.

Taylor, P.J. (2001), 'Specification of the world city network', *Geographical Analysis*, **33** (2), 181–194.

Taylor, P.J. (2004), *World City Network: A Global Urban Analysis*, London: Routledge.

Taylor, P.J. and B. Derudder (2016), *World City Network: A Global Urban Analysis* (2nd edition), London: Routledge.

Taylor, P.J., M. Hoyler and R. Verbruggen (2010), 'External urban relational process: Introducing central flow theory to complement central place theory', *Urban Studies*, **47** (13), 2803–2818.

Taylor, P.J., B. Derudder, J. Faulconbridge, M. Hoyler and P. Ni (2014), 'Advanced producer service firms as strategic networks, global cities as strategic places', *Economic Geography*, **90** (3), 267–291.

Taylor, P.J., P. Ni, B. Derudder, M. Hoyler, J. Huang and F. Witlox (eds) (2011), *Global Urban Analysis: A Survey of Cities in Globalization*, London: Earthscan.

Van Meeteren, M. and D. Bassens (2016), 'World cities and the uneven geographies of financialization: Unveiling stratification and hierarchy in the world city archipelago', *International Journal of Urban and Regional Research*, **40** (1), 62–81.

Van Meeteren, M. and D. Bassens (2018), 'Chasing the phantom of a "global endgame": The role of management consultancy in the narratives of pre-failure ABN AMRO', in M. Hoyler, C. Parnreiter and A. Watson (eds), *Global City Makers: Economic Actors and Practices in the World City Network*, Cheltenham, UK and Northampton, MA, USA: Edward Elgar Publishing, pp. 170–191.

Van Meeteren, M., B. Derudder and D. Bassens (2016), 'Can the straw man speak? An engagement with postcolonial critiques of "global cities research"', *Dialogues in Human Geography*, **6** (3), 247–267.

Vance, J.E. (1970), *The Merchant's World: The Geography of Wholesaling*, Englewood Cliffs, NJ: Prentice-Hall.

Watson, A. and J.V. Beaverstock (2014), 'World city network research at a theoretical impasse: On the need to re-establish qualitative approaches to understanding agency in world city networks', *Tijdschrift voor Economische en Sociale Geografie*, **105** (4), 412–426.

Wills, J., K. Datta, Y. Evans, J. Herbert, J. May and C. McIlwaine (2010), *Global Cities at Work: New Migrant Divisions of Labour*, London: Pluto Press.

Wójcik, D. (2013a), 'The dark side of NY-LON: Financial centres and the global financial crisis', *Urban Studies*, **50** (13), 2736–2752.

Wójcik, D. (2013b), 'Where governance fails: Advanced business services and the offshore world', *Progress in Human Geography*, **37** (3), 330–347.

Yamamura, S. (2018), 'The making of transnational urban space: Financial professionals in the global city Tokyo', in M. Hoyler, C. Parnreiter and A. Watson (eds), *Global City Makers: Economic Actors and Practices in the World City Network*, Cheltenham, UK and Northampton, MA, USA: Edward Elgar Publishing, pp. 106–123.

2. Producer service firms as global city makers: the cases of Mexico City and Hamburg

Christof Parnreiter

2.1 INTRODUCTION

In order to analyse global city makers and their practices, it is necessary to outline a theoretical understanding of what makes a 'global city'.[1] Such a conceptual definition is especially needed because since the publication of Sassen's (1991) seminal study, a large number of publications have appeared under the umbrella of 'global city' or 'world city' research. In light of the rapid spread of the respective terminology, it is of little surprise that the emerging literature is very heterogeneous (for a review see Parnreiter, 2013). Yet despite the proliferation of the global city literature we have not advanced satisfactorily in our understanding of the role of global cities in the world economy and, in particular, in the organization of globalization.

This is both surprising and problematic, because, as I see it, the global city model has been developed as an economic geography concept to comprehend the function and position of specific economic actors in certain cities in the management and, in particular, the 'command and control' of the world economy. Thus Sassen's (1991, p. 14) opening question is: 'What is the role of major cities in the organization and management of the world economy?' Yet, although Sassen's focus has been on the asymmetrical geographical distribution of strategic components such as producer services (PSs) and hence on 'questions of power and inequality' (Sassen, 2001, p. 351), relatively few studies have examined how producer service firms (PSFs) operate to articulate and control economic activities at various scales (for example, Hanssens et al., 2012; Jacobs et al., 2010; Jacobs, 2014; Parnreiter, 2010, 2015; Rossi et al., 2007).

Against this backdrop, in the next section I will outline my understanding of the key actors and practices in the making of global cities. Moreover, I suggest an operationalization of research on global city makers and their practices, proposing to conceptualize global cities as critical nodes in global commodity chains (GCCs) from where they are organized and, in particular, governed. To deepen this notion, I discuss global city formation in two non-prime global cities, namely Mexico City and Hamburg. Based both on quantitative and qualitative information, I argue that these two cities, while not belonging to the 'global elite' cities of which consultancies (for example AT Kearney, 2016) like to speak, nevertheless represent important places from where commodity chain governance is co-shaped. After discussing the reach and scope of Mexico City's and Hamburg's PSFs in economic governance, I finally reflect on the role of global cities in the making of uneven development.

2.2 KEY ACTORS AND PRACTICES IN THE MAKING OF GLOBAL CITIES

For me, the global city concept as proposed by Friedmann (Friedmann and Wolff, 1982; Friedmann, 1986) and Sassen (1988, 1991) consists of four interrelated claims (for a more detailed account see Parnreiter, 2014). Firstly, global cities are clusters for PSFs, which function, secondly, as centres for the management of the world economy and, thirdly, also as centres for its governance. Fourthly, PSFs are organized in a cross-border division of labour, and that is why global cities operate in a worldwide network (Taylor, 2001).

What implications for research on global city makers and their practices arise from the contention that the ultimate *raison d'être* of global cities is to provide inputs necessary for the management and the governance of the world economy? In line with Sassen's (1991) widely accepted premises, I assert that PSFs are the main global city makers, while their servicing of clients is the key practice underlying global city formation: the 'key indicator of global city status is whether a city contains the capabilities for servicing, managing, and financing the global operations of firms and markets. . . . *The question is whether coordination and specialized servicing of global firms and markets is taking place*' (Sassen, 2001, p. 359, p. 361; emphasis added).

Thus, for the smooth functioning and the governing of (cross-border) economic activities (or, in other words, of GCCs), functional intra- and inter-city linkages between PSFs and their clients have to exist. To conceptualize and to operationalize research on these linkages, Brown et al. (2010) proposed to integrate the literatures on global cities and on GCCs, arguing that '[a] world city can be seen as a critical node within commodity chains, precisely for its insertion of advanced services into the production process. Thus, every world city is a service node in and for a myriad of chains, thereby obtaining its overall centrality' (Brown et al., 2010, p. 23). A particular advantage of conceptualizing global cities as nodes within GCCs is that the literatures on GCCs, global production networks (GPNs) and global value chains (GVCs)[2] have advanced *a relational, actor-focused understanding of economic power.* Governance has proven to be a useful concept to operationalize research on economic power relations (cf. Bair, 2008; Coe, 2012; Gereffi et al., 2005; Gibbon et al., 2008; Henderson et al., 2002; Yeung, 2005), being more adequate for dealing with economic power than the somewhat vague notion of 'command and control' employed in much of the global city literature. Although Sassen has to my knowledge never used these two terms combined, they have become a kind of 'synopsis' of the global city concept. Nor has Sassen exactly defined 'command and control'. While 'command' is applied in *The Global City* rarely beyond the frequently cited passage 'highly concentrated command points in the organization of the world economy' (Sassen, 1991, p. 3), 'control' is used in combination with ownership or to denote 'the work of producing and reproducing the organization and management of a global production system and a global marketplace of finance' (Sassen, 1991, p. 6). Both notions are perfectly compatible with the idea of 'governance' as used in the literatures on GCCs, GVCs and GPNs.

Yet, while defining governance as the 'authority and power relationships that determine how financial, material and human resources are allocated and flow within a chain' (Gereffi, 1994, p. 97) would commit to analysing governance as multi-actor and multi-scalar relations, in reality most studies on GCCs, GVCs and GPNs have prioritized just one inter-firm link, namely the one between lead firms and key suppliers. Other possible actors such as PSFs, international organizations, national governments, unions and private standard setters have received far less attention (Brown et al., 2010; Ponte and Sturgeon, 2014; Yeung and Coe, 2015), for which reason governance studies still suffer from an all too simple conceptualization as 'dyadic' (Yeung and Coe, 2015, p. 31).

PSFs in particular have barely been analysed as key actors in chain or network governance (Coe, 2012), though their general importance has been recognized (Henderson et al., 2002; Rabach and Kim, 1994). Some authors have deepened this notion, signalling, for example, that PSFs might add the greatest share of the total value (Kaplinsky and Morris, 2002, p. 7), exercise 'dominant influence over the governance of GCCs' (Rabach and Kim, 1994, p. 125) or constitute organizations 'on which the corporation [the lead firm] depends' (Dicken, 2011, p. 135). More recently, however, increasing attention is being paid to the significant influence that

PSFs in general and financial firms in particular exercise on corporate strategies (Coe et al., 2014). For example, the consequences of lead firms' financialization have been discussed as regards the shape and extension of GCCs (Gibbon, 2002; Milberg, 2008) and the distribution of value amongst the different actors in a GCC (Palpacuer, 2008). On the other hand, Wójcik (2013) has highlighted that PSFs create and make accessible an offshore world, providing thereby critical support for their clients to escape the control of governmental or intergovernmental organizations.

These studies echo the findings of the broader literatures on financialization and transnational private governance that PSFs supply key inputs for economic governance, exerting thereby significant influence on how value is created in GCCs and, above all, how it is distributed. Yet, if PSFs are important actors in governance processes, then global cities, where these firms are clustered, are indeed central governance nodes in and for the world economy (Brown et al., 2010). As Sassen says (2001, p. 348): 'The global city network is the operational scaffolding of . . . the global economy.'

To support the notion that PSFs are key actors of global city formation and their servicing of clients the main underlying practice, in the next two sections I will provide some evidence of global city formation for non-prime global cities, namely Mexico City and Hamburg. Mexico City is, as a classical 'Third World megacity', a case of a city supposedly dropped off the global city map (Robinson, 2002). Hamburg was chosen because its port makes it a crucial hub in many GCCs (Hesse, 2006, 2018). Nevertheless, Hamburg's PS sector, although the second biggest in Germany, is relatively weakly integrated into the world city network (Taylor et al., 2011) – governance functions are hence less expected here than in Frankfurt/Main (Hoyler, 2011). To analyse whether these cities house a significant number of actors of global city making, namely global PSFs, I rely on information provided by the Mexican and the German statistical institutes, as well as on data by the Globalization and World Cities (GaWC) research network (Taylor and Derudder, 2016). To scrutinize the practices that underlie global city formation, I conducted semi-structured, open-ended interviews with professionals of global PSFs: 19 in Hamburg in 2013; 14 in Mexico City in 2007–08 and a further four in 2013 (for more detailed accounts see Parnreiter, 2010, 2015). The accountancy, advertising, finance and insurance, legal and management consultancy firms contacted were drawn from the GaWC list (Taylor et al., 2011). For most firms, clients with cross-border operations represent the lion's share of their business. Interviews lasted from 30 to 65 minutes, and were transcribed and analysed thematically. Quotes were translated by the author.

2.3 MEXICO CITY AS A FUNCTIONAL NODE IN GCCs

As previously noted, for Sassen (2001) participation in the management and control of GCCs is the key activity that makes a city a global city. Consequently, the actors involved in these tasks – PSFs – are the global city makers. An investigation of whether Mexico City fulfils global city functions in the world economy requires therefore verifying that there are global activities of companies to any significant degree. This is to some extent evidenced by the fact that the stock of foreign direct investment (FDI) in Mexico has grown by 11 000 per cent since the early 1980s, while annual exports increased by 1500 per cent (United Nations Conference on Trade and Development (UNCTAD), 2016). Moreover, the composition of exports has changed profoundly: while in the early 1980s, oil accounted for two thirds of all exports from Mexico, today manufacturing makes about three quarters of exports. Thus, companies in Mexico (and that is, in many cases, foreign companies in Mexico) are increasingly integrated into GCCs (World Bank, 2016). This raises the question: where is this production serviced, managed and governed? Does Mexico City play a significant role in this respect?

Mexico City has in fact a large producer service sector. In 2013, this sector provided services for US$80 billion, a number comparable to cities like Sydney or Munich (Euromonitor International, 2014). Moreover, Mexico City concentrates the majority of domestic production of business-oriented services: while more than two thirds of the value added in this sector in Mexico stems from Mexico City, in financial services the city's participation reaches even 81 per cent. It is also noteworthy that there is a similarly strong concentration of producer services *within* Mexico City: just four districts, namely Álvaro Obregón, Benito Juárez, Cuauhtémoc and Miguel Hidalgo, account for 71 per cent of all Mexican value added in financial services (Instituto Nacional de Estadísticas y Geografía (INEGI), 2016). Thus, the global city within Mexico City is clearly delineated, covering areas such as Santa Fe, Paseo de la Reforma, Polanco and the Avenida de los Insurgentes Sur (Parnreiter, 2009).

Yet, Mexico City not only has a large, but also a highly globalized sector of producer services. In 2013, more than half of the 175 globally active business-oriented service companies that make up the GaWC analysis (Taylor and Derudder, 2016) had an office in Mexico City. There are, however, significant differences between the subsectors: while all 25 global accounting firms are represented in Mexico City, only about half of the banks and financial institutions and only a quarter of global law firms have offices there. Nevertheless, some of the global banking and financial services maintain very high-ranking offices in Mexico City (such as BBVA, HSBC, Santander), along with some of the world's biggest PSFs such as, for example, the 'Big Four' of Deloitte, Ernst & Young, KPMG and PricewaterhouseCoopers.

Although a large sector of globalized PSFs is the prerequisite for a city to assume global city functions, it is still not sufficient proof. What about the demand side, that is, firms operating in GCCs? Can we assume that cities where manufacturing activities for automotive or electronic chains are carried out import producer services from Mexico City? This is very likely, given the pronounced functional and regional division of labour in Mexico. While producer services are, as indicated, highly centralized in Mexico City, this city contributes only marginally to the added value in manufacturing: only 3.5 per cent of total value added in the electronic industry and only 3.1 per cent of the value in the auto industry stem from Mexico City. The other side of this rigid spatial separation of economic functions is the absolute lack of producer services in most of Mexico's industrial cities. While just three *maquiladora* cities on the northern border, Ciudad Juárez, Tijuana and Reynosa, account for 43 per cent of the value in the electronics industry, and while just five cities (Cuautlancingo/ Puebla; Hermosillo, Ramos Arizpe and Ciudad Juárez in the North and Silao in the central region) produce 41.4 per cent of the value in the auto industry, none of these cities has a significant sector of business-oriented services. Together they make up only 1.4 per cent of the value of all business-oriented services, and even only 0.2 per cent of the financial and insurance services (INEGI, 2016).

These data very plausibly suggest that the companies related to the 'Mexican' sections of GCCs in the automotive and electronics industry obtain at least a part of their producer services from Mexico City. Places such as Mexico's *maquiladora* cities thus constitute what Robinson (2002, p. 547) has called with reference to export processing zones in general 'the other end of the command and control continuum of global city functions'. However, this assumption cannot be verified with census data, because the input–output matrices of the Mexican Institute of Statistics do not allow for regionalization. Service flows can be identified only between sectors, but not, for example, from Mexico City to Tijuana, Ciudad Juárez or Cuautlancingo. Thus, to scrutinize PSFs' practices of managing and governing their clients' GCCs, a turn to qualitative methods is necessary.

The respondents from global PSFs in Mexico City leave no doubt that, according to their view, Mexico City is a place where both Mexican and foreign firms obtain essential financial, insurance, legal, real estate and other consulting services. This means that Mexico City is a critical node in various commodity chains. Yet, interviewees also stress that the services provided by their company do not only 'grease' the global production lines of their clients. Rather, they point to their strategic influence via the pre-structuring of governance processes of the client's business. The partner of a global law firm in Mexico City, for example, suggests that:

> The lawyer . . . proposes a decision and influences it . . . Particularly in the case of corporations, the more institutionalized firms, in the sense that they are not family firms, but listed [at the stock exchange] . . . I believe that there really is a strong influence of *outsourcings* [external service providers] in the decision process on the level of decision makers.

As regards fields where they impact on business strategies and governance processes, the interviewed professionals mention in particular tax, labour and locational issues. In locational decisions, labour issues play a significant role because in Mexico workers' representation is organized based upon the 'closed shop' principle. A firm's locational choice is therefore closely related to the selection of a union with which to sign the collective bargaining agreement. Locational choices thus impact directly on chain governance:

> [The client] contracts you precisely for that. That you tell them which union is the most convenient one. . . . I think there's much influence one has. A good example . . . is the industrial branch x, the firm y. Y has closed plants, and has located other plants, only and exclusively because of the advice we have given . . . [They faced] problems with the union, because the union is very aggressive, because there used to be a contract, they had to pay certain, eh, benefits which were above the market standards. . . . *And who took the decision to relocate plants?* Well, . . . the client decides because it is their money, [but] based on the advice you give them. . . . If you tell them, the best place [to put the plant] is this one, it's unlikely that the client will opt for something else. (Partner, law firm)

This view is echoed by another lawyer: 'The one who takes the decision how things should be done, rather would be here, from the [law] firm. . . . I do believe that the one who makes the strategy, it's the partners of the law firm.'

Thus, interviewees in Mexico City say that PSFs influence, *through the services they provide*, how and where value in their clients' GCCs is created and how it is distributed. Of course, this is only one side – respondents might have overestimated their roles; they might see their importance in different areas than their clients; or they might even have downplayed their influence (suggesting, for example, that it is only *other* PSFs who influence governance). If governance evolves only as it is practised between actors (Allen, 2003), a critical assessment and triangulation of the findings through interviews with clients is still needed. Nevertheless, the numerous examples brought up in the interviews of how the services supplied influence governance relations in a way that clients' position in GCCs is improved clearly confirm that managing and governing others' businesses on various scales, including the global, is part of PSFs' daily job – even in a non-'prime' global city such as Mexico City.

2.4   HAMBURG AS A FUNCTIONAL NODE IN GCCs

As in the case of Mexico City, an investigation into Hamburg's global city functions requires showing both the economic activities to be articulated with the world market and the existence of a substantial globalized sector of PSs. Hamburg is one of the world's prime locations for maritime related producer services (Jacobs et al., 2010). As the world's second important 'world maritime city' behind Hong Kong (Verhetsel and Sel, 2009), the city houses headquarters of a number of large shipping companies (for example Hapag-Lloyd, Hamburg Süd). Moreover, as the 15th biggest container port in the world, and Europe's second biggest in 2014 (World Shipping Council, 2016), Hamburg is a critical node in numerous GCCs (Hesse, 2006).

In Germany, Hamburg has the second largest producer service sector as regards output, behind Berlin, but ahead of Munich or Frankfurt. Hamburg's PS sector generates nearly €30 billion, or a third of the city's total gross value added (GVA). Hamburg has about 300 000 employees in PSs, coming third in Germany behind Berlin and Munich (Volkswirtschaftliche Gesamtrechnungen der Länder, 2015). However, notwithstanding its size, Hamburg's producer service sector's global integration is relatively weak compared to other German cities. According to a recent analysis of global network connectivity (GNC) undertaken by GaWC (Hoyler, 2011; Taylor et al., 2011), Frankfurt/Main is Germany's best connected city (GNC 56.9, ranked 16th worldwide), followed by Munich (GNC 41.5) and Hamburg (GNC 38.4). The 54th most connected city worldwide, Hamburg is comparable in terms of connectivity to Cairo, Dallas or Düsseldorf. If we differentiate between subsectors of producer services, we find that Hamburg has a large cluster of legal services, accountancy firms and management consultancies; while its embeddedness in the networks of financial service firms is somewhat weaker (Hoyler, 2011; Taylor et al., 2011).

Such descriptive data are insufficient to assess global city functions in Hamburg, because the existence of a large and globally embedded producer service sector does not per se tell us anything regarding relevant practices. Are Hamburg's PSFs involved in the management and governance of cross-border economic activities? According to the interviewed professionals, this is clearly the case. In particular, respondents provide strong support for the assumption that PSFs have a shaping influence on their clients' GCC governance. Most of them agree with this notion either plainly or with the qualification that the impact depends on the service provided and on characteristics of the client (size, firm culture, market position). As the most obvious case of influencing clients' GCCs, respondents cite corporate governance, which even in its narrowest sense – compliance – leaves substantial room to manoeuvre for a better positioning of the client. Because there is always more than one way of adhering to the law, the PSF's task is to 'implement the law in our client's sense' (Partner, accountancy firm). In corporate governance's broader meaning – how a corporation is directed and controlled – PSFs' counselling implies an intervention in relationships between a company's board, managers, creditors, investors, shareholders and employees. Firm-intern restructuring, for example,

> [is not always] associated for each participant with a 100 per cent favourable result. That means that often such projects . . . are stuck because too many individual interests clash. And then it is our task (a) to moderate and (b) to make for a result. (Branch Head, consultancy firm)

Beyond corporate governance, a significant issue regarding PSFs' involvement in GCC governance is entry barriers. Expanding abroad means, for all firms, overcoming other firms' entry barriers in the target market in order to get access to their GCCs (or to replace them totally). No easy task – but more feasible with PSF support. Interviewees concur that they are contracted because of clients' needs to counter the deterrent effects of foreignness and opaqueness abroad. Relying on a global PSF, the target market 'becomes more accessible, that's fair to say, true. . . . I see the lawyer, the accountant, the tax advisor in an enabler function' (Business Development Manager, law firm). This is particularly, but not exclusively, true for small and medium-sized enterprises (SMEs), which 'have to face incredible hurdles . . . which after all are being reduced by service providers like us' (Partner, accountancy firm). One interviewed accountancy firm has developed, together with a leading German research institution, a tool to support clients' decision making-processes as regards the ways of going global: exports or FDI? Which countries for which option? Which legal form of the unit in which foreign country? Providing answers to these questions positions the PSF to proactively suggest strategies of globalization, including a restructuring of GCCs: 'we have done that, for example with a client who has three plants in Europe which are very similar, where we have proposed to relocate to the East for certain products' (Principal, accountancy firm).

PSFs also support their clients in erecting entry barriers. Developing standards, as consultancies and accountancy firms do, means designing the entrance ticket to the client's GCC. Advertisers are busy in erecting barriers through branding. Without it, 'I'd say that in many, many markets our client wouldn't be market leader. . . . We are . . . not only the creator of the brand, we also guide the brand' (Managing Director, advertiser). Lawyers, in turn, create entry barriers by striving to protect their clients' intellectual property. Advising the client in patent law is strategic, because it 'is of course very clear in order to prevent others from coming to the market. . . . Because intellectual property, very, very clearly leads to monopoly rights. And monopoly rights of course always serve to crowd out a competitor' (Office Managing Partner, law firm). Advice includes locational strategies because 'if in some place I don't have patent protection or not sufficient [protection], then the competition comes and takes [my product] away or modifies it or makes it cheaper. . . . And that is certainly very significant' (Partner, law firm).

Finally, providing or denying access to financing is a critical part of handling entry barriers. The head of the business centre of a finance firm reports that his firm occasionally includes his clients' suppliers in foreign markets in the financial schemes to increase the market power of the supplier vis-à-vis local competitors. This ties the supplier to the client and allows the latter to rely on more stable business relations.

Tax issues also show how PSFs influence clients' success in negotiating how 'resources are allocated and flow within a chain' (Gereffi, 1994, p. 97). Although respondents concur that a client's business cannot be assessed only as regards tax optimization, they also affirm that 'creative tax advice' (Partner, accountancy firm) constitutes an important field of their business:

> We see the organizational chart of a group, see how 40 companies are composed, . . . how there are, so to speak, tax flows, and then having such an account one can say, that is somehow suboptimal, one has to consider that, and here you could make a recommendation. (Partner, accountancy firm)

Such 'recommendations' are made quite pro-actively, because 'very few clients would develop such an [tax-saving] idea by themselves. Rather, it is us to provide the impetus. . . . The technical implementation is not the issue but rather the idea' (Partner, accountancy firm).

Labour relations constitute another field with 'much [potential for] shaping, according to the motto: what is the most reasonable [for my client]? . . . that clearly is a shaping task' (Partner, law firm). Referring to the closing of an industrial plant, the managing partner of another law firm emphasizes that 'we have been busy with that for four years . . . and practically everything, each move in the negotiations, bears our hallmark'.

Risk engineering is another typical field of PSFs' involvement with significant impact on GCC governance. Assessing all kinds of risks along the *whole* chain can, as the business development manager of a financial and insurance firm says, lead to proposals to restructure the GCC (if, for example, the assessment reveals vulnerabilities of a supplier), but it also can touch 'weak points in the [client] company' itself. This, then, would call for internal restructuring which, as noted above, is also guided by external PSFs. Moreover, the importance of PSFs in risk engineering is rising because financialization deepens the consequences of traditional risks. Referring to a fire in a steel mill, causing damage of €90 million and a further €1 million per day of business interruption, the human resources and financial manager of another financial and insurance firm maintains that the even bigger risk is that the company's stock prices go down due to these losses: 'And then, I'd say, in the course of solvency and operative risk management, this becomes more the focus, well, then you can exercise influence with this service'.

2.5   THE MAP OF ECONOMIC GOVERNANCE

The discussion of PSFs' practices in Mexico City and in Hamburg has shown that professionals, through the services they provide, make commodity chains function. Moreover, the interviews also make clear that PSF professionals exercise, at least in their view, economic governance because they influence how resources in the clients' GCCs are created and distributed: supplying services needed for corporate governance, for erecting or overcoming entry barriers, for optimizing tax burdens, for shaping labour relations, and for risk engineering. This implies that PSFs intervene in, and pre-structure, strategic processes and relations within the client firm and between the client and their business partners or other stakeholders. In the light of the conceptualization of global cities as centres of economic management and governance, this means that Mexico City's and Hamburg's professionals act as global city makers: it is the activities of PSFs that result in these two not so prominent cities being 'on the map' of global cities.

Respondents in both cities describe the relationships between their firm's offices globally as flat and functional. While all regional offices in Germany or Mexico provide a broad portfolio of more or less standardized services, specialized fields of knowledge are offered through specialized groups which are represented in fewer cities. In Germany, such regional specializations have emerged historically: the Frankfurt/Main offices are traditionally strong in finance, Munich has more high-quality professionals in IT, Stuttgart is strong in automotive industries, and Hamburg in shipping and logistics companies. Although the specialized groups have a head at the national, regional and global levels, respondents see neither a hierarchy between the specializations nor a general regional hierarchy in the sense that a professional specialized in finance and working in Frankfurt/Main could command colleagues in Hamburg.

Yet, offices are not of equal importance either. Firstly, there are differences in size. GaWC's connectivity values of cities are calculated on the basis of the number of global PSFs a city has and the size of their offices (Taylor, 2001; Taylor and Derudder, 2016). Thus, existing differences in the geographical distribution of offices and in their size can make the difference in the extent to which a city's office has impact on GCC governance. It is, however, important to note that according to the respondents in both Mexico City and Hamburg, the size differences between the offices stem from the size of the market in a given city (or country) and do not reflect weights in an intra-firm division of labour, and even less so hierarchies. Work with a client is usually organized through a Head of Account, and this is someone who usually comes from an office close to the client. Thus, who has the say in shaping the relations between a PSF's worldwide offices might in principle shift daily, depending on where clients come from. Yet, while this suggests a very flat structure, the geography of clients does impose a certain unevenness on the networks of PSFs: a Mexican partner of a global legal or accountancy firm will far more often have a Head of Account located in a US, German or Chinese city than their counterpart will have a Mexican colleague as Head. The same applies on a regional scale: a partner in Hamburg will have more Heads of Account from Frankfurt, simply because the market there is bigger.

It is exactly this structure that helps us to understand the role and reach of secondary global cities such as Mexico City or Hamburg. The organizational model of PSFs implies that there is the chain of command: while local cooperation is essential to do business in Mexico or to enter Europe via the port of Hamburg, the 'big' strategies are made by the lead partners. Thus, the more firms going global are in a specific market, the more lead partners an office of a PSF will have, the more deals this office will command and the more sales it will generate. To give one example from Mexico City: of the 3531 deals (1998–2008) of Holland & Knight in Mexico City, only 36.2 per cent originated in the country. The rest were brought through the law firm's offices in US cities, with Washington (26.5 per cent), Miami (13.3) and San Francisco (6.8) being the most important ones (Parnreiter, 2010). Thus, the existing unevenness of the world economy poses serious limitations to the development of governance functions in Mexico City.

2.6   GLOBAL CITIES AND UNEVEN DEVELOPMENT

Both the creation and distribution of values along commodity chains are marked by uneven geographies. While it is outside the scope of this chapter to discuss the various reasons and instruments for uneven development, I wish to draw attention to two mechanisms which are critical for creating and maintaining the unequal distribution of wealth. First, some actors in GCCs are able to appropriate a larger share of the value created than others, mainly because they manage to safeguard themselves behind barriers to entry. Because 'the primary returns accrue to those parties who are able to protect themselves from competition' (Kaplinsky and Morris, 2002, p. 25), those behind entry barriers enjoy monopoly rents. Second, uneven development may result from a 'geographical transfer of value' (Hadjimichalis, 1984) in which value produced at one location is being transferred to another. In both cases commodity chains will be shaped in a way that some nodes will receive more wealth for consumption and further accumulation, while others are characterized by the outflow of resources.

I have emphasized these two mechanisms of uneven development because, in both, professionals of PSFs are key actors: as the above mentioned quote from the partner of a global law firm in Hamburg clearly reveals, law firms play a critical role in creating entry barriers. Thereby, they provide their clients with the possibility of reaping extra profits, namely monopoly rents. Yet, there are many more ways through which PSFs protect their clients against competitors. Consultancies and accountancy firms, for example, design the entrance ticket to GCCs through the development and implementation of standards, and advertisers erect entry barriers through branding (Faulconbridge et al., 2011). Banks may or may not grant financing. An example brought up in an interview in Hamburg refers to the opening of the lead firm's credit lines for a local supplier in Asia, which increases the latter's market power vis-à-vis local competitors, ties them to the German lead firm and allows the latter to drive down the supplier's prices. As regards the geographical transfer of value, the practices involved – from profit repatriation and transfer-pricing to tax evasion and foreign direct investment – fall within the core competencies of PSFs (Sikka and Willmott, 2010). Moreover PSFs are, as developers of taxation, transfer pricing and profit repatriation strategies, key actors in shaping geographies of de- and re-investment.

The critical point here is that a shift of wealth in commodity chains towards certain actors and regions or cities requires the 'servicing help' of PSFs professionals. Because of this indispensability of PSFs' involvement in the unequal distribution of resources, global cities – and, amongst them, places such as Mexico City or Hamburg – are strategic sites for the organization of uneven development. While I think that such reasoning has been the critical gist underlying the development of the global city concept, the goal of analysing the role of specific cities and the dominant elites in them in the making of uneven development has been lost over the years (Parnreiter, 2014). Nevertheless, for me, the objective of global city research is the same as the one Roberts (1986, p. 459) defined 30 years ago. Criticizing that, for some authors in the then upcoming global city literature, '[r]elationships of inequality are taken as a given, . . . [while] the mechanisms by which power is exercised and reproduced are not fully examined', he suggested focusing particularly on 'how cities and the classes within them achieve control over other regions'. The task is, thus, to add an explicit urban dimension to Hadjimichalis's (1984) concept of the 'geographical transfer of value' – something which has not been achieved, neither in critical (development) geography nor in world-systems analysis. What that could look like has been roughly suggested nearly half a century ago by Andre Gunder Frank in his geographical vision of the 'development of underdevelopment'. According to Frank (1969, p. 6), the making of centre-periphery relations works through inter-city networks: '[A] whole chain of constellations of metropoles and satellites relates all parts of the whole system from its metropolitan center in Europe or the United States to the farthest outpost in the Latin American countryside . . . we find that each of the satellites . . . serves as an instrument to suck capital or economic surplus out of its own satellites and to channel part of this surplus to the world metropolis of which all are satellites.'

2.7   CONCLUSIONS

This chapter's concern has been to analyse key actors in global city formation and their practices in two secondary global cities: Mexico City and Hamburg. Departing from Sassen's (1991) notion of global cities as centres for the management and the governance of the world economy, I have asserted that PSFs are the main global city makers, while their servicing of clients is the key practice underlying global city formation. In order to operationalize research on the functional intra- and inter-city linkages between PSFs and their clients, I have proposed integrating the literatures on global cities and on GCCs: every global city is a service and governance node in and for a myriad of commodity chains, precisely because of the input of PSs which are needed by firms in GCCs. A particular advantage of conceptualizing global cities as nodes within GCCs is that the literatures on GCCs, GPNs and GVCs have advanced a relational, actor-focused concept of economic governance, one which has proven to be a very useful concept to operationalize research on economic power relations.

Furthermore, I have used two not so prominent, but nevertheless important global cities to scrutinize the practices that underlie global city formation. Both Mexico City and Hamburg have sizeable clusters of globalized PSFs, and in both cities respondents to interviews are very clear in stating that their services provide critical support to their clients in conducting global business. Professionals of global PSFs in both cities thus fulfil 'management functions' for their clients' global operations and that is why Mexico City and Hamburg are critical nodes in many GCCs. As regards the notion that global cities are 'highly concentrated command points in the organization of the world economy' (Sassen, 2001, p. 3), the interviews do provide support for the claim that PSFs have impact on the governance of their clients' GCCs. Most respondents agree that servicing the clients involves influence on decision-making processes, and they provide a number of examples where this is the case. Thus, what Faulconbridge (2007, p. 928) argues in the case of lawyers in London and New York can be generalized beyond these particular cities and services to places such as Mexico City and Hamburg: PSF professionals 'provide commercially sensitive advice to clients that is designed to provide positive business outcomes'.

A key task for further global city research is to better grasp the role global cities play in the production and reproduction of uneven relations in the world's divisions of labour. In particular, there is a need to better understand how PSFs in global cities help to realize the geographical transfer of value towards the centres, and the practices through which professionals of PSFs contribute to shifting wealth along GCCs towards their clients (and themselves).

NOTES

1. While some authors use the terms 'global city' and 'world city' interchangeably, others have stressed the conceptual differences behind these terms (Derudder, 2006). In this chapter I will adopt the respective terminology of the authors I refer to. Where I allude to the general debate, I use the term 'global cities', since my own work draws strongly on Sassen's (1991) *The Global City*.
2. The concepts of GCCs, GVCs and GPNs share conceptualizations of how production and consumption are organized and governed as interconnected and often cross-border operations. Although I am aware of the conceptual differences between these literatures, for the purpose of this chapter they are of minor importance.

REFERENCES

Allen, J. (2003), *Lost Geographies of Power*, Oxford: Blackwell.
Arbeitskreis Volkswirtschaftliche Gesamtrechnungen der Länder (ed.) (2015),

Bruttoinlandsprodukt, Bruttowertschöpfung in den kreisfreien Städten und Landkreisen der Bundesrepublik Deutschland 2000 bis 2013, Stuttgart: Statistisches Landesamt Baden-Württemberg.

AT Kearney (2016), *Global Cities 2016*, accessed 1 July 2016 at www.atkearney.com/research-studies/global-cities-index.

Bair, J. (2008), 'Analysing economic organization: Embedded networks and global chains compared', *Economy and Society*, **37** (3), 339–364.

Brown, E., B. Derudder, C. Parnreiter, W. Pelupessy, P.J. Taylor and F. Witlox (2010), 'World city networks and global commodity chains: Towards a world-systems' integration', *Global Networks*, **10** (1), 12–34.

Coe, N.M. (2012), 'Geographies of production II: A global production network A–Z', *Progress in Human Geography*, **36** (3), 389–402.

Coe, N.M., K.P.Y. Lai and D. Wójcik (2014), 'Integrating finance into global production networks', *Regional Studies*, **48** (5), 761–777.

Derudder, B. (2006), 'On conceptual confusion in empirical analyses of a transnational urban network', *Urban Studies*, **43** (11), 2027–2046.

Dicken, P. (2011), *Global Shift: Mapping the Changing Contours of the World Economy* (6th edition), London: Sage.

Euromonitor International (2014), *Passport Cities*, London: Euromonitor International.

Faulconbridge, J.R. (2007), 'Relational networks of knowledge production in transnational law firms', *Geoforum*, **38** (5), 925–940.

Faulconbridge, J.R., J.V. Beaverstock, C. Nativel and P.J. Taylor (2011), *The Globalization of Advertising: Agencies, Cities and Spaces of Creativity*, London: Routledge.

Frank, A.G. (1969), *Latin America: Underdevelopment or Revolution. Essays on the Development of Underdevelopment and the Immediate Enemy*, New York: Monthly Review Press.

Friedmann, J. (1986), 'The world city hypothesis', *Development and Change*, **17** (1), 69–83.

Friedmann, J. and G. Wolff (1982), 'World city formation: An agenda for research and action', *International Journal of Urban and Regional Research*, **6** (3), 309–344.

Gereffi, G. (1994), 'The organization of buyer-driven global commodity chains: How U.S. retailers shape overseas production networks', in G. Gereffi and M. Korzeniewicz (eds), *Commodity Chains and Global Capitalism*, Westport, CT: Praeger, pp. 95–122.

Gereffi, G., J. Humphrey and T. Sturgeon (2005), 'The governance of global value chains', *Review of International Political Economy*, **12** (1), 78–104.

Gibbon, P. (2002), 'At the cutting edge? Financialisation and UK clothing retailers' global sourcing patterns and practices', *Competition and Change*, **6** (3), 289–308.

Gibbon, P., J. Bair and S. Ponte (2008), 'Governing global value chains: an introduction', *Economy and Society*, **37** (3), 315–338.

Hadjimichalis, C. (1984), 'The geographical transfer of value: Notes on the spatiality of capitalism', *Environment and Planning D: Society and Space*, **2** (3), 329–345.

Hanssens, H., B. Derudder and F. Witlox (2012), 'Managing organizational and geographical complexity: The "positionality" of advanced producer services in the globalizing economies of metropolitan regions', *Erdkunde*, **66** (1), 45–55.

Henderson, J., P. Dicken, M. Hess, N. Coe and H.W-C. Yeung (2002), 'Global production networks and the analysis of economic development', *Review of International Political Economy*, **9** (3), 436–464.

Hesse, M. (2006), 'Global chain, local pain: Regional implications of global distribution networks in the German North Range', *Growth and Change*, **37** (4), 570–596.
Hesse, M. (2018), 'Focal firms, grand coalitions or global city makers? Globalization vs. new localism in Hamburg's maritime network', in M. Hoyler, C. Parnreiter and A. Watson (eds.), *Global City Makers: Economic Actors and Practices in the World City Network*, Cheltenham, UK and Northampton, MA, USA: Edward Elgar Publishing, pp. 151–169.
Hoyler, M. (2011), 'External relations of German cities through intra-firm networks – a global perspective', *Raumforschung und Raumordnung*, **69** (3), 147–159.
INEGI (2016), *Censos Económicos 2014. Resultados Definitivos*, accessed 21 June 2016 at www.inegi.org.mx/est/contenidos/proyectos/ce/ce2014/.
Jacobs, W. (2014), 'Rotterdam and Amsterdam as trading places? In search of the economic–geographical nexus between commodity chains and world cities', *Tijdschrift voor Economische en Sociale Geografie*, **105** (4), 483–491.
Jacobs, W., C. Ducruet and P. De Langen (2010), 'Integrating world cities into production networks: The case of port cities', *Global Networks*, **10** (1), 92–113.
Kaplinsky, R. and M. Morris (2002), *A Handbook for Value Chain Research*, accessed 18 February 2016 at www.prism.uct.ac.za/papers/vchnov01.pdf.
Milberg, W. (2008), 'Shifting sources and uses of profits: Sustaining US financialization with global value chains', *Economy and Society*, **37** (3), 420–451.
Palpacuer, F. (2008), 'Bringing the social context back in: Governance and wealth distribution in global commodity chains', *Economy and Society*, **37** (3), 393–419.
Parnreiter, C. (2009), 'Global-City-Formation, Immobilienwirtschaft und Transnationalisierung. Das Beispiel Mexico City', *Zeitschrift für Wirtschaftsgeographie*, **53** (3), 138–155.
Parnreiter, C. (2010), 'Global cities in global commodity chains: Exploring the role of Mexico City in the geography of global economic governance', *Global Networks*, **10** (1), 35–53.
Parnreiter, C. (2013), 'The global city tradition', in M. Acuto and W. Steele (eds), *Global City Challenges: Debating a Concept, Improving the Practice*, Houndmills: Palgrave Macmillan, pp. 15–32.
Parnreiter, C. (2014), 'Network or hierarchical relations? A plea for redirecting attention to the control functions of global cities', *Tijdschrift voor Economische en Sociale Geografie*, **105** (4), 398–411.
Parnreiter, C. (2015), 'Managing and governing commodity chains: The role of producer service firms in the secondary global city of Hamburg', *Die Erde*, **146** (1), 1–15.
Ponte, S. and T. Sturgeon (2014), 'Explaining governance in global value chains: A modular theory-building effort', *Review of International Political Economy*, **21** (1), 195–223.
Rabach, E. and E.M. Kim (1994), 'Where is the chain in commodity chains? The service sector nexus', in G. Gereffi and M. Korzeniewicz (eds), *Commodity Chains and Global Capitalism*, Westport, CT: Praeger, pp. 123–143.
Roberts, B. (1986), 'Review of Timberlake, M., Urbanization in the World-Economy', *International Journal of Urban and Regional Research*, **10** (3), 458–459.
Robinson, J. (2002), 'Global and world cities: a view from off the map', *International Journal of Urban and Regional Research*, **26** (3), 531–554.
Rossi, E.C., J.V. Beaverstock and P.J. Taylor (2007), 'Transaction links through cities: "Decision cities" and "service cities" in outsourcing by leading Brazilian firms', *Geoforum*, **38** (4), 628–642.

Sassen, S. (1988), *The Mobility of Labor and Capital: A Study in International Investment and Capital Flow*, Cambridge: Cambridge University Press.

Sassen, S. (1991), *The Global City: New York, London, Tokyo*, Princeton, NJ: Princeton University Press.

Sassen, S. (2001), *The Global City: New York, London, Tokyo* (2nd edition), Princeton, NJ: Princeton University Press.

Sikka, P. and H. Willmott (2010), 'The dark side of transfer pricing: Its role in tax avoidance and wealth retentiveness', *Critical Perspectives on Accounting*, **21** (4), 342–356.

Taylor, P.J. (2001), 'Specification of the world city network', *Geographical Analysis*, **33** (2), 181–194.

Taylor, P.J. and B. Derudder (2016), *World City Network: A Global Urban Analysis* (2nd edition), London: Routledge.

Taylor, P.J., P. Ni, B. Derudder, M. Hoyler, J. Huang and F. Witlox (eds) (2011), *Global Urban Analysis. A Survey of Cities in Globalization*, London: Earthscan.

UNCTAD (2016): *UNCTADSTAT Foreign Direct Investment*, accessed 20 June 2016 at unctadstat.unctad.org/wds/ReportFolders/reportFolders.aspx?IF_Activ ePath=P,5.

Verhetsel, A. and S. Sel (2009), 'World maritime cities: From which cities do container shipping companies make decisions?', *Transport Policy*, **16** (5), 240–250.

Wójcik, D. (2013), 'Where governance fails: Advanced business services and the offshore world', *Progress in Human Geography*, **37** (3), 330–347.

World Bank (2016), *World Development Indicators*, accessed 20 June 2016 at databank.worldbank.org/data/reports.aspx?source=world-development-indicators.

World Shipping Council (2016), *Top 50 World Container Ports*, accessed 20 June 2016 at www.worldshipping.org/about-the-industry/global-trade/top-50-world-container-ports.

Yeung, H.W-C. (2005), 'Rethinking relational economic geography', *Transactions of the Institute of British Geographers*, **30** (1), 37–51.

Yeung, H.W-C. and N.M. Coe (2015), 'Toward a dynamic theory of global production networks', *Economic Geography*, **91** (1), 29–58.

3 Commodity traders as agents of economic globalization

Wouter Jacobs

3.1 INTRODUCTION

> Using Jacobs [1969, 1984, 2000] encourages thinking beyond contemporary globalisation, and in particular the agency of advanced producer service firms in this period. The latter can be interpreted as a current mechanism for facilitating inter-city trade; prior to globalisation there will have been other such mechanisms. Braudel (1982, 1984), for instance, for the period 1400 to 1800 mentions merchant banks, trading houses, dispersed family firms, specialist ethnic diasporas, maritime insurance and other ways of sharing geographical risks as means for facilitating trade. (Taylor, 2014, p. 391)

Despite the explicit recognition by world city scholars of the importance of merchant trade in the pre-modern formation of inter-city networks (Taylor, 2004; Taylor et al., 2010; Verbruggen, 2011), current practices of merchants, the very sophistication of trading operations in physical goods (commodities) and, indeed, the global span of control of the contemporary trading houses have gone almost entirely unnoticed. As I argued elsewhere (Jacobs, 2014) and highlighted above by Peter Taylor, there is value in looking beyond the conventional study of globalization through the lens of advanced producer services (APS) firms. Moreover, I argue here that many such 'other mechanisms' than APS, thus the trading houses, merchant banks and the like of pre-modern times, continue to play a significant and understudied role in contemporary globalization and global network formation. By empirically focusing on the contemporary trade in physical commodities, three conceptual issues in the study of world cities and world city networks come to the fore.

The first issue is the importance of specialization of actors that constitute inter-city linkages, most notably APS. Specialization is the product of unique development paths of firms, often at specific locations, in which interactions with value chain partners produce experience and trust that allow for further business development. Specialization is both a choice and an outcome that results in unique capabilities of firms within niche markets that can be global. The second issue relates to the physicality of global networks. The world economy is as much about the physical trade in commodities and merchandise as it is about the financial transactions and the amount of data circumventing the globe. This trade reconciles geographical mismatches in supply and demand. Logistics have been referred to as an APS that copes with this global demand in transportation and shipping. Yet logistics have consequently been analysed as a categorical APS in itself (O'Connor, 2010; O'Connor et al., 2016; Lüthi et al., 2010; Coe, 2014), without considering possibilities of specialization into particular trades and without reconciling the linkages that exist between logistics services providers and other industries such as finance, insurance and risk management (Jacobs et al., 2011). The third issue has become more prominent of late and relates to the lack of theoretical and empirical understanding of the role of agency in shaping inter-city network formation in the world economy (Watson and Beaverstock, 2014). This issue concerns what agents do to make or produce the 'global' or 'world city', in what we loosely define as the aggregated capacity of locations to link up with other places and markets across the globe through intra- and interfirm connections and to coordinate and govern these connections from these places.

We tackle these three conceptual issues by looking at commodity trade, an industry that has been overlooked by scholars in world city research (Jacobs, 2014). Commodity trading involves the global sourcing, transportation, processing and distribution of raw materials and natural resources that are crucial inputs in various manufacturing industries. Next to the physical trade, there is also a 'paper trade', which concerns the trade in financial derivatives (in essence, delivery contracts) that are used by commodity traders to mitigate price risks and, more controversially, by investment funds for speculation on capital markets. Commodity traders are thus specialized intermediate firms in global networks that can be considered advanced since they manage highly information-intensive transactions and coordinate complex physical supply chains (Pirrong, 2014). The largest commodity traders have a global footprint with presence on all continents, including down- and midstream physical operations and assets such as grain elevators, storage facilities, port jetties and refineries. The latter are often in places not regarded to be part of the world city network, but which can be considered as crucial points of physical exchange and information in the wider trading operation. Yet, it is the trading desks that possess the agency to link supply and demand of commodities globally and manage the various risks involved. And these trading desks are concentrated in only a few places across the world, including Geneva, Singapore and London (Jacobs, 2014).

The structure of this chapter is as follows. In the next section we revisit the literature on world city network formation by advanced producer services and discuss the three conceptual issues mentioned above. Addressing these three issues allows for a nuanced appreciation of the practices and capabilities of specialized agents, commodity traders, to transact internationally and coordinate long distance exchange from concentrated places while securing the necessary physical supplies (grains, energy, metals and minerals) that literally feed the planet and power the world economy. In the third section we revisit the work of James Vance (1970) and his eloquent thesis on 'the mercantile model of settlement'. What makes his thesis unique is that it represents one of the few studies in economic geography that has engaged theoretically with wholesale trading (as opposed to retailing) in explaining urban settlement structures, particularly in the US. Even more important is that he places particular emphasis on the role of agency that trading merchants possess in linking distant markets through the flow of information and knowledge they control and diffuse across time and space. The insights derived from Vance are still relevant today in order to understand the current practice of commodity trading firms and in explaining the evolutionary trajectories of cities and urban systems from the perspective of commodity trading. In the fourth section the agency of present day commodity trading firms will be discussed and how they manage geographically dispersed supply chains and the associated risks while connecting various places and actors across the world through their trading activities. In the fifth section we look more closely at the world's leading trading places and the tendency of agency to coordinate global exchange and transactions from concentrated places (i.e. world cities). The main hypothesis is that in order for commodity traders to act as global agents they prefer the concentrated agglomeration benefits offered by (world) cities. In doing so, traders subject various other places that facilitate the very real extraction, production and distribution of the commodities traded to the logic of the world city.

3.2   WORLD CITY NETWORKS AND ADVANCED PRODUCER SERVICES AS INTERLOCKING AGENTS

Central to the formation of world cities and the connections between them are APS. These are business-to-business services provided mainly to transnational corporations (TNCs). Since large TNCs have globalized operations in various jurisdictions, they are in the need of services that can help them run their business and overcome the problem of the 'liability of foreignness' (Goerzen et al., 2013, p. 431). These services are advanced, as they are highly knowledge intensive, often intangible and tailored to the complex needs of the globally operating client firm. The providers of these services are capable of synthesizing knowledge domains, while customizing and de-contextualizing their client-specific solutions (Strambach, 2008). Above all, APS are capable of providing these services globally; this is what makes them significant to the operations of a TNC or multinational enterprise (MNE). This in turn requires a presence in the markets where the client TNC operates and in which proximity benefits matter (Bennett et al., 2000). Many of the world's leading APS firms are therefore TNCs themselves. They have internationalized following their clients or in search of a global client portfolio and access to particular geographical markets (Sassen, 2001). Much like other TNCs, these APS have centralized certain mandates and managerial powers into corporate head offices (see, however, Jones' (2002) critique of the 'myth of "global management"' in transnational service firms). The geographical concentration of the functions of the largest APS firms constitutes the 'world city' status of particular places. The aggregated linkages of these firms, based upon their worldwide office distribution, constitute the global network connectivity of world cities and are, arguably, a relational source of power within the world economy (Alderson and Beckfield, 2004).

The type of services considered to be APS in empirical studies varies. Typically included are banks, insurance companies, law firms, accountancies/tax advisories, management consultancies and marketing firms: those included in key studies by the Globalization and World City (GaWC) research network (www.lboro.ac.uk/gawc; e.g. Taylor et al., 2011). Other studies have included logistics firms in the population of global APS (Hoyler et al., 2008; Lüthi et al., 2010) or have argued to include them as important intermediaries within global production networks (Hesse, 2013; Coe et al., 2008; Coe, 2014). This inclusion makes sense at least for those firms that actually evolved from simple transportation service providers (shipping) into third-party logistics (3PL) service provision including all kinds of internalized (advanced) services such as customs clearance, terminal handling and warehousing, planning of multi-modal hinterland distribution and the risk- and repair management (O'Connor, 2010; O'Connor et al., 2016) on behalf of the TNC client. The focus on logistics, and with it the shipment of physical or material goods, also highlights three neglected points in the existing world city network literature. One is the importance of specialization, a second the physicality of global networks, and a third concerns agency.

The specialization of advanced producer service firms has been somewhat overlooked by most conventional research on world city networks. Arguably the most globalized APS firms have, next to a wide geographical coverage, also a wide client portfolio with varying degrees of sector expertise. Indeed, key for large APS firms is that they hold both horizontal and vertical knowledge domains (Strambach, 2008) which they can customize and 'commodify' (Sassen, 2010) across geographical markets. Some can be highly globalized niche players without making it into the lists of the largest APS firms, while others remain rather localized yet have large TNCs as main clients. Sector specialization of APS is indeed recognized conceptually (Beaverstock et al., 2002), but empirically studied only marginally. APS firms as units of analysis are already characterized by their heterogeneity (e.g. banks, legal firms, insurance companies, advertising agencies, or indeed logistics services), and this is exacerbated when taking into account that they can specialize vertically into specific client sectors (e.g. maritime law, marine insurance, ship finance in the case of global shipping). This heterogeneity has an impact on the geographical constellation of the world city networks studied, as some of the leading APS firms have a strong presence in certain client sectors, with the corporate mandates and specialized workforce distributed along only a few offices relevant to this specific client sector, whereas other places might have historically been important places in certain sectors and therefore have a relatively large concentration of specialized APS firms.

The second aspect concerns the physicality of global networks. Physicality in terms of APS firms is reduced to the office space they occupy in cities or the travel and labour mobility of professionals that make up the APS firm. Hence the importance given to international airports and airport linkages as an aggregate in explaining world cities and the facilitation of business between those cities (Derudder and Witlox, 2005), or as critical infrastructure that can offer temporary proximities between geographically dispersed professionals, partners and clients to engage in business (Rychen and Zimmermann, 2008). Yet economic globalization is as much about the ease of executive (labour) mobility and of transmitting data and intelligence as it is about shipping material goods across markets. Indeed, both technological revolutions in information and communication technology (ICT) and in transportation (the ocean shipping container) have facilitated the disintegration of production and the integration of world trade since the 1980s (Feenstra, 1998; Levinson, 2006) in which logistics and supply chain management can be considered as critical spin-offs of such an industrial and economic transition. Yet the role of APS in the facilitation of global shipping and the role of shipping networks in servicing the urbanized global economy have been hardly studied by world city researchers (but see Jacobs et al., 2011). More fundamental is the functional relationship between the physical movement of goods and the governance of these commodity supply chains (Hall and Hesse, 2012; Parnreiter, 2010, 2018). As argued by Parnreiter (2010) through the example of Mexico City,

APS are involved in various trade and supply functions, backwardly and forwardly in the value chains that make up Mexico's external trade relationships, yet the agglomeration of foreign-based APS takes place near central city functions.

The third aspect relates to agency. As argued recently by Watson and Beaverstock (2014) and Derudder and Parnreiter (2014) there is a need to reconsider the concept of agency in the empirical understanding of world city formation. For Taylor (2014), it is APS firms that act as the agents, yet much of the research has since focused on hierarchies at the expense of what agents really do. As asserted by Watson and Beaverstock (2014) there is a need for the development of grounded theory on agency within world city network formation. They borrow from economic geography, most notably the works of Allen (2003) and the global production networks scholars (Dicken et al., 2001; Coe et al., 2004; Yeung, 2005), who view agency from a relational perspective (Bathelt and Glückler, 2003; Jacobs and Lagendijk, 2014). The relational approach 'allows us to avoid the two polarized frameworks in contemporary economic geography – actor networks and institutional structures' (Yeung, 2005, p. 38), and thus to 'identify the complex relational geometry comprising *local* and *non-local* actors, *tangible* and *intangible* assets, *formal* and *informal* institutional structures, and their interactive power relations' (Yeung, 2005, p. 48). Power in a relational sense refers not to 'power over' such as the command of resources, but more to 'the power to' in which such resources (including networked relationships) are employed strategically in multi-actor games or, as Dicken et al. (2001, p. 93) define: 'the *capacity to exercise* that is realized only through the process of exercising'. To illustrate this point from a trading perspective: it is not so much the number of tank terminals that a global trading company such as Vitol owns that provide it with power in the world's energy markets, rather it is to employ such assets to manage price movements and to deliver the volumes to customers at the right time for the right price. Indeed, typical for commodity traders is that they possess agency to link global markets and to transform commodities in time (through storage), space (through logistics) and form (through processing) (Pirrong, 2014).

3.3 VANCE'S MERCHANT'S WORLD AND THE AGENCY OF TRADE

In order to develop a thorough understanding of the role of commodity traders in the world city network, we revisit the work of James Vance (1970) and his eloquent thesis on the historical economic geography of wholesaling. Vance developed a 'mercantile model of settlement' using Central Place Theory (CPT) (Christaller, 1933 [1966]) as his starting point. However, this only gained wider currency in the Anglo-American geographical literature in the late 1960s. Vance criticized CPT for being essentially focused on endogenic change within a territorially 'closed system' and with no consideration of external (i.e. international trading) relationships that might exist with the outside world and of exogenous forces (e.g. transportation revolutions) that impede on such relationships. According to Vance, Christaller's model might have worked well for the towns, villages and countryside that made up Southern Germany at the time of study, but it was unfit to analyse the evolution of the urban settlement structure of North America into the nineteenth and early twentieth century. In addition, Christaller's model is confined to retail trade, which has a far more limited geographical reach, supplies fewer industries and is run by a different business model compared with wholesale trade. Other geographers of the time like James Bird (1973) and Andrew Burghart (1971) shared his criticism of CPT through their focus on the development of 'gateway cities': cities of commerce that developed out of bulk-breaking transport nodes such as seaports and that prospered because of the 'command of the connections between the tributary area and the outside world' (Burghart, 1971, p. 269). But unlike his peers Vance introduced the role of agency in making external linkages through wholesale trade:

> We may logically suppose that some group of persons, at some point in time, learns to produce goods in an abundance greater than the parochial need. The ability would father the desire to expand trade beyond the local area; but to secure that expansion it would be necessary (1) to familiarize the outside consumers with the abundance and its location, and (2) to familiarize the producer with the location of external scarcity in the good. (Vance, 1970, p. 5)

The merchant or wholesale trader thus acts as the knowledge broker in the geographical transfer of information on supply and demand and in such a way contributes to price setting or the creation of markets. It is through the flow of knowledge on supply and demand (S&D) beyond the 'parochial needs' (localized demands) that CPT is made open and subject to exogenous change. In order to capitalize on the information asymmetry between S&D, the successful merchant needed to penetrate deep into the 'tributary areas' of supply, while carefully monitoring demand and maintaining customer relationships in the imperial capital and 'central city'. No wonder that successful merchants were highly mobile and were closely aligned with seafaring communities (Glaeser, 2005; Jones, 1998). The successful merchant also had to bear all kinds of operational risks in order to ultimately fulfil the physical delivery. Therefore the merchant's entrepreneurial skills were put to the test:

> The experienced merchant has the organization and the enterprise to undertake new lines, thus following the New England dictum that true entrepreneurs should "trye all ports" and risk all freights. Thus, when innovation is under consideration, it is quite reasonable to hold that it will take place where entre-preneurial activity is most highly developed. (Vance, 1970, p. 152)

To 'trye all ports' and 'risk all freights' is indeed a dictum that runs deep into the contemporary commodity traders' routines, as we argue later when discussing optionality, whether it concerns 'fair trade' products, mainstream commodity trade or illicit commodity trades such as of narcotics: the principles remain the same. The innovations that merchants pressed for at the time were plentiful. One important innovation was the establishment of commodity exchanges (e.g. Chicago Board of Trade, New York Mercantile Exchange, Kansas Board of Trade, London Metals Exchange) that were founded at places in need of price discovery and transparency, often closely linked to the commercialized information to be obtained from the break-bulking and entrepôt functions of the gateways where physical deliveries and exports arrived and left.

Other innovations resulting from trade dealt with specialized insurance, standardization of shipping contracts, law practices and financial services. Derived from these practices came the earliest forms of financializa-tion: innovations in the form of contracts that allowed for hedging and speculations on the future supply and demand.

Vance (1970, p. 156) continues by distinguishing three inter-related vari-able exogenous factors that affect the dynamics of the wholesale industry. First, this concerns the commercial intelligence flows closely attached to the entrepôt function of a city and which will 'extend outward as far as the limits of commercial intelligence available to that city's merchants'. As a consequence, improvements in intelligence flows will tend to expand the trade areas of the larger wholesale centre at the expense of smaller ones. Second, Vance mentions technological improvements in transportation, as distinct from information communication, that may also provide 'weapons to allow the traditional trading structure to maintain itself' (Vance, 1970, p. 157). The third factor relates to the commodity product itself: 'Once supply innovation occurs, the conditions obtaining at the beginning of any trade are reintroduced. Thus, a new set of supply-intelligence flow-demand conditions is established' (Vance, 1970, p. 157). Such supply-based innovations still hold when considering the contemporary markets such as liquefied natural gas (LNG) or biofuels.

The 'mercantile model of settlement' as proposed by Vance is ultimately driven by information exchange brokered by merchants. Merchants had the agency to source supplies in 'the interior' that are in demand in the overseas markets. In return, merchants were able to gain an informational advantage on the availability of new tools and finished goods available at those markets and procure these for use back in 'the interior'. In doing so, the merchant was able to increase productivity in the intermediate trading place from which they ran their operations, allowing these places to grow and expand into their own interior and gaining 'central city' status.

The thesis of Vance is largely historical economic geography, yet it became implicitly endorsed by influential economists grouped around the Nobel Prize laureate Paul Krugman in what is now known as New Economic Geography (NEG). The essence of the NEG is that it explains the agglomeration of economic activity from increasing returns as a result of trade. Such increasing returns derive from the premise that 'manufactures production will tend to concentrate where there is a large market, but the market will be large where manufactures production is concentrated' (Krugman, 1991, p. 486). The initial concentration of manufactures is driven by transport costs, hence the concentration around transport nodes such as seaports. Based upon formalized mathematical modelling, Fujita and Mori (1996) therefore argued that many ports spurred the development of cities despite initial transportation cost advantages disappearing (e.g. a deepwater seaport or other critical infrastructures). Increasing returns to scale lock in 'self-reinforcing' mechanisms of agglomeration that in combination with transport cost advantages explain why so many 'great cities' have been borne out of ports and why this model 'fits well for the regions of the world which developed out of colonial expansion' (Fujita and Mori, 1996, p. 97).

3.4 COMMODITY TRADERS AS INTERLOCKING AGENTS IN THE GLOBAL ECONOMY

How do commodity trading firms (CTF) act as interlocking agents in a system of world cities and how do they relate to the material goods economy which is the very real extraction, distribution and production of commodities that power the world economy?

Let us start with a practical example (drawn from a CTF's in-house newsletter provided to the author) of a particular supply chain of soybeans harvested in Nebraska, USA. A local farmer has sold his seasonal harvest of soybeans to a CTF. The farmer sends the beans to a nearby grain elevator owned by the trader located along a railway track owned and operated by one of America's main freight railroad companies. The elevator can load a 110-car unit shuttle train in about ten hours. From there the soybeans start their journey to the destination market in Beijing. The 110–120 car fleets are secured by the trader through auction processes administrated by the railroad company (e.g. BNSF), which gives the trader the right to run shuttles and incur the fees to move rail cars. First stop is an export terminal, jointly owned by the trader and a farmers' collective in the port of Tacoma. The terminal is one of three export facilities the trader owns in the Pacific Northwest. This provides the trader with logistical flexibility and allows for both substitutions between, and combinations of, various related agricultural commodity products (soybeans, grains, corn). It takes about four to five days to reach the terminal from Nebraska and one day to unload the soybeans. Securing rail shuttle car concessions and making sure that the trains arrive on time at the terminal are the responsibility of the rail freight trade and logistics division Western USA of the CTF, based in Chicago.

Next, the soybeans are loaded into a voyage-chartered Panamax vessel by the Ocean Freight division of the CTF based in Geneva, Switzerland at the port of Tacoma for shipment to the port of Qingdao in China (an 18–20-day voyage). Once it arrives in the port of Qingdao, market spreads are determined for shipment from Qingdao to other ports in China where the CTF has crush plants for further processing and for final delivery to clients. The soybeans originating from Nebraska have been bought by the CTF's merchandizing team based in Shanghai. The Shanghai team bought the soybeans two months ago for further processing in the CTFs crush plants in the ports of Nantong and Dongguan and have delivery contracts with animal feed manufacturers based in Beijing capital region and other customers in Korea and Japan. The whole transaction and supply chain is coordinated from the CTFs global trading unit based in Geneva, Switzerland. The global trading unit role is to secure supplies for customers while minimizing price risk and locking in a price differential between US-sourced soybeans and Asian benchmark prices for soybeans on delivery two months later. Based upon the freight rates provided by the Chicago-based rail logistics team and by the Geneva-based ocean transportation team, which in the end are the real costs incurred by the CTF to ship the soybeans from the American interior to the Chinese market, and based upon the price differential per bushel on the markets as set on exchanges in Chicago and Dalian (China), the global trading unit in Geneva determines the offering price for the Nebraska originating soybeans for the merchandize desk of the CTF in Shanghai. To summarize: the demand invoice comes from the Shanghai team, which sends the information midday to Geneva to coordinate price movements who in turn send the intelligence to the Chicago office that buys the soybeans supplied from Nebraska on behalf of the Shanghai team in real-time.

What becomes clear from this simple example is that one particular commodity trade locks in many different places across the world through which information is shared and from which decisions are taken. Information exchange and intelligence are crucial for managing these physical networks across time zones. A key factor in the business model for the commodity trader is optionality: the value created by having choice. An example of such optionality is the choice between particular raw materials or substitutes (e.g. sugar or corn sweetener) as ingredients or as input in manufacturing processes (e.g. the production of soft drinks or biofuels). The driver for the final choice of one raw material vs. another is their relative price. Relative prices reflect the relative scarcity and hence convey important information about availability. The optimal composition of the (commodity) input is usually arrived at via least-cost formulation or linear programming. Optionality in commodity supply chains further includes ocean freight and the arbitrage between, for example, using bigger size vessels vs. parcelling the cargo into smaller size vessels, or the origin of specific commodities and the arbitrage between various origins or between reception points (e.g. ports), depending on freight economics. Many factors affecting prices, supply and demand need to be taken into account when considering optionality in trading, such as the weather, foreign currency exchange rates, strategic inventories held, vessel chartering rates, government policies (in terms of tariffs, quota and sanctions), local incidents and accidents, and so on.

In order to mitigate price risks, the commodity trader is also involved in the paper trade of financial derivatives (including forward contracting, futures, options and swaps). The trader runs a price risk since they buy the commodities at a certain time and place for a certain price and sell it to a buyer at a different time and place for a different price (preferably with a margin) with an obligation for physical delivery. The latter element is crucial to differentiate between the CTF and other participants in the financial derivative markets such as investment banks, private equity funds and institutional investors (e.g. sovereign wealth funds) that only speculate on price volatility without physical delivery obligations (Labban, 2010). Commodity prices vary over geographical space (providing arbitrage opportunities) but, indeed, can plummet suddenly due to various S&D shocks, leaving the CTF with a loss or with an excess inventory which it hopes to sell when prices recover. The forward contract is the simplest derivative and its origins date back to the Dutch trading republic of the seventeenth century whereby fishermen sold the herring for a certain price prior to catch. Forward contracting is still common today in many commodity product groups and allows CTFs to lock in price differentials across geographical space. More sophisticated are the futures contracts (specifying a certain amount of physical commodities to be delivered at some place in the future). In the futures markets, traders can take long and short positions and use these instruments to manage the price risk. In a long position, somebody expects the rise of prices whereas in a short position somebody expects a decline in prices in the future.

To illustrate the latter with a practical example, once again provided as a business case to the author by a large CTF, imagine a typhoon hitting the Philippines during the weekend, wiping out the coconut production almost entirely, including all transport infrastructure (coconut oils are used for producing oleochemicals that are in turn used for producing shampoo and that are mostly procured from the Philippines). The leading trading desk in Europe has a problem on Monday morning. This shock in supply will affect prices and the CTF has existing delivery contracts with buyers (e.g. Unilever or Palmolive) three months into the future. The trading desk will first monitor existing inventories of coconut oils, while calling customers across the globe to ask whether they will accept substitutes in the form of palmkernel oils from Malaysia not affected by the typhoon. The price of coconut oil will initially rise due to shortage of supplies vis-à-vis its substitute palmkernel oil (referred to as market spread). The trading strategy on Monday morning is then 'to go long' on palmkernel oils (its price is likely to rise as many other buyers will move into this market due to the shortage of coconut oils), while immediately 'going short' on positions of coconut oils (while price initially rises, it will drop as demand moves elsewhere). Losses in existing delivery contracts due to an instant rise of coconut oil prices are in such a way mitigated (for an elaboration of this case, see Jacobs and Horster, forthcoming).

In addition to price, CTFs need to mitigate other risks more directly linked to physical operations of the supply chain. Cargo can get lost or damaged in traffic or in storage. Cargo can be delivered too late, counter parties can fail to oblige financial or other contractual agreements. If that is the case it needs proper specialized legal support in the respective jurisdiction. Many of these risks are managed by specialized insurance products offered at the Lloyd's market in London and via contracts with preferred legal services suppliers. Finally, traders need banks to finance their transactions. Specialized banks are involved by issuing letters of credit to the CTFs in support of the transaction, and whereby the value of the commodities serve as collateral, known as structured finance, and in which the bank takes temporary ownership until delivery (often in ports) as specified in the bills of lading. For large transactions many banks are involved, who are invited by the lead arranger of the transaction. There are only a handful of globalized specialists that frequently act as lead arranger, such as BNP Paribas and Société Générale from France, Standard Chartered from the UK and the Dutch banks ING Bank, ABN AMRO Bank and to lesser extent Rabobank. The trade finance teams of these banks are located often in close proximity to the trading desks of the CTFs, such as in Geneva and Singapore. In addition, investment banks (e.g. Goldman Sachs, JPMorgan Chase, Morgan Stanley) are involved in the financial derivatives markets in which they hedge prices for their clients (often large industrials or companies with large exposure to commodity price risks such as airline companies) and for speculation. Some banks have also controversially been involved in so-called 'proprietary trading' in the past, in which they held physical stocks. Such practices are now heavily discouraged by financial regulators in the US and EU and many banks have sold off their proprietary trading teams. More common these days are large commodity traders directly involved in trade financial structures whereby supply guarantees for fixed prices are transacted for cash to extraction companies to invest in productivity.

Thus, today, like in Vance's historical analysis, it is traders that possess agency, a dynamic capability to couple local supplies with distant demands through finance, risk management and logistics in order to overcome the barriers of time and space, manage various disruptions in the supply chain and benefit from information asymmetry fundamental to international trade.

3.5   THE WORLD'S TRADING PLACES

Commodity traders thus play a crucial role in directing worldwide physical flows of raw materials, while managing risks and transactions. While the physical flows, and with them possession and exchange, occur across a vast and indeed global geographical space and along various connecting points in a supply chain, the coordination of trade as transaction remains concentrated in only a few trading places (Jacobs, 2014). Defining a trading place is not so much about the volumes that move through ports (e.g. Rotterdam) or pipeline junctions (e.g. Cushing in Oklahoma for West Texas Intermediate oil or Henry Hub in Texas for US gas), nor is it even about the trades cleared through a commodity exchange (e.g. Chicago Mercantile Exchange or the InterContinental Exchange), but more about the value of the transactions that are kept in the books of the individual commodity trader. In other words, it is the location of the trading desk in relation to its operations and assets that is crucial for understanding the 'command and control' points in the commodity trading system. Command and control is a relational position in this context. CTFs do not 'command and control' prices, nor their customers, suppliers or regulators. Rather, they continuously anticipate price volatilities, risks and behaviour (buying and call-off decisions of customers). Within the CTF, the trading desk does have the mandate to buy, sell and hold up stocks, leading the entire global or regionalized operation. The trading desk carefully coordinates with the origination (sourcing) and (merchandize) sales desks (destination), the logistics team and the in-house procurement teams (in the case of a firm supplying its own processing facilities) on a peer-to-peer basis at locations in the world's major time zones.

Data regarding the trading books and the value of transactions are very scarce and hard to come by because of confidentiality. The secret of the trade is in the trade. Nonetheless, it is no secret that the majority of global trades in commodities are coordinated from only a few major hubs (Figure 3.1) that cover the world's macro-regions (Asia, EMEA, the Americas). The two leading trading places in Asia are the two city-states Singapore and Hong Kong, while Tokyo remains the main hub of the

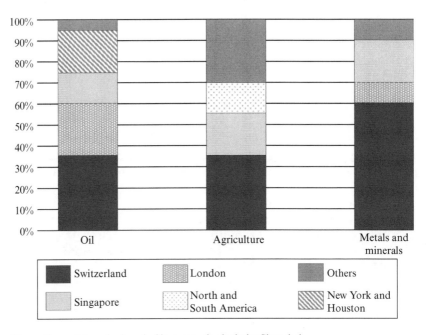

Note: For metals and minerals, Singapore also includes Shanghai.

Source: Swiss Academies of Arts and Sciences (2016).

Figure 3.1   Market share of main commodities hubs

major Japanese trading conglomerates (*sogo shosha* such as Marubeni or Mitsui) with Shanghai increasingly challenging Asia's status quo. In Europe (and the Middle East and Africa) the leading hubs are the Greater Geneva Lake region and London, followed by 'niche players' such as Hamburg (coffee), Rotterdam (grains), Amsterdam (cocoa) and Paris (sugar). Dubai in the United Arab Emirates (UAE) is aggressively positioning itself as the leading hub for the Middle East, Africa and the Indian Subcontinent. In the Americas, New York and Chicago remain the main hubs, with, however, a major role in the energy markets for Houston, Texas. Sourcing the commodities from 'originations' in commodity-rich South America is largely coordinated from its leading 'world city' São Paulo (Jacobs and van Bergen, 2014; KPMG, 2015; Swiss Academies of Arts and Sciences, 2016).

So despite the fact that traders are more or less footloose – they can execute the transaction and book the trade from more or less any place – the business still remains highly concentrated in only a few major hubs across the world. Particularly striking is the position of Switzerland, which is responsible for 35 per cent of the global trade in crude oil, 35 per cent in agricultural commodities and over 60 per cent in metals and minerals (Swiss Academies of Arts and Sciences, 2016). Within Switzerland, Geneva is the main trading place but other cantons such as tiny Zug (home to for example Glencore Xstrata) and Lugano also have their fair share. According to the Swiss Trading and Shipping Association (STSA), the trading industry in the Greater Geneva region is home to about 500 firms generating 10 000 jobs in 2014 (STSA, 2016). This leading position is remarkable since Geneva (and Switzerland) is not endowed with any significant natural resources, it is landlocked with no port facilities to historically develop entrepôt functions the way Amsterdam or London did, it is not home to a commodity exchange and, finally, Switzerland is a rather small home market (see also Jacobs, 2014).

3.6   CONCLUSION: TRADING PLACES AS WORLD CITIES?

Trade is the connection of supply and demand in time and space. Trade is about connecting markets and markets are driven by the productive economies of cities. Merchants and wholesalers have been what Vance (1970) called 'pioneers in space', connecting markets and hinterlands through information at least since the early days of modern day capitalist America and, as argued by Verbruggen (2011), way before that in Europe. It was also international trade that spurred the development of earlier forms of APS such as marine insurance, contracting, stock and commodity exchanges and merchant banking (trade finance), and, indeed, the foundation of the modern corporation (see also Hall, 1966; Taylor, 2004). Nonetheless, the contemporary commodity trading industry has been overlooked conceptually and empirically by scholars in world city research.

In this chapter I have argued that by empirically looking at commodity traders we can contribute to debates on world cities by emphasizing three important conceptual concerns. First, I have demonstrated that contemporary commodity traders possess agency to interlock various places and firms, including APS, across the globe. Second, CTFs to a large degree take responsibility for the physical supply of commodities to customers worldwide, for which they accept and manage the various risks in the ultimate physical delivery. Third, commodity traders are specialized global firms, often trading only a few commodities that have been able to foster globalization through their trades while continuously adapting to the factors that are shaping it.

The scope of the CTF's operation is global and often reaches deep into the lands of origination, but the governance or coordination of the trade transaction is run by the trading desks that are currently highly concentrated in only a few places in the world. Of these 'trading places', most have a physical trading history as 'gateway' or 'entrepôt' such as London, New York, Singapore, Hong Kong or Shanghai, all of which are cities that are considered 'world cities' in the conventional literature. So the world's leading trading places indeed mirror 'world cities'. Yet, the chapter twists the argument around. As shown by the thesis of Vance (1970) and by economists such as Paul Krugman (1991), it had largely been places of trade and physical exchange that possessed an initial advantage to develop into centres of commerce, innovation and growth, exactly because of the persistency of transaction costs. Such a perspective suggests that contemporary world cities have uniquely evolved from the practices and the physicality of their origins as 'trading places'.

REFERENCES

Alderson, A.S. and J. Beckfield (2004), 'Power and position in the world city system', *American Journal of Sociology*, **109** (4), 811–851.
Allen, J. (2003), *Lost Geographies of Power*, Oxford: Blackwell Publishing.
Bathelt, H. and J. Glückler (2003), 'Toward a relational economic geography', *Journal of Economic Geography*, **3** (2): 117–144.
Beaverstock, J.V., M.A. Doel, P.J. Hubbard and P.J. Taylor (2002), 'Attending to the world: Competition, cooperation and connectivity in the world city network', *Global Networks*, **2** (2), 111–132.

Bennett, R.J., W.A. Bratton and P.J.A. Robson (2000), 'Business advice: The influence of distance', *Regional Studies*, **34** (9), 813–828.

Bird, J.H. (1973), 'Of central places, cities and seaports', *Geography*, **58** (2), 105–118.

Braudel, F. (1982), *The Wheels of Commerce*, London: Collins.

Braudel, F. (1984), *The Perspective of the World*, London: Collins.

Burghart, A.F. (1971), 'A hypothesis about gateway cities', *Annals of the Association of American Geographers*, **61** (2), 269–285.

Christaller, W. (1933 [1966]), *Central Places in Southern Germany*, trans. C.W. Baskin (1966), Englewood Cliffs, NJ: Prentice Hall.

Coe, N.M. (2014), 'Missing links: Logistics, governance and upgrading in a shifting global economy', *Review of International Political Economy*, **21** (1), 224–256.

Coe, N.M., P. Dicken and M. Hess (2008), 'Global production networks: Realizing the potential', *Journal of Economic Geography*, **8** (3), 271–295.

Coe, N.M., M. Hess, H.W-C. Yeung, P. Dicken and J. Henderson (2004), '"Globalizing" regional development: A global production networks perspective', *Transactions of the Institute of British Geographers*, **29** (4), 468–484.

Derudder, B. and C. Parnreiter (2014), 'The interlocking network model for studying urban networks: Outline, potential, critiques, and ways forward', *Tijdschrift voor Economische en Sociale Geografie*, **105** (4), 373–386.

Derudder, B. and F. Witlox (2005), 'An appraisal of the use of airline data in assessing the world city network: A research note on data', *Urban Studies*, **42** (13), 2371–2388.

Dicken, P., P.F. Kelly, K. Olds and H.W-C. Yeung (2001), 'Chains and networks, territories and scales: Towards a relational framework for analysing the global economy', *Global Networks*, **1** (2), 89–112.

Feenstra, R.C. (1998), 'Integration of trade and disintegration of production in the global economy', *Journal of Economic Perspectives*, **12** (4), 31–50.

Fujita, M. and T. Mori (1996), 'The role of ports in the making of major cities: Self-agglomeration and hub-effect', *Journal of Development Economics*, **49** (1), 93–120.

Glaeser, E.L. (2005), 'Reinventing Boston: 1630–2003', *Journal of Economic Geography*, **5** (2), 119–153.

Goerzen, A., C.G. Asmussen and B.B. Nielsen (2013), 'Global cities and multinational enterprise location strategy', *Journal of International Business Studies*, **44** (5), 427–450.

Hall, P. (1966), *The World Cities*, London: Weidenfeld and Nicolson.

Hall, P.V. and M. Hesse (eds) (2012), *Cities, Regions and Flows*, London: Routledge.

Hesse, M. (2013), 'Cities and flows: Re-asserting a relationship as fundamental as it is delicate', *Journal of Transport Geography*, **29**, 33–42.

Hoyler, M., T. Freytag and C. Mager (2008), 'Connecting Rhine-Main: The production of multi-scalar polycentricities through knowledge-intensive business services', *Regional Studies*, **42** (8), 1095–1111.

Jacobs, J. (1969), *The Economy of Cities*, New York: Vintage.

Jacobs, J. (1984), *Cities and the Wealth of Nations*, New York: Vintage.

Jacobs, J. (2000), *The Nature of Economies*, New York: Vintage.

Jacobs, W. (2014), 'Rotterdam and Amsterdam as trading places? In search of the economic-geographical nexus between commodity chains and world cities', *Tijdschrift voor Economische en Sociale Geografie*, **105** (4), 483–491.

Jacobs, W. and R. Horster (forthcoming), 'Commodity supply   networks as complex adaptive systems: How commodity and freight markets respond to a supply shock in coconut oils', in G. Wilmsmeier and J. Monios (eds), *Geographies of Maritime Transport: Transition from Transport to Mobilities*, Cheltenham, UK and Northampton, MA, USA: Edward Elgar Publishing.

Jacobs, W. and A. Lagendijk (2014), 'Strategic coupling as *capacity*: How seaports connect to global flows of containerized transport', *Global Networks*, **14** (1), 44–62.

Jacobs, W. and T. van Bergen (2014), 'Understanding the economic geography of commodity trade', *Port Technology International*, **61**, 31–33.

Jacobs, W., H. Koster and P. Hall (2011), 'The location and global network structure of maritime advanced producer services', *Urban Studies*, **48** (13), 2749–2769.

Jones, A. (2002), 'The "global city" misconceived: The myth of "global management" in transnational service firms', *Geoforum*, **33** (3), 335–350.

Jones, G. (1998), 'Multinational trading companies in history and theory', in G. Jones (ed.), *The Multinational Traders*, London: Routledge, pp. 1–21.

KPMG (2015), *Commodities Trading: Transforming with Agility*, Switzerland: KPMG Holding AG/SA.

Krugman, P. (1991), 'Increasing returns and economic geography', *Journal of Political Economy*, **99** (3), 483–499.

Labban, M. (2010), 'Oil in parallax: Scarcity, markets, and the financialization of accumulation', *Geoforum*, **41** (4), 541–552.

Levinson, M. (2006), *The Box. How the Shipping Container Made the World Smaller and the World Economy Bigger*, Princeton, NJ: Princeton University Press.

Lüthi, S., A. Thierstein and V. Goebel (2010), 'Intra-firm and extra-firm linkages in the knowledge economy: The case of the emerging mega-city region of Munich', *Global Networks*, **10** (1), 114–137.

O'Connor, K. (2010), 'Global city regions and the location of logistics activity', *Journal of Transport Geography*, **18** (3), 354–362.

O'Connor, K., B. Derudder and F. Witlox (2016), 'Logistics services: Global functions and global cities', *Growth and Change*, **47** (4), 481–496.

Parnreiter, C. (2010), 'Global cities in global commodity chains: Exploring the role of Mexico City in the geography of global economic governance', *Global Networks*, **10** (1), 35–53.

Parnreiter, C. (2018), 'Producer service firms as global city makers: The cases of Mexico City and Hamburg', in M. Hoyler, C. Parnreiter and A. Watson (eds), *Global City Makers: Economic Actors and Practices in the World City Network*, Cheltenham, UK and Northampton, MA, USA: Edward Elgar Publishing, pp. 23–40.

Pirrong, C. (2014), *The Economics of Commodity Trading Firms*, Houston, TX: Bauer College of Business, University of Houston.

Rychen, F. and J.-B. Zimmermann (2008), 'Clusters in the global knowledge-based economy: Knowledge gatekeepers and temporary proximity', *Regional Studies*, **42** (6), 767–776.

Sassen, S. (2001), *The Global City: New York, London, Tokyo* (2nd edition), Princeton, NJ: Princeton University Press.

Sassen, S. (2010), 'Global inter-city networks and commodity chains: Any intersections?' *Global Networks*, **10** (1), 150–163.

Strambach, S. (2008), 'Knowledge-Intensive Business Services (KIBS) as drivers of multilevel knowledge dynamics', *International Journal of Services Technology and Management*, **10** (2–4), 152–174.

STSA (2016), *Swiss Trading and Shipping Association*, accessed 3 August 2016 at https://stsa.swiss/.

Swiss Academies of Arts and Sciences (2016), 'Switzerland and the commodities trade: Taking stock and looking ahead', *Swiss Academies Factsheets*, **11** (1), accessed 11 May 2018 at https://naturalsciences.ch/service/publications/58677-switzerland-and-the-commodities-trade---taking-stock-and-looking-ahead.

Taylor, P.J. (2004), *World City Network: A Global Urban Analysis*, London: Routledge.

Taylor, P.J. (2014), 'A research odyssey: From interlocking network model to extraordinary cities', *Tijdschrift voor Economische en Sociale Geografie*, **105** (4), 387–397.

Taylor, P.J., M. Hoyler and R. Verbruggen (2010), 'External urban relational process: Introducing central flow theory to complement central place theory', *Urban Studies*, **47** (13), 2803–2818.

Taylor, P.J., P. Ni, B. Derudder, M. Hoyler, J. Huang and F. Witlox (eds) (2011), *Global Urban Analysis: A Survey of Cities in Globalization*, London: Earthscan.

Vance, J.E. (1970), *The Merchant's World: The Geography of Wholesaling*, Englewood Cliffs, NJ: Prentice-Hall.

Verbruggen, R. (2011), *World Cities Before Globalisation: The European City Network A.D. 1300–1600*, PhD thesis, Loughborough University.

Watson, A. and J.V. Beaverstock (2014), 'World city network research at a theoretical impasse: On the need to re-establish qualitative approaches to understanding agency in world city networks', *Tijdschrift voor Economische en Sociale Geografie*, **105** (4), 412–426.

Yeung, H.W-C. (2005), 'Rethinking relational economic geography', *Transactions of the Institute of British Geographers*, **30** (1), 37–51.

4 Real estate and global capital networks: drilling into the City of London

Colin Lizieri and Daniel Mekic

4.1 INTRODUCTION

There is a growing awareness in urban social science of the importance of commercial real estate as a medium by which major cities are embedded within global capital networks (Guironnet and Halbert, 2014; Halbert et al., 2014a, 2014b) and a 'rediscovery' of real estate as a topic for critical urban analysis (Christophers, 2010; Dörry and Handke, 2012; Gotham, 2006; Guironnet and Halbert, 2014). In particular, city centre transformations, driven by office developers and investors and focused on financial and business services firms, serve to tie cities into international employment cycles while the capital sunk into the real estate locks those cities into global capital markets through investment ownership and the finance and funding of the built environment (Lizieri, 2009). This trend is most pronounced in developed world cities whose focus is on financial services – international financial centres – or who aspire to create a financial sector.

In this chapter, we examine the changing patterns of office ownership in the City of London: the financial heart of an archetypical global city. We show that real estate investors play a critical role in creating the functional form of the city and its dynamic operation. Further, the nature and character of those investors has changed over time. Not only has there been a significant shift from domestic to international owners; the type of investor has also changed away from traditional landlords and institutional investors to a more varied pattern of ownership. As the type of investor changes, so too does the motivation for holding real estate, with potentially profound impacts on urban development and city planning – a critical fact that has tended to be ignored in the urban social science literature. We document these changes and consider their implications for the City and our wider understanding of global urban processes.

London's role as the pre-eminent international financial centre in Europe has created a depth and breadth of markets that underpins demand for office space in the City and its surrounding sub-markets. Within London, the City's main competition comes from lower cost business centres in Canary Wharf and South Bank, as well as the West End.[1] The City of London forms the largest complex of office space in Europe, with the Corporation of London estimating the total floorspace in the City at some 8.6 million square metres as at March 2014 (City of London, 2014). The building of office space and the investment in commercial real estate, as well as the functional specialization, has long historical antecedents (Devaney, 2010; Scott, 1996).

Office real estate within global cities provides the physical infrastructure that allows financial and business services actors to operate international service networks worldwide, while at the same time acting as an important investment vehicle. Global cities with the highest concentration of office investment are found to be most exposed to risk associated with international financial markets (Lizieri and Pain, 2014). With such an evident link, the global financial instability that began in 2007 led to a resurgence of interest in financial crises, systemic risk and contagion effects from real estate (Aalbers, 2009; Ashton, 2009; McDowell, 2011); for some, commercial property was at the heart of explanations of the origins of the crisis (BoE, 2013). Systemic risk arises through the process of real estate investment within and across such cities due to the locking together of occupational markets (functionally specialized in financial services activities), investment markets (through acquisition of offices), supply markets (both through demand drivers and the supply of finance for development), and real estate finance (through property as collateral for lending) – see Lizieri (2009) for a more detailed discussion.

While urban research has identified these tendencies, the nuances of market processes and the role of specific actors are often lost in portmanteau categorizations such as 'international financial capital', 'finance capital investors' (Attuyer et al., 2012), 'property developers' and 'now dominant financial clientele' (Guironnet and Halbert, 2014). In practice, there is considerable diversity in the nature of office investors, and that diversity can lead to substantial differences both in their motivations for building international real estate portfolios and in the potential impacts of that investment for the cities concerned. We examine this diversity in the context of the City of London's office market. The empirical content of this chapter is based on the fifth update of a proprietary database that tracks the office ownership in the City of London from 1972.

The database documents the change in ownership in the City office market over the 1980s and 1990s in response to financial deregulation,

Global city makers

propelled by the 'Big Bang' – the financial deregulation that was part of the macro-economic policy shifts in the Atlantic neo-liberal era (Baum and Lizieri, 1998; Lizieri et al., 2001). That deregulation helped establish the City as a global financial centre with foreign banks establishing offices and buying domestic firms. The database shows that it took over a decade for foreign ownership to increase sharply: real estate was left behind in the first round of globalization. Since then, the updates of the dataset show an increasing share of foreign ownership, even in the midst of the global financial crisis (Lizieri et al., 2011).

Investment in the London office markets is increasingly international in nature. CBRE estimates suggest that in the ten years from 2005 to 2014, 63 per cent of office acquisitions in central London and 68 per cent of acquisitions in the City of London were by non-UK investors. This is part of a wider globalization of office investment; starting mainly in the late 1980s, and gaining pace in the first decade of the twenty-first century. Real Capital Analytics data for top 1000 office deals in each year from 2007 to 2014 show that 30 per cent of transactions and 35 per cent of the value of those transactions were cross-border. That investment is strongly concentrated, with just 20 cities accounting for over 67 per cent of those deals by value. London, with $107 billion of office transactions, was clearly the major target market over that period, ahead of New York, Paris and Tokyo. Major global investors play a key role in this process (the top ten ranked individual investment funds were involved in $151 billion of trans-actions, 12 per cent of the total) as do international chains of brokers and agents (the top ten brokerage firms were involved in some 57 per cent of sales; the headquarters of those firms are predominantly in major global cities).

We proceed as follows: the next section will provide a discussion of the financialization of the urban space, which highlights some of the chal-lenges for the urban environment to anchor mobile capital. This is followed by a focused review of the influx of investment to the City of London, touching upon the many hypotheses that explain the disproportionate interest, given apparently poor investment performance. Following this, key investors and their possible style strategies are summarized. This is followed by two sections reviewing the methodology and results from the proprietary *Who Owns the City* [of London] database. Here the changes in the ownership are analysed, in terms of both nationality and type of owner, to highlight the globalization of ownership and trends in the type of owner, using supporting third-party data that show investment and occupier trends. The chapter intends to highlight the many nuances in the investment trends that show waves of interest that have built up the non-domestic ownership of London and the changes in the type of investors, driven by domestic policy and global trends in deregulation and economic development.

4.2   INVESTORS AND THE FINANCIALIZATION OF URBAN SPACE

With the trend of globalization, neo-liberalism and financialization, economic transactions within and between countries have dramatically risen (Baker et al., 1998, Chapter 1), driving transnational investment across economic sectors. Owing to this trend, and often relating to specific case studies, the role of finance at the urban scale has attracted much attention (Coq-Huelva, 2013; Corpataux and Crevoisier, 2005; Corpataux et al., 2009; Fields, 2015; Halbert et al., 2014a; Ó Riain, 2012; Weber, 2010). Many countries have adopted finance-friendly policies, such as reducing capital controls and the political oversight of central banks (Polillo and Guillén, 2005), while broadening the scope of allowed investments for historically domestic actors. Overall, this has spurred on a structural shift that has supported financialization, defined as 'the increasing role of financial motives, financial markets, financial actors and financial institutions in the operation of the domestic and international economies' (Epstein, 2005, p. 3). Much of the literature has focused on new urban projects and the role of private finance; however, capital is also directed towards existing property – the investment rationale based on an assumption of future capital appreciation of that existing stock.

Financialization is a trend supported by state actors and international policy to create markets for investment in real estate, which is a philosophy increasingly adopted by policy makers in the post-World War II era. In the USA, the Federal Government implemented policies to increase liquidity in real estate by creating new forms of property and tax incentives to invest in real estate (Weber, 2002). The securitization of mortgages connected real-estate credit markets to the nation's general capital markets and provided an effective end to geographical segmentation (Schill, 1999). From the 1960s, the USA led the way to establishing a new type of tax efficient investment vehicle for real estate (McWilliam, 2015), real estate investment trusts (REITs), which, in their more liberalized, post-1980s format, have been replicated in many countries in varying forms.

In the new financialized paradigm, development and/or construction firms are often interlocutors between sources of finance and local actors:

> they are capable of evaluating and translating the multiple dimensions of a project and certain sustainability challenges into financial terms, in a way that permits the anchoring of capital in the city. In parallel, the issue of sustainability

depends greatly on the capacity of the local actors to negotiate with the promoters of urban projects. (Theurillat and Crevoisier, 2014, p. 501)

Developers and construction companies need to balance the demands
of local actors (e.g. local authorities) and those of funders (e.g. pension
funds) to permit the 'anchoring of capital'. Such roles of agents may take
different forms depending on locality (Gerber et al., 2011; Halbert and
Rouanet, 2014; Lizieri et al., 2000). This suggests a level of disengagement
of funders from the development process, as well as potentially from the
active management of assets. This observation is indicative of the capabilities and motivations of capital to influence the urban landscape, as agents
that negotiate with local actors have an important mediating role.

The motivations of capital are potentially an important component
in the financialization of the urban environment, as it determines how
the capital may impact its formation. The asset needs to be attractive to
financial investors (Theurillat and Crevoisier, 2014). However, the dimension of *type* of investor has been largely neglected in the financialization
literature, where there has been a tendency to treat all financial players as
if they are homogenous. It is important, therefore to note that investors
have different goals, as well as having funds or sources of equity capital
with divergent investment objectives. Some investor types (such as pension
funds) are risk-averse, seeking long-term cash returns; others (such as
ultra-high net worth investors) may be seeking safe havens and capital
preservation; still others (private equity real estate funds for example) are
motivated by short-run capital gains. Furthermore, the ownership of the
City is dynamic with fluctuations in the ownership proportions of different
investor groups (Lizieri et al., 2011). Despite literature on different time
periods (Corpataux and Crevoisier, 2005; Weber, 2010), the dynamics of
ownership have not been addressed. There is insufficient recognition that
the financial actors in the urban landscape are changing. The *Who Owns
the City* database provides a unique long term view on the ownership of
the Square Mile, mapping the ownership of office space from 1972 to 2014.

4.3   THE DOMINANCE OF LONDON FOR INVESTMENT

By giving some economic players privileged access to capital and to money
creation, the development of the financial markets brings with it dualization:
on one side, the characteristic organizations of the *global city* (large companies,
financial institutions, major banks, financial services, etc); on the other side,
industrial systems made up of SMEs [small and medium-sized enterprises],
regional and local banks, and tourist regions – all with only indirect access to

those financial channels, but all with heavy needs for long-term investment. (Corpataux and Crevoisier 2005, p. 332)

The ability to attract mobile capital and the negotiating power of global financial centres has been discussed by a number of scholars (Corpataux and Crevoisier, 2005; Halbert et al., 2014a; Theurillat and Crevoisier, 2014). This has led to a supposition of dualization between global cities and regional centres, where the global cities are advantaged in their ability to attract capital. This, it is suggested, has led to a disparity where relatively less capital flows to regional centres, where investment is often needed, in comparison to global cities.

With post-crisis investor emphasis on perceived high quality, low risk assets such as gold[2] or triple-A Government bonds, the focus of investors on prime real estate and major urban markets could be seen as a flight to safety. However, commonly accepted risk measures, such as Sharpe ratios, do not support the idea that large city office markets are inherently safer. Empirical evidence suggests that the City of London provides poor risk-adjusted returns when compared to other European cities and to UK regional markets. On the other hand, in a recent Investment Property Forum (IPF)-sponsored report, different valuation methodologies implied that the City was under-valued (Burston and Burrell, 2015) for investors with longer intended hold periods, despite historically low yields. The relatively higher valuation for longer-term investors stems from lower annualized transaction costs and risk/liquidity premiums – emphasizing that benefits will vary across actors in real estate investment space. Commercial property markets exhibit both rational and path dependent decision making (Fuchs and Scharmanski, 2009). Thus, the high concentration of investment in major centres reflects behavioural and social biases, alongside investor preferences for liquidity, economies of scale and presence of assets that define their benchmark (i.e. constituents of indices or proxies). Motivations vary by type of investor: however, the City of London, by virtue of its size and scale of its commercial real estate markets, has been able to meet the objectives of a wide range of investors. Nonetheless, the changing nature of investors as actors transforms the relationship between real estate and risk in the urban economy.

The city-making process associated with institutional and property investors and their advisors in commercial office markets is a social process. This is associated with long-term regional variations in the spatial relationship between property investment and the pattern of economic activity in the UK (Henneberry and Mouzakis, 2014). Henneberry and Mouzakis see evidence of 'mis-pricing', or 'pricing inaccuracies' in UK commercial real estate on account of a supposed 'bias' of actor networks

toward the London market. This bias in property investment decisions is
a supposed outcome of 'familiarity' on the part of not only investors but
also their professional investment advisors. Investments are decided by
what is, according to Henneberry and Mouzakis (2014, p. 535), a 'relatively
small, long-established, dominant network of portfolio managers and
professional advisers and intermediaries based in London'. Familiarity is
one explanation for the fact that investor and broker decisions continue to
favour global city markets that are observed as likely to offer returns 'that
are low relative to risk' (Lizieri, 2009, p. 180) apparently uninfluenced by
studies pointing to market price imperfections.

Lizieri and Pain (2014) suggest that the flight of global investors to the
largest markets with higher unit prices and greater transaction volume at
the expense of other cities represented a 'flight to liquidity' (saleability)
even though, as Henneberry and Mouzakis (2014) note, liquidity as
measured by transactions' rates is higher in 'peripheral' than in 'core' office
property markets (see also Lizieri and Bond, 2004). Liquidity may have
been confused with a flight to quality, borrowing ideas from bond market
literature (Beber et al., 2009; Longstaff, 2002). Liquidity also implies ability to place capital quickly without moving the market price: for the largest
global investors such as sovereign wealth funds, this may only be feasible in
major global cities where very large capital sums can be invested in single
'trophy' assets, again emphasizing the importance of type of investor.

As noted in the various *Who Owns the City* reports, non-domestic investors
play a significant role in owning central London office space. Diversification,
following Markowitz's portfolio theory, is a convenient argument for holding
non-domestic real estate. Investing in foreign real estate has been found to offer
more diversification benefits than foreign equities. Foreign real estate was
found to have a lower correlation with US stocks than foreign stocks (Conover
et al., 2002). Nonetheless, the role of currency movements and hedging
exchange rate risk remains problematic (Sirmans and Worzala, 2003), without
a clear path for resolution. However, while national indices of commercial real
estate may exhibit low correlation, the practical investment strategies followed
by investors may fail to deliver that diversification, if the assets acquired are
heavily concentrated in prime offices and global cities driven by common
economic drivers such that financial shocks may create downside risk across
the whole portfolio (Lizieri, 2009; Lizieri and Pain, 2014).

4.4   INVESTORS IN THE URBAN ENVIRONMENT

In broad terms, the anchoring of mobile financial capital can take place
in the form of equity or debt, which the investors or promoters determine

as the funding sources for their developments or acquisitions. They may use consortiums and special purpose vehicles to acquire and manage the assets. In the *Who Owns the City* database, the emphasis is on the beneficial owner, as explained further below. Thus, investors are assumed to have a significant interest in how their building is owned and maintained in the urban environment of the City (their propensity to develop, type of tenant, etc.). In addition, they have an indirect effect on other actors as buyers of commercial offices, as such actors (e.g. promoters of urban projects) will seek to design the urban environment in a manner that attracts funding and finance.

Central to our concerns in this chapter, it should not be assumed that all investors have the same characteristics, motivations or attitudes to risk. For example, investment activity in real estate is often classified into three broad investment styles, reflecting risk and return exposure: core, value-added and opportunistic (NCREIF and The Townsend Group, 2009). Grade A or prime buildings with AAA tenants, such as offices in the City, are typically considered as the mainstay of core investment activity (Prescott, 2015). While funds and owner are not classified by investment style in the database, it is important to keep in mind this range of styles active in the market since attitudes to risk and return will determine decision-making with respect to the real estate assets held.

In recent times, sovereign wealth funds have attracted publicity, owing to their link to national interests and evident interest in real estate (Bernstein et al., 2013; Chambers et al., 2012; Mason et al., 2015). They are typically categorized as stabilization funds, savings funds, pension reserve funds, or reserve investment corporations (Hammer et al., 2008). Many of these funds are either savings funds for future generations or fiscal stabilization funds, and only those funds with long-term investment horizons would be expected to invest in real estate (Kunzel et al., 2011).

Domestic public bodies, livery companies and charities were historically a significant owner of City of London office space. In addition, the Corporation of London still retains many of its freehold interests, ostensibly for planning purposes. Charities may own properties as owner-occupiers or as investments to fund their work – these tending to be characterized as long-term buy-and-hold investors. The historic livery companies have mainly retained freeholds to properties, while disposing of the long-term leasehold interests to extract value.[3]

Unlike many sovereign wealth funds, pension funds generally have defined and immediate liabilities (Baum and Hartzell, 2012, p. 6). Pension funds, along with insurance companies and wealth managers, are aggregators of retail capital. Insurance companies often also manage funds for pension funds. Real estate in the portfolio may be used as a hedge against inflation, as there is evidence to suggest that real estate returns are correlated with expected inflation. In particular, rent reviews help ensure that income increases along with inflation, providing a link to the liabilities of pension funds.[4] Sovereign wealth funds, pension funds and insurance companies are therefore expected to be long-term investors in real estate. They may refurbish and optimize their investments, with the use of developers and agents that may provide missing expertise. Even within the pension fund sector, a distinction needs to be drawn between defined benefit and defined contribution schemes (with the former more concerned with liabilities matching than the latter) and between mature and immature funds (with the latter being more growth-oriented), affecting their portfolio allocation decisions, in terms of exposure to real estate and to different forms of real estate.

Private equity real estate funds and property companies are expected to be more active managers of properties (Prescott, 2015) since they must deliver short-run performance from their real estate activities. Such active managing and development has been a route for many investors to improve on the low yields available in the City; however, these naturally increase risk through that development activity and through use of higher leverage. Fund managers and promoters offer different forms of exposure, risk and expected returns to investors which affects their policies towards their real estate holdings. For example, a highly geared, finite life closed end real estate fund has to focus on short-run growth in capital value in order to redeem the debt and return capital to its investors. This necessarily affects the type of asset sought and the management policies pursued, resulting in behaviour that is likely to differ from that of a long-term investor such as an endowment or sovereign wealth fund, which can adopt a more passive approach.

While acquisition of city centre office buildings has predominantly been a professional investment activity, there is evidence of a growth of commercial real estate investment among high net worth individuals. For individuals, the main investment policy decision is the degree of risk that they wish to take in their portfolio (Black, 1976), suggesting variation within this group of investors.[5] Variation is likely to exist in all investor groups, owing to differing objectives and implementation strategies. Investors are categorized to show changes in ownership structure, so that inferences can be drawn about implications for the urban space.

4.5   THE *WHO OWNS THE CITY* DATABASE

The pivotal data for our analysis is the sample database of City of London offices used in the previous *Who Owns the City* reports.[6] The database contains information on 126 core buildings (representing currently 14 per cent of the City's office floorspace) and a further 65 newly constructed (or subject to significant major refurbishment and expansion) properties in the period 2001–2014. The newly constructed properties were identified from the Corporation of London's Development Schedules. This chapter focuses on the 126 properties that have been tracked back to 1972, since we wish to trace the changing tides of ownership on the existing built structure of the City. Ownership is quantified by the net floor area of the buildings; capital values are not available historically. By applying conservative assumptions on rents and yields we can estimate that the capital value of the 'historic' offices in the database is in the range £8.5 billion – £10.5 billion.[7] Given the new developments in the database and, at time of writing, escalating capital values, this may be an underestimate.

The concept of ownership is complex. When determining ownership two principal factors are considered. The first is the flow of benefits received: that is, where the cashflow received is clearly linked to performance of the underlying office(s). This factor excludes conventional bondholders and lenders as owners and would define a long leaseholder paying a fixed or stepped ground rent (or peppercorn rent), rather than the freeholder, as the beneficial owner. In the latest update of the database, the freeholder with a long lease is apportioned a 1 per cent share of ownership, as a notional stake in the building.

The second factor is effective control. A shareholder in a listed REIT or a property company owns rights to the firm's assets and residual cashflow but, typically, has very limited decision-making influence. Thus, a listed property company (with a reasonable free float) is classified as a single owner, domiciled where its shares are principally listed. Similarly, a private real estate fund pooling investment from multiple sources is typically classified by the nationality of the general partner, promoter or fund manager. However, a private equity vehicle such as a limited partnership with a restricted number of investors is different in nature: particularly if the vehicle is the medium for joint venture or club investment. Here, the ownership classification would reflect the characteristics of the major investors. Wherever possible, ownership has been apportioned amongst the partners according to their share of capital invested; where it is not possible to find this information, equal shares are assumed.

Ownership structures and regulatory structures (including changes in property taxes) have made tracking ownership more complicated. With traditional property market structures, attribution of ownership was a relatively straightforward task, since most buildings were owned by a single organization or individual (with legal restrictions constraining multiple ownership), on either a freehold or a long leasehold basis. Long leaseholds generally carried a fixed or infrequently reviewed ground rent. Similarly, debt structures were typically full recourse, chargeable to the company. The significance of foreign investors in UK property makes identifying nationality a challenge. While much of the investment has been direct and under the parent company name, other investors have established or acquired UK-registered and domiciled vehicles to channel investment or have used joint-venture structures. In markets dominated by financial service firms, this international activity is further complicated by global mergers and acquisitions activity (such that a property can remain under the same effective management yet pass through three or four legal ownerships with different parent nationalities as a result of corporate restructuring).

4.6   TRENDS IN CITY OFFICE OWNERSHIP

In 1980, only 10 per cent of space in the City was owned by non-domestic investors (including owner-occupiers). Following 'Big Bang', foreign ownership began increasing, driven by financial deregulation and the removal of entry barriers for both occupiers and investors. The initial influx of foreign owners came largely from Japan and mainland Europe. By 2000, with the growth of global real estate investment and the expansion of private real estate fund vehicles, a third of all space on the database was owned by non-UK investors. By the onset of the global financial crisis, some 50 per cent of floorspace in the database was in foreign ownership. The 2014 update shows the continuing decline in UK ownership of City of London offices, with nearly two thirds of the space being in foreign hands (see Figure 4.1). This result is considered more robust for larger, prime office space; it is probable that the proportion of foreign owners in smaller, older, secondary and tertiary space is lower. Assuming the proportion holds over the whole of stock, the result implies that foreign investors own approximately 5.8 million square metres of City office space. In Figure 4.2, the ownership of the newly built/refurbished offices (excluding older buildings in the database) is shown. By 2014, this sub-sample comprised some 60 buildings. Figure 4.2 shows that, since 2006, the newer office stock is 50 per cent in non-domestic ownership, reinforcing the findings from the core part of the database.

Foreign interest does not appear to have abated following the great recession; far from causing capital flight, the market downturn appears to have *increased* the extent of non-domestic ownership. This effect is more pronounced than the slight increase observed following the 1989/1990 downturn. Foreign ownership increased between 2007 and 2011 in the aftermath of the financial crisis, despite the falling capital values and weak

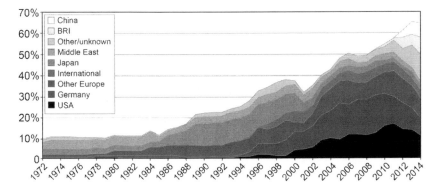

Source: *Who Owns the City* database, core sample.

Figure 4.1 *Non-UK ownership of City offices, 1972–2014*

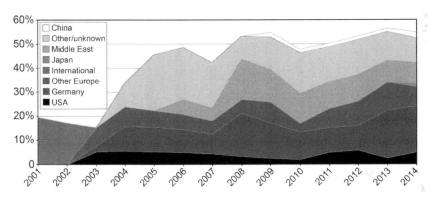

Source: *Who Owns the City* database, new and redeveloped sub-sample.

Figure 4.2 *Non-UK ownership, new and redeveloped City offices, 2001–2014*

return performance (see Figure 4.3). Using CBRE market data, we can examine the relative performance of European office markets, although it is important to acknowledge the risk of over-interpretation of comparative data based on the views of local market agents.[8]

Examining those Western European office markets where rental, yield and capital value data are available over the period 1995 to 2014, the City of London ranks 13th of 35 markets in terms of mean capital value growth, but sixth in terms of capital value *volatility* as a proxy for risk. It experienced the fourth largest fall in capital values during the financial

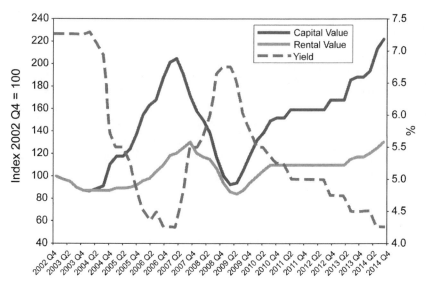

Source: Authors' calculations from CBRE Central London Office Market data.

Figure 4.3   City of London offices: rents, capital values and yields

crisis, although it has rebounded strongly post-crisis (this rebound driven by falling yields rather than rising rental values). Estimating synthetic returns using the rental value and yield data, the City ranks 30th of 35 European markets on a risk-adjusted return (Sharpe ratio) basis. Over that period, real, inflation-adjusted rental value growth is negative – indeed, real rental values per square metre in the City remain below their 1988 levels, before the 1990 crash. This evidence suggests that the City of London office market's reputation as a safe haven for investment is misplaced, for all the continued evidence of the City as a key target market for global real estate investors. As can be seen, capital value falls were far sharper than rental value falls, emphasizing the importance of investment flows on total return performance. From 2011 to 2014, the trend continued with the new arrivals from the BRICs (Brazil, Russia, India, China), despite falling yields and rising capital values.

Since the *Who Owns the City* database is a sample, results regarding individual national holdings should not be over-interpreted. However, there do appear to be shifts in regional ownership over time: for example, the growth and then decline in Japanese holdings (which peak at around 11 per cent in the early 1990s); the rise of German investment from the late 1990s led by the German open ended funds; and the small but significant growth

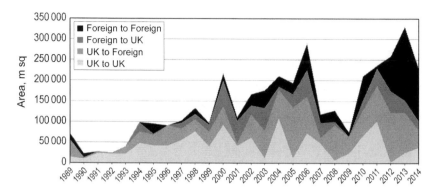

Source: *Who Owns the City* database, core sample.

Figure 4.4   Transaction activity, City offices, 1989–2014

of 'international' investment funds that pool capital from multiple national sources. The BRIC nations enter the database decisively in 2012, driven by significant investment from Chinese sovereign wealth funds and private individuals. Since 2011, German and US investors have divested their share of the floorspace, potentially explained by more attractive opportunities elsewhere and by deleveraging following the financial crisis. There is a significant rise in unknown investors, potentially explained by the rise in private investment by very high net worth individuals and family offices.[9]

Figure 4.4 illustrates the importance of foreign ownership to the maintenance of the liquidity of the City of London office market, one of the market's key investment advantages. Transactions activity provides a stream of information, reducing pricing uncertainty and giving investors confidence that they will be able to enter and exit the market according to their required portfolio strategy. The data illustrates how vital foreign players are in maintaining that activity. In the decade 2001–2010, less than a third of transactions were between UK buyers and UK sellers; 19 per cent of sales were between foreign purchasers and sellers. Following the dramatic increase in foreign ownership, only 16 per cent of sales 2011–2014 were UK to UK; but 33 per cent were UK to foreign, with 14 per cent foreign to UK. Sales of UK to foreign may be plateauing as 2011–2014 and 2001–2010 have similar proportions of such sales. Supporting further rises in liquidity, transaction volumes have consistently increased from decade to decade.

Overall, turnover rates for the properties on the *Who Owns the City* database fell sharply in the downturn. Turnover peaked in 2006 with nearly 20 per cent of the floorspace on the database changing hands; the numbers

of investors anxious to enter the market was matched by investors taking
profits near the top of the market. Turnover then fell sharply away, with
very low levels of activity in 2009; however, it sharply increased thereafter,
as companies de-levered or divested for other reasons. The liquidity crunch
of 2009 may be due to the lack of sellers, as the limited sales were from
sellers with pressure to realize losses.[10] The recent large extent of foreign
to foreign sales supported the non-domestic ownership with proportion-
ally few sales being to UK investors. The relatively low foreign to UK
sales show that there is little sign of the trend to non-domestic ownership
reversing.

Turning from nationality to type of owner (Figure 4.5), the trend
observed in previous *Who Owns the City* reports was of a shift away from
traditional ownership by livery companies, institutions and established
property companies, characterized by a single freehold owner, low turnover rates and passive buy-and-hold investment strategies, towards a more
financial form of ownership by financial service firms, specialist real estate
funds, non-domestic investors and private vehicles, often with ownership
split between different funds and vehicles. However, reversing this trend, in
the recent period, the Finance, Insurance, Real Estate (FIRE) sector has
decreased its share of the office market control from 2011 to 2014, thought

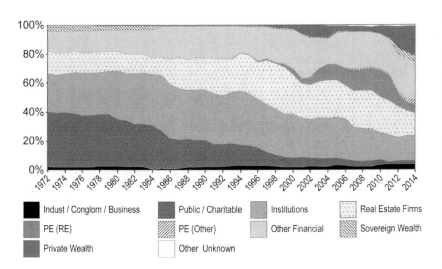

Note: PE = Private Equity; RE = Real Estate.

Source: *Who Owns the City* database, core sample.

Figure 4.5   Ownership by type of investor, 1972–2014

be linked to seeking more attractive yields elsewhere and, possibly, being outbid by new arrivals in the City.

The database detects the growth of two types of investor that are new to the *Who Owns the City* analysis: the individual private investor and sovereign wealth funds. While there has been a long tradition of private ownership of commercial real estate by high net worth investors, this has been less evident in the prime segment of the City office market. However, we now are recording private ownership of significant buildings, totalling 21 per cent of floorspace in the database. This high number should not be over-interpreted as it is biased by one single large purchase. However, it might even be an underestimate, given that the 'unknown' category may well contain more individuals reluctant to be in the public eye and harder to trace through standard searches. Moreover, our analysis suggests that the majority of these private owners are non-UK individuals, although the domicile of many ultra-high net worth individuals is not always easy to define.

The high holdings of office space by investors from the financial services sector are broadly matched by the Corporation of London's analysis of the Business Register and Employment Survey (BRES) data for 2009, which shows 75 per cent of employees in the City working in finance (41 per cent), real estate or professional services (28 per cent) or information and communications technology (ICT) (6 per cent), with much of that ICT and professional service employment being focused on international financial services (City of London, 2011). Once again, this emphasizes how functionally specialized the City is. This represents a strength for London: that specialization produces the breadth and depth of markets that sustains the City. However, it is also a source of potential risk, as discussed in *Towers of Capital* (Lizieri, 2009) and in previous *Who Owns the City* reports, in locking the fortunes of the City to the volatility of international capital markets and financial systems.

Many of the more recent arrivals, notably the sovereigns and the ultra-high net worth investors have long investment horizons and, as a result, are able to tolerate short-run volatility. For such investors, the London office market has benefits in as far as it enables them to place large amounts of capital rapidly and is a safe haven in the sense that there are few restrictions on investment and little concern over expropriation. Whether or not such investors have expectations of real rental and capital value growth, the long investment horizon enables them to exploit redevelopment options and benefit from intensification of land-use and land value impacts.[11] To this extent, they may be less passive investors than the traditional institutional investors of the 1980s, who relied on long leases and upward only rent review clauses to deliver the solid income returns needed to meet liabilities and match inflation, and may have some similarities to the traditional London landed estates with an emphasis on place-making and value increase from stewardship. However, since many of these investors are non-domestic (and may have relatively small investment teams), initial management is more likely to be passive and to make coordinated action across different ownership interests more difficult.

Such long-term investors should be contrasted with private equity funds and listed property companies who have much shorter horizons, often tied to debt maturity, with finite time horizons for many closed fund entities and, above all, with the need to deliver short-run promised or expected returns to their ultimate investors and stakeholders. The appetite for risk and, hence, investment behaviour, will vary across fund types: more opportunistic investors using higher leverage and promising higher returns are more vulnerable to short-term market volatility and cyclical downturns than lower-geared core investors, particularly those with more control over the timing of exit. These more financially-oriented funds are more likely to lock a city's office market into global capital market instability. This will be particularly the case for larger international investors whose real estate portfolios are more likely to be exposed to other global city markets and are thus more vulnerable to systemic contagion effects. However, the very size of those funds pushes them towards investing in the larger markets in order to place capital quickly without moving prices.[12]

4.7 CONCLUSIONS

The growth of foreign investment in the City of London office market is part of an overall trend towards a more global and financialized real estate market which, in turn, has been driven by the development of a more open and interlinked international financial system across the late twentieth century and the early part of the twenty-first. London has remained the principal target for office investment in Europe and stands alongside New York globally. The ownership of the office space, a core constituent of the urban environment, is continually evolving, illustrating the diminishing ownership of domestic companies. Those non-domestic owners are, in turn, continually evolving according to their own domestic environments, such as changes in home country regulations and accumulation of surplus capital. As ownership patterns change, so too do attitudes to risk and return, with implications for the management and performance of the office space in the City.

There has been little evidence of significant capital flight from the City in the aftermath of the market downturn. Nonetheless, that global investment has occurred despite poor historic real estate market performance. The City of London office market has not delivered real rental or capital value growth over the long term and has been more volatile than other UK regional markets or cities in mainland Europe (at least to the extent that available statistics are considered robust). Foreign ownership has not remained static; there is active trading of floorspace, as certain countries decrease their share and others increase it.

What advantages does the City offer, then, which might counterbalance the apparent poor investment performance? One contender is enhanced liquidity. We noted above that global investors have underpinned liquidity over the cycle. Transaction activity fell sharply in the downturn: but a very high percentage of the deals that did take place involved non-UK parties – and very few of those sales were by non-UK owners selling to UK buyers. There are two key features that might lead investors to conclude that the City has greater liquidity: first, that even in a market crisis, they will probably be able to find a buyer: and, second, that if they seek to sell – or buy – they are unlikely to have a pricing impact, given the scale of the market. Even though this has not been tested with comparisons to other cities or regions, this is considered to be a symptom of the dualization and focus on global cities, which provides a continual draw to mobile capital, in particular for those larger actors such as the sovereign wealth funds or globalizing pension funds and insurance companies.

Another key feature for the attraction of mobile capital is transparency. The size of the market leads to a high volume of rental and sales transactions, irrespective of the turnover rate. In turn, this provides a flow of information to investors, which provides greater confidence, reducing required risk premia. The extensive research available on this market provides a further source of confidence. The presence of global brokerage firms with (relatively) standardized practices provides a key benefit to investors building global portfolios. In turn, though, this will tend to direct investors to the same set of markets, increasing competition for available assets (and, hence, potentially forcing down yields) and potentially directing investors away from the greater diversification potential in other markets. Thus, brokers, as actors in the commercial real estate markets, may influence the flows of capital across cities (see Scofield, 2018).

In considering liquidity and transparency, the differentiation between types of investors and the changing characteristics of ownership become critical. Liquidity and transparency depend on transaction activity and monitoring. If the market has seen a shift away from investors with shorter time horizons to those with longer, this might imply a reduction in transaction activity, if holding periods lengthen and investors seek to exploit more distant redevelopment options and to be more interested in long-term stewardship of their urban estates. As such, long-term investors may be more prepared to cooperate with city planners and in regeneration schemes (provided that these provide some alignment with their investment interests) than private equity or opportunistic investors with short-run performance motivations.

Our analysis did identify some new features of the market. The shift away from UK ownership masks a trend away from continental European ownership (particularly if German investors are excluded), with an increasing share taken by US, Middle Eastern and, more recently, non-Japanese Asian investors. The long-run data show that there are waves of regional investment, so it may be too early to see this as a structural shift, but the capital market and current account imbalances between the Atlantic economies and the emerging Asian and Middle Eastern economies may lead to an increase in inward investment over time.

The database also reveals shifts over time in the nature of investors, which suggests that an over-simplified categorization of 'financial capital investors' or similar fails to accommodate the nuances of ownership. In the early period, we see substantial holdings from traditional investors and institutions, typically with relatively passive investment strategies grounded in the long 'institutional' lease giving cashflow security. The rise of private equity real estate investors and other investors using leverage and with shorter investment horizons puts more emphasis on short-run returns and capital appreciation (and in large measure contributes both to greater potential market volatility and systemic risk).

More recently, the growing presence of sovereign wealth funds, private investors and family trusts may mark a shift back to a longer perspective on the City, albeit one perhaps more grounded in capital preservation than income return. Different types of investor have different time horizons, risk appetites and objectives: consequently, their impact on the functioning of the City cannot be collapsed into a single dimension. These changes in investor type need to be overlaid on the shifts in the nationality of ownership to understand market dynamics and the way in which investment patterns serve to integrate the City into global financial and urban networks and assist or frustrate efforts at city planning and management.

Understanding current and future investor needs is critical to maintaining the successes of the City of London in its ability to anchor foreign capital. The influx of capital and the appetites of investors provide funds for real estate development and acquisition that can help build up and maintain the office stock to a standard that meets the changing needs of occupiers but also locks the City into global financial markets with implications for overall economic performance and volatility. In the aftermath of the financial crisis and after the sharp downturn in commercial property prices, capital values rebounded sharply and yields have been compressed, despite the track record of poor risk adjusted returns. The City of London appears to attract continued non-domestic interest: local policy makers and planners have an integral role in managing the office stock and the needs of different investors and need to interact with each wave of investor type. The *Who Owns the City* database highlights the rising tide of foreign ownership and temporal changes in investor types, whose needs and preferences differ. The challenge for policy makers is to manage the increasing mobile capital flows to the economic advantage of the urban space, using the different levers within each investor group while considering the impact of these investment flows and ownership patterns for the functioning and stability of the City economy.

NOTES

1. Rental values per square metre are higher in the West End than in the City of London, but this has not prevented the emergence of specialist financial services clusters, for example of hedge fund managers.
2. The idea that gold is a safe haven is deeply embedded but weakly empirically grounded. For example, between 1974 and 2014, gold produced lower annual average returns than the US equity market but with higher volatility.
3. These typically would have been long building leases with a fixed ground rent payment, reflecting an assumption or expectation of low inflation and little real growth in rent or value. Hence, the long leaseholder would have extracted any value uplifts from rental or capital growth until reversion and thus can be considered as the beneficial owner. More contemporary ground leases have rent review clauses to capture some of any increase in market rent.
4. This is particularly the case for defined benefit pension schemes where pension payouts are linked to salaries and inflation. The shift to defined contribution schemes makes precise liabilities matching less critical. Defined contribution schemes may be more drawn to listed real estate than direct ownership, as this provides liquidity and daily pricing. This would, once again, represent a shift in the nature of commercial ownership.
5. See also Lizieri and Jalali (2014).
6. Earlier *Who Owns the City* research was supported by Development Securities plc. We acknowledge the role of Andrew Baum in establishing the database and the researchers who helped build the historic records.
7. Including the newer developments in the database, we have coverage of some £21–24 billion of office space.
8. It should be noted, though, that CBRE are a major global real estate advisor whose views will influence global investors. While local market offices have some autonomy, some level of common practice and uniformity is imposed by the global network.
9. In addition some of our data sources, such as Estates Gazette interactive, typically do not publish the names of private individuals on their databases.
10. Anecdotal evidence from a round table discussion at the Cambridge Real Estate Principal Investor Club 6 and 7 July 2015, Trinity Hall College, University of Cambridge.
11. This is not to say that they will realize such options and indeed may take profits and exit early: the point is that they do not have an immediate pressure to deliver high returns.
12. This also applies equally to most sovereign wealth funds, contributing to investment pressure on yields.

REFERENCES

Aalbers, M.B. (2009), 'The sociology and geography of mortgage markets: Reflections on the financial crisis', *International Journal of Urban and Regional Research*, **33** (2), 281–290.

Ashton, P. (2009), 'An appetite for yield: The anatomy of the subprime mortgage crisis', *Environment and Planning A*, **41** (6), 1420–1441.

Attuyer, K., A. Guironnet and L. Halbert (2012), '"Turning pumpkins into carriages": Sustainable urban development and the financialization of "green" commercial real estate in France', *Articulo – Journal of Urban Research*, **9**, accessed 16 September 2016 at http://articulo.revues.org/2155.

Baker, D., G. Epstein and R. Pollin (1998), *Globalization and Progressive Economic Policy*, Cambridge: Cambridge University Press.

Baum, A. and D. Hartzell (2012), *Global Property Investment: Strategies, Structures, Decisions*, Chichester: John Wiley & Sons.

Baum, A. and C. Lizieri (1998), *Who Owns the City?* London: Development Securities plc.

Beber, A., M.W. Brandt and K.A. Kavajecz (2009), 'Flight-to-quality or flight-to-liquidity? Evidence from the euro-area bond market', *The Review of Financial Studies*, **22** (3), 925–957.

Bernstein, S., J. Lerner and A. Schoar (2013), 'The investment strategies of sovereign wealth funds', *Journal of Economic Perspectives*, **27** (2), 219–237.

Black, F. (1976), 'The investment policy spectrum: Individuals, endowment funds and pension funds', *Financial Analysts Journal*, **32** (1), 23–31.

BoE (2013), *Bank of England Quarterly Bulletin*, **53** (1), accessed 16 September 2016 at http://www.bankofengland.co.uk/publications/Pages/quarterlybulletin/default.aspx.

Burston, B. and A. Burrell (2015), *What is Fair Value?*, London: Investment Property Forum.

Chambers, D., E. Dimson and A.S. Ilmanen (2012), 'The Norway model', *Journal of Portfolio Management*, **38** (2), 67–81.

Christophers, B. (2010), 'On voodoo economics: Theorising relations of property, value and contemporary capitalism', *Transactions of the Institute of British Geographers*, **35** (1), 94–108.

City of London (2011), *Employment Trends, BRES Data 2009*, London: City of London Corporation.

City of London (2014), *Offices in the City of London*, Section 1 of 4: Introduction and B1 Office Floorspace, London: City of London Corporation.

Conover, M., S. Friday and S. Sirmans (2002), 'Diversification benefits from foreign real estate investments', *Journal of Real Estate Portfolio Management*, **8** (1), 17–25.

Coq-Huelva, D. (2013), 'Urbanisation and financialisation in the context of a rescaling state: The case of Spain', *Antipode*, **45** (5), 1213–1231.

Corpataux, J. and O. Crevoisier (2005), 'Increased capital mobility/liquidity and its repercussions at regional level: Some lessons from the experiences of Switzerland and the United Kingdom (1975–2000)', *European Urban and Regional Studies*, **12** (4), 315–334.

Corpataux, J., O. Crevoisier and T. Theurillat (2009), 'The expansion of the finance industry and its impact on the economy: A territorial approach based on Swiss pension funds', *Economic Geography*, **85** (3), 313–334.

Devaney, S. (2010), 'Trends in office rents in the City of London: 1867–1959', *Explorations in Economic History*, **47** (2), 198–212.

Dörry, S. and M. Handke (2012), 'Disentangling the geography of finance and real estate: Competing space-times of decision-making and uneven spatial development', *Articulo – Journal of Urban Research*, **9**, accessed 16 September 2016 at http://articulo.revues.org/2149.

Epstein, G.A. (2005), 'Introduction: Financialization and the world economy', in G.A. Epstein (ed.), *Financialization and the World Economy*, Cheltenham, UK and Northampton, MA, USA: Edward Elgar Publishing, pp. 3–16.

Fields, D. (2015), 'Contesting the financialization of urban space: Community organizations and the struggle to preserve affordable rental housing in New York City', *Journal of Urban Affairs*, **37** (2), 144–165.

Fuchs, M. and A. Scharmanski (2009), 'Counteracting path dependencies: "Rational" investment decisions in the globalising commercial property market', *Environment and Planning A*, **41** (11), 2724–2740.

Gerber, J.D., S. Nahrath, P. Csikos and P. Knoepfel (2011), 'The role of Swiss civic corporations in land-use planning', *Environment and Planning A*, **43** (1), 185–204.

Gotham, K.F. (2006), 'The secondary circuit of capital reconsidered: Globalization and the U.S. real estate sector', *American Journal of Sociology*, **112** (1), 231–275.

Guironnet, A. and L. Halbert (2014), 'The financialization of urban development projects: Concepts, processes, and implications', *Working Paper*, 14-04, accessed 16 September 2016 at https://hal-enpc.archives-ouvertes.fr/hal-01097192/document.

Halbert, L. and H. Rouanet (2014), 'Filtering risk away: Global finance capital, transcalar territorial networks and the (un)making of city-regions: An analysis of business property development in Bangalore, India', *Regional Studies*, **48** (3), 471–484.

Halbert, L., J. Henneberry and F. Mouzakis (2014a), 'The financialization of business property and what it means for cities and regions', *Regional Studies*, **48** (3), 547–550.

Halbert, L., J. Henneberry and F. Mouzakis (2014b), 'Finance, business property and urban and regional development', *Regional Studies*, **48** (3), 421–424.

Hammer, C., P. Kunzel and I. Petrova (2008), 'Sovereign wealth funds: Current institutional and operational practices', *IMF Working Paper*, 08/254, accessed 16 September 2016 at http://www.imf.org/external/pubs/cat/longres.aspx?sk=22453.

Henneberry, J. and F. Mouzakis (2014), 'Familiarity and the determination of yields for regional office property investments in the UK', *Regional Studies*, **48** (3), 530–546.

Kunzel, P., Y. Lu, I. Petrova and J. Pihlman (2011), 'Investment objectives of sovereign wealth funds – a shifting paradigm', *IMF Working Paper*, 11/19, accessed 16 September 2016 at https://www.imf.org/external/pubs/cat/longres.as px?sk=24598.0.

Lizieri, C. (2009), *Towers of Capital: Office Markets and International Financial Services*, Oxford: Blackwell-Wiley.

Lizieri, C. and S. Bond (2004), 'Defining liquidity in property', in C. Lizieri (ed.), *Liquidity in Commercial Property Markets*, London: Investment Property Forum, pp. 7–21.

Lizieri, C. and R. Jalali (2014), 'Real estate: Risk, return and diversification', in A. Rudd and S. Satchell (eds), *Quantitative Approaches to High Net Worth Investment*, London: Risk Books, pp. 171–200.

Lizieri, C. and K. Pain (2014), 'International office investment in global cities:

The production of financial space and systemic risk', *Regional Studies*, **48** (3), 439–455.

Lizieri, C., A. Baum and J. Reinert (2011), *Who Owns the City 2011? Change and Global Ownership of City of London Offices*, Cambridge and London: University of Cambridge and Development Securities plc.

Lizieri, C., A. Baum and P. Scott (2000), 'Ownership, occupation and risk: A view of the City of London office market', *Urban Studies*, **37** (7), 1109–1129.

Lizieri, C., M. Oughton and A. Baum (2001), *Who Owns the City 2001? An Examination of Office Ownership in the City of London*, Reading: University of Reading and Development Securities plc.

Longstaff, F.A. (2002), 'The flight-to-liquidity premium in U.S. Treasury bond prices', *NBER Working Paper*, 9312, accessed 16 September 2016 at http://www.nber.org/papers/w9312.

Mason, L., A. Bensted and O. Senchal (2015), 'Sovereign wealth funds investing in real estate', *Real Estate Spotlight*, **9** (3), 2–5.

McDowell, L. (2011), 'Making a drama out of a crisis: Representing financial failure, or a tragedy in five acts', *Transactions of the Institute of British Geographers*, **36** (2), 193–205.

McWilliam, P.R. (2015), 'United States REIT structure and real estate assets', *Ilkam Law Review*, **31**, 35–61.

NCREIF and The Townsend Group (2009), 'Policies', accessed 16 September 2016 at https://www.ncreif.org/public_files/NCREIF_Townsend_Policies.pdf.

Ó Riain, S. (2012), 'The crisis of financialisation in Ireland', *The Economic and Social Review*, **43** (4), 497–533.

Polillo, S. and M.F. Guillén (2005), 'Globalization pressures and the state: The worldwide spread of central bank independence', *American Journal of Sociology*, **110** (6), 1764–1802.

Prescott (2015), 'Real estate equity investment categories', accessed 16 September 2016 at http://prescott-group.com/iamCat.asp?section=2&subs=5.

Schill, M.H. (1999), 'Impact of the capital markets on real estate law and practice', *The John Marshall Law Review*, **32** (2), 269–288.

Scofield, D. (2018), 'Global cities, local practices: Intermediation in the commercial real estate markets of New York City and London', in M. Hoyler, C. Parnreiter and A. Watson (eds), *Global City Makers: Economic Actors and Practices in the World City Network*, Cheltenham, UK and Northampton, MA, USA: Edward Elgar Publishing, pp. 83–105.

Scott, P. (1996), *The Property Masters: A History of the British Commercial Property Sector*, London: Spon.

Sirmans, C.F. and E. Worzala (2003), 'International direct real estate investment: A review of the literature', *Urban Studies*, **40** (5–6), 1081–1114.

Theurillat, T. and O. Crevoisier (2014), 'Sustainability and the anchoring of capital: Negotiations surrounding two major urban projects in Switzerland', *Regional Studies*, **48** (3), 501–515.

Weber, R. (2002), 'Extracting value from the city: Neoliberalism and urban redevelopment', *Antipode*, **34** (3), 519–540.

Weber, R. (2010), 'Selling city futures: The financialization of urban redevelopment policy', *Economic Geography*, **86** (3), 251–274.

5 Global cities, local practices: intermediation in the commercial real estate markets of New York City and London

David Scofield

5.1 INTRODUCTION

This chapter examines the particular market practices of advanced producer services firms, as both investors and intermediaries, in the commercial real estate markets of New York and London. Often viewed as two sides of the same transatlantic global city 'NY-LON' (e.g. McGuire and Chan, 2000; Smith, 2012; Taylor et al., 2014), New York and London have jockeyed for top position in global finance since at least the mid-twentieth century. Today, they are of near equal importance as primary circuits of global capital, and serve as key nodes of financial confluence wherein capital of different forms is combined and transformed (Wójcik, 2013). The market behaviours that underlie the definition of these cities as global cities are not identical, but rather retain unique differences that result in actors in similar positions operating differently.

Key to the global primacy of New York and London are the dense concentrations of producer services firms (Sassen, 1991, 1999). These corporate clusters embody 'professional knowledge' in order to process 'specialized information', knowledge comprising 'the only source of their competitive success' (Hall and Pain, 2006, p. 113). In the commercial real estate investment markets of New York and London, advanced producer service firms occupy both sides of the investment equation, operating as both buyers and sellers of commercial real estate. Other producer services firms (or sometimes different branches of the same firms) provide a number of other real estate services, including asset valuation, management and intermediation. It is intermediation in the form of brokerage that is the focus of this chapter. Fixed in place and embedded in local market cultures, real estate are foundational assets that provide sources of value from which financial innovation can proceed (Lizieri, 2009; Lizieri and Mekic, 2018; see also Leyshon and Thrift, 2007). The broker (agent) intermediary is a key catalyst in the conversion of liquid capital into real estate assets, and vice versa, assuming a pivotal role in the placement, switching and distribution of knowledge drawn from individuals working at the margins of the market (Clark and Monk, 2013).

The costs to investors when transacting commercial real estate are high due to the private nature of the markets in which the exchange occurs (and attendant information asymmetry), the heterogeneity of real assets, and the time it takes to acquire and dispose of property. Brokers provide knowledge of the asset, the market and the counterparty to the transaction and by doing so can increase trust between parties and improve market efficiency. However, while a single broker representing the seller may benefit the search process in ways which offset the not insubstantial costs of brokerage, the advantages provided by the more expensive system of double brokerage (whereby both buyer and seller have individual broker representation) and the conditions in which it occurs are far less understood.

This chapter will explore how local practices of broker intermediation (one, two or none) and the individual social networks of highly placed investment managers/directors correspond in the commercial real estate investment markets of New York and London. Evidence of a feedback effect is found, whereby local practice impacts social network development which, in turn, reinforces local practices. As well, broker intermediaries use individual and collective agency to establish and maintain networks for knowledge procurement throughout the market. It is through these linkages that knowledge is transferred to facilitate investment in commercial real estate in New York and London.

The chapter proceeds in four parts. Section 5.2 provides an empirical examination of brokerage in the commercial real estate markets of New York and London. It explores the role and prevalence of brokers in the respective markets by isolating common trends in brokerage during different market periods. Section 5.3 concerns the network implications of different forms of brokerage. Section 5.4 provides an examination of the social networks of investors active in New York and London and explores linkages between network form and the type of intermediation typically practised in each market. A summary of findings and concluding comments are found in the final section.

5.2 BROKERAGE IN NEW YORK AND LONDON

Commercial real estate assets are large, 'lumpy' and heterogeneous. Acquisition and sale occurs over an extended period typically lasting weeks or months. The extended time to transact coupled with other aspects of the asset combine to increase risk to investors which usually prompts some form of broker intermediation (Devaney and Scofield, 2013).

To uncover the forms of brokerage typically practised in different market environments in New York and London, a unique dataset of commercial real estate transactions was consulted.[1] A sample of 9338[2] transactions were analysed with all transactions placed into one of four categories: (1) No broker involved; (2) Broker for seller only; (3) Broker for buyer only; (4) Broker for both parties. This was to facilitate econometric analysis of what distinguishes transactions where brokerage is observed,[3] and those cases where each party is represented by a separate broker.

The data confirms that the volume of commercial real estate transactions varies with oscillations in the market and the wider economy. Three broad phases falling between Q4 2001 and Q4 2011 across both cities were identified: a period of low transaction activity (2001–2004), a period of strong growth and high transaction volumes (2005–2007) and, finally, a significant market correction starting mid- to end-2007 (the beginning of the global financial crisis) that is accompanied by a fall in the number of transactions (Figure 5.1).

It is clear that the role and prevalence of brokers remained largely consistent over the market cycle in both cities. Despite significant changes in the way other investment assets are traded (e.g. Hall and Pain, 2006; Hoyler et al., 2008), and despite growth in the availability of performance data (e.g. RCA, CoStar, MSCI) and enhanced networking opportunities (e.g. Society of Property Researchers; Investment Property Forum; Association of Foreign Investors in Real Estate), the form of brokerage practised in each market also remained relatively consistent over the period. The data shows that single broker transactions are more prevalent in New York than London, while buyer representation (double brokerage) is significantly higher in London, occurring in 63 per cent of transactions as compared to only 9 per cent of cases in New York (Table 5.1). Distinctions persist when comparisons are made between sectors of properties (e.g. offices) and investor types (e.g. financial institutions) suggesting the difference is not due to the mix of assets and investors in each city.

In order to control the effect of different variables on broker use while other factors are held constant, Probit regression models were used. Three sets of models of core commercial real estate (office, retail and industrial) in each city were estimated: one set that examines the decision by sellers to use brokers, another set that examines the decision to use brokers by buyers of real estate assets, and a final set that explores the use of brokers by both parties. New York and London were modelled separately to see whether similar factors are influential to decisions to use brokers in each

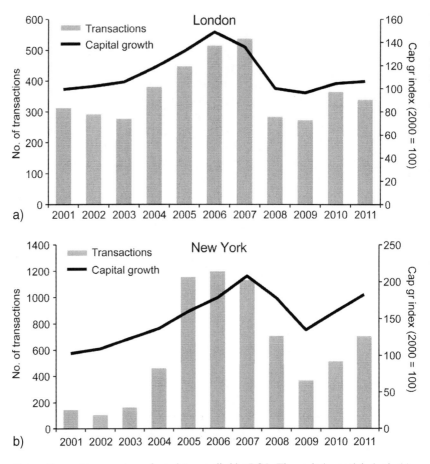

Note: Transaction counts are from data supplied by RCA. The capital growth index in (a) is the IPD UK quarterly index and in (b) is the Moody's/RCA CPPI for US Major Markets. In both cases, these are 'All Property' series.

Source: Devaney and Scofield (2013).

Figure 5.1 Number of transactions in London and New York and wider market conditions

case, notwithstanding the clear difference in brokerage between the cities overall.

Among a number of findings (see Devaney and Scofield, 2013) results indicate that when institutional buyers (e.g., banks, pension funds, life funds, etc.) acquire commercial real estate in London they are more likely to use brokers than any other type of buyer; the effect of their involvement

Table 5.1 *Use and form of brokerage – London and New York City*

	No broker	For seller only	For buyer only	Broker for both	Total	Seller represented	Buyer represented
Number of transactions							
London	460	782	389	1754	3385	2536	2143
New York	3398	2011	54	490	5953	2501	544
Percentage by number							
London	14	23	11	52	100	75	63
New York	57	34	1	8	100	42	9
Value ($ bn)[a]							
London	34.4	48.5	22.7	117.6	223.2	166.1	140.3
New York	55.6	101.9	4.0	15.7	177.2	117.6	19.7
Percentage by value[b]							
London	15	22	10	53	100	75	63
New York	31	57	2	9	100	66	11

Notes:
a. US$ in December 2000 terms.
b. Based on deflated local currency values.

Source: Devaney and Scofield (2013).

increases the probability of buyer brokerage by 10 per cent. In contrast, when the same type of investor acquires real estate in New York they are less likely to use brokers, their involvement reducing the probability of buyer brokerage by 7 per cent. Unlike London, New York findings suggest that transaction complexity, prompted in part by information asymmetry, and the relative knowledge and experience of different buyer types operating there affect the investor's decision to use a broker when buying property.

Overall, the findings show that the use of brokers and the form of brokerage persist over the study period, seemingly immune to the state of the market and the advent of new forms of information and communication technologies and the digitization of finance that has affected other investment markets. As well, double brokered transactions, a hallmark of the London market, remain despite representing significantly higher economic costs (transaction costs) compared to other forms of brokerage – type of real estate and national provenance of the investment firm notwithstanding. This is in contrast to typical broker intermediation practice in New York where transactions are significantly less likely to involve two brokers, and when this does occur, is likely to involve a foreign buyer with potentially less experience and reduced networks of market contacts.

The making of the global city, the institutions and practices that comprise it, takes on different forms in different contexts, even within a very specialized type of transaction as shown here. Findings so far demonstrate in sharp relief the difference in the use of brokerage in leading global cities.

5.3   THE *TERTIUS*

For commercial real estate investors, two brokers effectively doubles the cost of intermediation, *ceteris paribus*,[4] and may have a negative impact on asset liquidity. But, observable benefits to the buyer that would outweigh the additional cost of double brokerage have largely proven elusive.[5]

Common forms and practices of broker intermediation can encourage two distinct *tertius* roles (Simmel, 1950): *tertius gaudens*, the middle (dyad) that benefits (Burt, 1997; Reagans and Zuckerman, 2008); and, *tertius iungens*, the one who brings together facilitating exchange (Baker and Obstfeld, 1999, Obstfeld, 2005), the matchmaker. When two brokers work a deal (seller – broker ↔ broker – buyer) a 'tri-dyad' network is created. This is in contrast to the dyad created when seller and buyer exchange directly (seller ↔ buyer); and, the triad formed when the seller retains a broker while the buyer acts alone (seller – broker ↔ buyer), the practice most common in New York City. The tri-dyad creates a hole, or gap, between seller and buyer presenting conditions in which the broker dyad that works between the seller and buyer enjoys access to, and control of, information (knowledge) pertaining to all aspects of the investment, including the preferences of both parties to the transaction. Disconnected investment firms communicate exclusively through their respective broker intermediaries, underscoring the value of this network form to the intermediaries involved (e.g. Ahuja et al., 2012; Burt, 1992; Marsden, 1982). Brokers use individual and collective agency to maintain networks of relations and reproduce market practices that embed them at the centre of the investment process.

A broker intermediary trades on social capital (Burt, 1992; Lin, 2001) in order to extract knowledge embedded in networks of interpersonal relationships that span and connect the investment community (Kilduff and Brass, 2010; Zenger et al., 2011). The tri-dyad reflects the social network priorities of the market actors who employ them – i.e. investment managers prioritize the benefits of constrained networks (i.e. rule enforcement, trust building) but use brokers to off-set the consequences of constrained networks, allowing them access to new pools of information unavailable to them through their own social networks. The tri-dyad is a distinctive feature of the London commercial real estate investment market, and is largely unaffected by market cycles, asset quality, or investor knowledge and market experience. Though brokers often help mitigate uncertainty during economic exchange, the tri-dyad network formed when two brokers 'work a deal' may actually increase information asymmetry among investors and reduce asset liquidity while increasing transaction costs.

5.4 SOCIAL NETWORKS AND BROKERAGE

Findings so far clearly show that practices of broker intermediation vary significantly between New York and London. It has been described that a particular form of brokerage (double) has a strong impact on information asymmetry creating a *tertius gaudens*; and, this form is significantly more likely to occur in London, in deals involving highly sophisticated institutional investors. In this section, the social networks of a small group of investment managers/directors who represent major commercial real estate investment firms active in New York and London are explored in order to understand how brokerage corresponds with social network attributes and priorities.

Due to information asymmetry between sellers and buyers, and other risks, in the private commercial real estate markets of New York and London, brokers are frequently consulted and it is logical the social networks of investment managers who instruct the brokers would reflect the form of intermediation most common in each market. For example, where single/no broker is the typical form, investment managers would be expected to exhibit less constrained networks, while the opposite would be true where double brokerage is typical. In this section, the social networks of a small group of investment managers/directors who represent major commercial real estate investment firms active in New York and London are explored in order to understand whether brokerage corresponds with social network attributes and priorities.

Social capital network theories (e.g. Burt, 1992; Granovetter, 1973) offer a framework for measuring the attributes of social networks and their association with the movement of knowledge and dissemination of practices, in different market environments. What follows is analysis of the individual (ego-centric) social capital networks of three senior investment managers/directors, each of whom is directly responsible for the acquisition of commercial real estate on behalf of major investment firms based in the US or the UK. The three were chosen based on the size of the firms they represent (greater than US$5 billion equivalent under management), and the scope of their investment roles within their respective firms. Analysis was conducted to map each network as mobilized in the instrumental action of real estate investment. The names of the parties participating and the firms they represent have been redacted to preserve the anonymity of those involved.

5.4.1 Name Generation/Interpretation

To isolate those individuals most instrumental to the professional success of the investment manager, 11 questions were posed to each subject (Burt, 1997; Völker and Flap, 2004). The individuals who emerge through this process are termed 'alter'. Once defined, the next step is to interpret relations between the investment manager (ego) and network members (alter), as well as between the alter. The questions are designed to uncover: (a) attributes of network members (i.e. age, education, race/ethnicity, location); (b) properties of the relationship (tie) between the ego and members of their network (i.e. frequency of contact, duration of acquaintance, intensity); and (c) intensity of ties between members (pairs of alter) (e.g. Marsden, 1990).

The results provide an inventory of each alter in the ego network, the relationship (duration, frequency) between the ego and the alter, as well as the strength of ties between alter. Together, average tie strength, the characteristics of the alter, communication activity, network range and density are key determinants of network structure and constraint within networks (Marin and Hampton, 2007). The respondent (ego) is asked to indicate emotional closeness between themselves and each alter using a four-point scale (1–4, weakest to strongest). To determine the strength of relations between pairs of alter, the ego is asked to define their relations on a three-point scale: especially close, distant, or somewhere in-between.

Network analysis then proceeds as follows: the strength of relations (Z_{ij}) between ego (i) and each alter (j) is measured for each pair of people in the ego network, including the ego. For the purposes of the model they are symmetric ($Z_{ij} = Z_{ji}$), and vary from a minimum of 0 to a maximum of 1 (Scott, 2000). A network characterized by strong, reciprocal ego–alter and alter–alter ties is indicative of a dense network. Meanwhile, constraint varies with three factors: network size (larger networks are less constraining), density (networks of more strongly interconnected contacts are more constraining), and hierarchy (networks in which all contacts are exclusively tied to a single contact are more constraining).[6] The model is as follows:[7]

Investment manager 'i' (ego) is:

$$C_{ij} = (P_{ij} + \Sigma_q P_{iq} P_{qj})^2$$

for $q \neq i, j$ where P_{ij} is the proportion of i's relations invested in contact j, and the total in parenthesis is the proportion of i's relations that are directly or indirectly invested in the connection with contact j. The sum of C_{ij} is determined from across contacts (j) to arrive at the constraint value (C) (see Burt, 2000, for a detailed discussion).

Within the ego network, the extent to which alter, 'j', constrains ego, 'i', is a multiplication of (a) 'i's investment in 'j' (closeness – various measures); and (b) the lack of structural holes around j. The constraint measure is a function of the network size, density and hierarchy (networks in which all contacts are exclusively tied to a dominant contact), and is designed to measure the extent to which the focal ego lacks structural holes. Structural holes suggest a network characterized by low density wherein the ego is the sole connection between others (Völker and Flap, 2004). The higher the constraint score, the fewer structural holes in the network. Constraint is also expected to correlate with broker practice: i.e. when investment managers with more constrained social networks acquire commercial real estate they are more likely to engage the services of a broker to represent them.

5.4.2 Exploring Networks

A series of interviews were conducted in the UK and the US commencing in the spring of 2007 and concluding in the fall of 2008. The subjects whose contacts form the basis of the ego-centric analysis that follows were part of an interview group of 34 (UK: 25; US: 9) (see Scofield, 2011). These individuals were asked to provide their insights into commercial real estate investment processes and practices in the UK and the US.

Firm A

The first subject (ego) is a senior director and head of acquisitions for a UK-based investment firm. He was 40 years old and had been with the firm for ten years at the time of the interview. The subject holds a graduate degree in real estate investment, and membership in the Royal Institution of Chartered Surveyors (RICS) and the Investment Property Forum (IPF). His investment remit includes commercial real estate investments in London and throughout the UK. He was asked to provide a list of individuals (alter) in response to an initial list of 11 questions.

He indicated 16 contacts, including three family members who were removed from the study. The subject was next asked to describe using a four-point scale (1 being strongest, 4 weakest) the level of emotional closeness between himself (ego) and his contacts (alter). Following on, the subject was tasked with defining the level of closeness between each of the alter on a three-point scale: 1 = especially close; 0 = not close at all, distant; or blank indicating a level of closeness somewhere between 1 and 0.

The results indicate that all alter are male and have an average age of 39 years. The subject network (E) is comprised of 13 alter; all work in London with the exception of 'A4' (Manchester), a trusted contact (Figure 5.2). The effective degree score is 8.325, indicating that 8 alters are not strongly tied

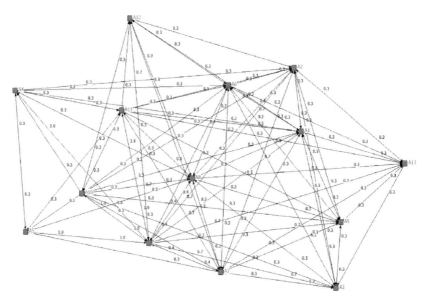

Note: See Appendix A5.1.

Figure 5.2   Ego–alter and alter–alter tie strength, Firm A

to any other, 38 per cent less than the total network. Ties that comprise the effective network measure are crucial in that they enable access to information outside the subject's immediate network. Seven alter were listed as his most trusted, valuable, professionally impactful contacts. The constraint score, a measure of the degree to which the ego is tied to others who are connected to each other, is 24.6. Interestingly, and despite the subject's investing responsibilities lying both within and beyond London, all alter but one live and work within the greater London area. This is indicative of a dense network with limited geographical reach outside the global city London.

Firm B

The second subject is male, was 37 years old at the time of the interview and has a graduate degree. He is an investment manager and director of fund management, and works for a UK-based investment firm that maintains a large portfolio of commercial real estate assets in London and around the UK. He is a member of the RICS and the IPF and had been with the firm for seven years at the time of the interview. His investment remit includes commercial real estate properties in London and throughout the UK.

The same questions were put to the subject. As in the first case, family members were excluded unless they were directly involved in the subjects' investment activities. Sixteen contacts were listed and two family members were removed.

The contacts are male, with an average age of 38 which is very similar to the first subject. All work in London with the exception of 'A8' (Edinburgh) (Figure 5.3). This individual is also among the subject's most trusted contacts. The effective degree measure is 8.36 indicating 8 alter are not strongly tied to any other alter in the network, 43 per cent less than the total network. In response to questions about the identity of his most trusted, valuable contacts, and those who have contributed most to his professional development, seven individuals were listed. The constraint score for this network is 25.5 suggesting a marginally more constrained network than Firm A (24.6).

Of the 27 alter provided across both case studies, two reside outside the London region. Though both of the UK-based subjects (ego) are responsible for investments in London and throughout the UK, 93 per cent of alter, and 86 per cent of their most trusted contacts, reside in London.

Firm C

The third subject is a senior vice-president, director of acquisitions for a major investment firm based in the US. The subject was 43 years old and had been with the firm for five years at the time of the interview. He has a graduate degree in real estate and is a member of REIAC (Real

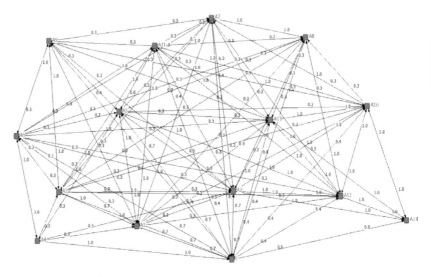

Note: See Appendix A5.2.

Figure 5.3 Ego–alter and alter–alter tie strength, Firm B

Estate Investment Advisory Council) and the CCIM Institute (Certified Commercial Investment Members). His investment remit includes New York City and other areas in the northeast and mid-west of the US. The subject was presented with the same questions as the UK participants.

As in the UK studies, 100 per cent of the alter are male while the average age is slightly older at 46. In sharp contrast to the UK cases, 50 per cent of alter reside outside the subject's home location across the subject's investment area. A total of 23 individuals were listed, with no family members included. The scale (degree) of the network is clearly considerably larger than either of the UK cases (13 and 14 respectively) (Figure 5.4). The effective size measure is 20.8 (21) indicating 21 contacts are not closely tied to one another in this network. This is more than double either of the previous studies; the effective size is only 9 per cent less than the total network size. Six were indicated as most valuable, trusted and professionally important to the subject. The constraint score (0.11) indicates a network less than half as constrained as either of the previous cases.

Moreover, while 93 per cent of alters indicated in the UK studies reside in the same place as the subject, in the US study 50 per cent of alter reside outside the subject's home location. Among his most trusted contacts, 67 per cent reside outside his home location.

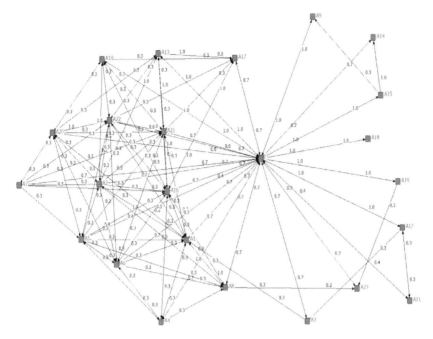

Note: See Appendix A5.3.

Figure 5.4 Ego–alter and alter–alter tie strength, Firm C

Network constraint and location – all firms

Table 5.2 shows the strength of ties between alter in each network; higher constraint scores indicate alter who are more closely tied to each other. The US-based investment manager at Firm C has a constraint score of 0.111, which is less than half the constraint of either of the UK-based investors (Firm A: 0.246; Firm B: 0.255).

As a proportion of each network, Firm C (US) is 55 per cent less constrained than Firm A (UK), and 57 per cent less constrained than Firm B (UK). Investment manager social networks in Firms A and B indicate fewer structural holes effectively reducing the flow of new knowledge to the investment manager. Meanwhile, the less constrained, larger (degree and effective size) network outlined by the investment manager at Firm C has more structural holes offering more opportunities to access distant information pools outside his immediate environment. In addition to significant differences in constraint, Table 5.3 shows the networks found in Firms A and B are also much more homogenous in terms of shared location.

Table 5.2   Constraint between firms

Firm C vs. Firm A	11.1 vs. 24.6	↓ 55% constraint
Firm C vs. Firm B	11.1 vs. 25.5	↓ 57% constraint
Firm B vs. Firm A	25.5 vs. 24.6	↓ 4.5% constraint

Note: On a scale of 0–100, the constraint variation was indicated between institutions.

Table 5.3   Ego–alter location

Firm A – Location density	
Density*	No. of ties
0.8571	156
Firm B – Location density	
Density	No. of ties
0.7363	156
Firm C – Location density	
Density	No. of ties
0.3388	187

Note: * On a scale of 0–1, 1 representing the highest density.

Levels of density (i.e. ego–alter living/working in the same locale) vary greatly across the cases. Networks of both UK investment managers exhibit location density levels of 85.7 (0.8571) and 73.6 (0.7361) respectively, while the US investment manager network is half as dense with a score of 33.8 (0.3388). This is in line with other findings that point to higher density and constraint in the social networks of UK investment managers.

Network density was further explored by analysing the location charac-teristics of a limited network for each case. This limited network sample was defined as the most trusted contacts of each subject (ego) (Table 5.4).

The proportionality of the constraint measures is largely retained, though the number of key alter equalizes somewhat across the cases. The second column (Table 5.5) shows the revised density measure as determined through analysis of only those indicated as most trusted/ important.

While the greatest decrease in network density was found in the social network of the investment manager surveyed at Firm B, it is interesting that location density decreased across all networks. Moreover, Firm B

Table 5.4   Ego–alter location – most trusted (most important to the investment)

Firm A – Location: most trusted
Alter: A2, A9, A4, A10, A11, A12 and A13. The following density measures were noted:

Density	No. of ties
0.7500	42

Firm B – Location: most trusted
Alter: A1, A7, A2, A6, A8, A9 and A10. The following density measures were noted:

Density	No. of ties
0.5455	30

Firm C – Location: most trusted
Alter: A11, A12, A1, A2, A7 and A6. The following density measures were noted:

Density	No. of ties
0.2857	12

Note: * On a scale of 0–1, 1 representing the highest density.

Table 5.5   Whole versus partial network density change

Institution	Whole network density	Partial network density	Density change (%)
Firm A	0.8571	0.7500	↓ 13
Firm B	0.7363	0.5455	↓ 26
Firm C	0.3388	0.2857	↓ 16

Note: * On a scale of 0–1, 1 representing the highest density.

continues to exhibit almost twice the density of the network in Firm C when only the most trusted network is considered.

Table 5.6 shows the occupations of the most trusted contacts. The occupations ranged similarly across subjects, as did the population of each role as a percentage of the network as a whole.

Each manager/director performs the same role, at similar firms, and is individually responsible for commercial real estate investment across regions distant from their home location. Though the subjects clearly have much in common, there are a number of significant variations in their respective networks which reflect typical brokerage practices in their respective markets. First, the degree of the Firm C network (the total number of alter listed) is far greater than that found in either UK case (Firm A: 13; Firm B: 14; Firm C: 23). As well, the effective size

Table 5.6   Alter occupation

Institution	Proportion fund or asset managers	Proportion agents/ brokers and surveyors	Proportion other
Firm A	14% (1/7)	71% (5/7)	14% (1/7)
Firm B	43% (3/7)	57% (4/7)	0% (0/7)
Firm C	33% (2/6)	50% (3/6)	17% (1/6)

of each network varies similarly (Firm A: 8.33; Firm B: 8.36; Firm C: 20.8), and the likelihood of ego and alter sharing the same location is also greatly reduced in Firm C, indicating greater geographical reach than either A or B. The constraint measures tell the same story (Firm A: 0.246; Firm B: 0.255; Firm C: 0.111). The network outlined for Firm C is clearly less constrained and has a greater number of structural holes than either of the UK networks by a large degree. This suggests the investment manager at Firm C would have more opportunities to source knowledge independent of a third-party broker when acquiring commercial real estate as compared to his UK counterparts at Firms A and B. Results further suggest that investment managers who typically rely on third-party brokers will prioritize constrained, dense networks conducive to rule enforcement and trust building. However, when the search responsibility remains within the firm, the investment manager will prioritize a less constrained, more geographically expansive social network.

Though these results are based on a very small sample of social networks, they do support the chapter's assertion that city making practices in commercial real estate markets vary between top global cities in ways not obviously related to qualities of the real estate, nor experience of the investor. Brokers summon individual and collective agency to reproduce and maintain practices of intermediation that become internalized in the network priorities of the managers who represent investment firms. Additional ego-centric network studies were contemplated, but time constraints during the US portion of the study and difficulty in finding senior investment managers/directors willing to get involved in a time-consuming audit of their personal social network rendered further analysis impossible.

5.5   CONCLUSION

Through careful analysis of a large sample of data pertaining to commercial real estate transactions in New York City and London over a ten-year period and examination of the social networks of a small mix of investment managers active in each city, this chapter explored the linkages between common forms of broker intermediation and the social networks of investment managers/directors who acquire commercial real estate for large investment firms.

Broker intermediaries tap social networks to locate information (knowledge) and facilitate exchange between investors, a prerequisite to the movement of capital into commercial real estate in each city. When investors acquire commercial real estate in New York City, the role of buyer intermediary is typically absorbed within the investment firm. In London, on the other hand, buyer intermediation is more likely to be contracted out to third-party brokers external to the firm. Brokers are found to exercise agency both individually and collectively to maintain and reproduce practices of intermediation in London that are different to those found in New York. Divergent practices persist despite higher transaction costs, offering the London broker a unique *tertius* role in global city making.

Evidence of a feedback effect whereby practices of intermediation impact the social network priorities of investment managers which, in turn, reinforce local broker practice is also found. Indeed, social networks reflect the institutions of practice particular to each market (e.g. North, 1991), and those practices become embedded in the social network priorities of individual investment actors and are reproduced through the individual and collective agency. The results challenge assertions of homogeneity in the market systems of global cities; among markets for different financial assets – i.e. real estate – predictions of an 'end of geography' have been greatly exaggerated (O'Brien, 1992).

It is important to note that while findings regarding typical brokerage practice are robust and statistically significant across the study period, caution must be exercised in drawing broad conclusions from the social networks of three investment managers/directors. While not generalizable across the population of investors active in the commercial real estate markets of New York City and London, the network analysis attempted in this chapter contributes to our understanding of how social networks and agency impact market practice and global city making.

There are any number of possible extensions to this work, including expansion along the lines of what is presented here, and parallel studies of the social networks of commercial brokers. As well, studies of broker networks in, and between, global cities would provide unique insight into how these networks embed and reproduce practices. It would also be beneficial to broaden the focus of future work to include city making in a wider range of countries so we might better understand how social networks embed institutions of practice, and better recognize the subtle forces shaping economic actors and practices across global cities.

NOTES

1. This was provided by Real Capital Analytics (RCA), a research organization that collects and analyses data on real estate investment transactions in all major real estate markets across the globe. For properties over US$2.5 million in the US and US$10 million or greater elsewhere RCA estimates their coverage to be 95 per cent above these thresholds. Transactions span the period Q1 2001 to Q4 2011.
2. From 10 687 transactions provided by RCA. Records pertaining to development sites, and incomplete records, were removed from the study leaving 9338 transactions, or 87.4 per cent of the original.
3. Transactions involving institutional sellers of commercial real estate that do not indicate broker representation for the seller fall outside normal market practice as described during interviews with US investors (Scofield, 2011) and are likely to be recording errors. For a portion of transactions involving private, non-institutional buyers/sellers the use of a limited liability company (LLC) in New York City among investors seeking liability protections and potential preferential tax treatment can obscure both the identity of the principals and intermediaries involved.
4. Brokerage fees typically range around 1 per cent of the sale price of the asset, each.
5. For example, the form of brokerage had no bearing on other aspects of asset liquidity in London – e.g., the time taken to buy and sell commercial real estate (Devaney and Scofield, 2015).
6. Though included in the constraint score calculation, hierarchy scores are not shown for each case.
7. Constraint and density measures were compiled and illustrated using UCINET 6 for Windows (Borgatti et al., 2002).

REFERENCES

Ahuja, G., G. Soda and A. Zaheer (2012), 'The genesis and dynamics of organizational networks', *Organization Science*, **23** (2), 434–448.
Baker, W.E. and D. Obstfeld (1999), 'Social capital by design: Structures, strategies, and institutional context', in R.T.A.J. Leenders and S.M. Gabbay (eds), *Corporate Social Capital and Liability*, Boston: Kluwer Academic, pp. 88–105.
Borgatti, S.P., M.G. Everett and L.C. Freeman (2002), *Ucinet for Windows: Software for Social Network Analysis*, Harvard, MA: Analytic Technologies.
Burt, R.S. (1992), *Structural Holes: The Social Structure of Competition*, Cambridge, MA: Harvard University Press.
Burt, R.S. (1997), 'A note on social capital and network content', *Social Networks*, **19** (4), 355–373.
Burt, R.S. (2000), 'The network structure of social capital', in B.M. Staw and R.I. Sutton (eds), *Research in Organizational Behavior, Volume 22*, Greenwich, CT, USA: JAI Press, pp. 345–423.
Clark, G.L. and A.H.B. Monk (2013), 'Financial institutions, information, and investing-at-a-distance', *Environment and Planning A*, **45** (6), 1318–1336.
Devaney, S. and D. Scofield (2013), 'Broker use and the cost of liquidity in commercial real estate investment', *Journal of European Real Estate Research*, **6** (3), 279–302.
Devaney, S. and D. Scofield (2015), 'Liquidity and the drivers of search, due diligence and transaction times for UK commercial real estate investments', *Journal of Property Research*, **32** (4), 362–383.

Granovetter, M.S. (1973), 'The strength of weak ties', *American Journal of Sociology*, **78** (6), 1360–1380.

Hall, P. and K. Pain (eds) (2006), *The Polycentric Metropolis: Learning from Mega-City Regions in Europe*, London: Earthscan.

Hoyler, M., R.C. Kloosterman and M. Sokol (2008), 'Polycentric puzzles – emerging mega-city regions seen through the lens of advanced producer services', *Regional Studies*, **42** (8), 1055–1064.

Kilduff, M. and D.J. Brass (2010), 'Organizational social network research: Core ideas and key debates', *The Academy of Management Annals*, **4** (1), 317–357.

Leyshon, A. and N. Thrift (2007), 'The capitalization of almost everything: The future of finance and capitalism', *Theory, Culture & Society*, **24** (7–8), 97–115.

Lin, N. (2001), *Social Capital: A Theory of Social Structure and Action*, Cambridge: Cambridge University Press.

Lizieri, C. (2009), *Towers of Capital: Office Markets & International Financial Services*, Chichester, UK: Wiley-Blackwell.

Lizieri, C. and D. Mekic (2018), 'Real estate and global capital networks: Drilling into the City of London', in M. Hoyler, C. Parnreiter and A. Watson (eds), *Global City Makers: Economic Actors and Practices in the World City Network*, Cheltenham, UK and Northampton, MA, USA: Edward Elgar Publishing, pp. 60–82.

Marin, A. and K.N. Hampton (2007), 'Simplifying the personal network name generator: Alternatives to traditional multiple and single name generators', *Field Methods*, **19** (2), 163–193.

Marsden, P.V. (1982), 'Brokerage behavior in restricted exchange networks', in P.V. Marsden and N. Lin (eds), *Social Structure and Network Analysis*, Beverly Hills, CA: Sage, pp. 201–218.

Marsden, P.V. (1990), 'Network data and measurement', *Annual Review of Sociology*, **16**, 435–463.

McGuire, S. and M. Chan (2000), 'The NY-LON life', *Newsweek-International Edition*, 13 November, 40–46.

North, D.C. (1991), 'Institutions', *Journal of Economic Perspectives*, **5** (1), 97–112.

O'Brien, R. (1992), *Global Financial Integration: The End of Geography*, London: Chatham House.

Obstfeld, D. (2005), 'Social networks, the *tertius iungens* orientation, and involvement in innovation', *Administrative Science Quarterly*, **50** (1), 100–130.

Reagans, R.E. and E.W. Zuckerman (2008), 'Why knowledge does not equal power: The network redundancy trade-off', *Industrial and Corporate Change*, **17** (5), 903–944.

Sassen, S. (1991), *The Global City: New York, London, Tokyo*, Princeton, NJ: Princeton University Press.

Sassen, S. (1999), 'Global financial centres' *Foreign Affairs*, **78** (1), 75–87.

Scofield, D. (2011), *Risk, Cost and Capital: Liquidity and Transaction Cost Pricing in Commercial Real Estate Investment*, unpublished PhD thesis, University of Sheffield.

Scott, J. (2000), *Social Network Analysis*, London: Sage.

Simmel, G. (1950), *The Sociology of Georg Simmel*, trans. and ed. K.H. Wolff, New York, USA, London, UK: The Free Press.

Smith, R.G. (2012), 'NY-LON', in B. Derudder, M. Hoyler, P.J. Taylor and F. Witlox (eds), *International Handbook of Globalization and World Cities*, Cheltenham, UK and Northampton, MA, USA: Edward Elgar Publishing, pp. 421–428.

Taylor, P.J., B. Derudder, J. Faulconbridge, M. Hoyler and P. Ni (2014), 'Advanced producer service firms as strategic networks, global cities as strategic places', *Economic Geography*, **90** (3), 267–291.

Völker, B. and H. Flap (2004), 'Social networks and performance at work: A study of the returns of social capital in doing one's job', in H. Flap and B. Völker (eds), *Creation and Returns of Social Capital*, London: Routledge, pp.172–196.

Wójcik, D. (2013), 'The dark side of NY-LON: Financial centres and the global financial crisis', *Urban Studies*, **50** (13), 2736–2752.

Zenger, T.R., T. Felin and L. Bigelow (2011), 'Theories of the firm-market boundary', *The Academy of Management Annals*, **5** (1), 89–133.

APPENDIX A5.1   CONSTRAINT MEASURES, FIRM A

		Degree	EffSize	Efficiency	Constraint
E	(London)	13.000	8.325	0.640	0.246
A1	(London)	12.000	5.950	0.496	0.335
A2	(London)	12.000	5.847	0.487	0.339
A3	(London)	9.000	3.518	0.391	0.427
A4	(Manchester)	8.000	3.476	0.435	0.516
A5	(London)	6.000	2.335	0.389	0.734
A6	(London)	12.000	6.662	0.555	0.322
A7	(London)	12.000	6.606	0.551	0.333
A8	(London)	13.000	7.614	0.586	0.307
A9	(London)	10.000	4.160	0.416	0.393
A10	(London)	12.000	5.425	0.452	0.373
A11	(London)	12.000	5.545	0.462	0.380
A12	(London)	8.000	3.099	0.387	0.481
A13	(London)	9.000	3.465	0.385	0.430

Notes:
EffSize = size of network minus redundancy in network.
Efficiency = effective size / actual size of network.
Constraint = summary measure that taps the extent to which ego's connections are to others
who are connected to one another. More in network connection equals higher constraint.

APPENDIX A5.2 CONSTRAINT MEASURES, FIRM B

		Degree	EffSize	Efficiency	Constraint
E	(London)	14.000	8.360	0.597	0.255
A1	(London)	13.000	7.224	0.556	0.312
A2	(London)	14.000	8.188	0.585	0.293
A3	(London)	13.000	7.297	0.561	0.301
A4	(London)	6.000	3.002	0.500	0.604
A5	(London)	13.000	6.829	0.525	0.318
A6	(London)	12.000	7.132	0.594	0.313
A7	(London)	12.000	5.773	0.481	0.338
A8	(London)	11.000	4.843	0.440	0.361
A9	(Edinburgh)	10.000	5.028	0.503	0.403
A10	(London)	12.000	6.203	0.517	0.360
A11	(London)	12.000	5.792	0.483	0.327
A12	(London)	12.000	6.424	0.535	0.304
A13	(London)	13.000	6.906	0.531	0.332
A14	(London)	5.000	1.384	0.277	0.723

Notes:
EffSize = size of network minus redundancy in network.
Efficiency = effective size / actual size of network.
Constraint = summary measure that taps the extent to which ego's connections are to others who are connected to one another. More in network connection equals higher constraint.

APPENDIX A5.3   CONSTRAINT MEASURES, FIRM C

		Degree	EffSize	Efficiency	Constraint
E	(Atlanta)	23.000	20.828	0.906	0.111
A1	(Chicago)	11.000	6.737	0.612	0.362
A2	(Chicago)	12.000	7.343	0.612	0.342
A3	(Atlanta)	3.000	1.381	0.460	1.218
A4	(Chicago)	6.000	2.131	0.355	0.611
A5	(Chicago)	11.000	6.717	0.611	0.352
A6	(Chicago)	10.000	5.570	0.557	0.387
A7	(Minneapolis)	7.000	3.734	0.533	0.515
A8	(Chicago)	8.000	4.237	0.530	0.473
A9	(Atlanta)	2.000	1.000	0.500	1.286
A10	(Atlanta)	7.000	4.162	0.595	0.524
A11	(Atlanta)	2.000	1.000	0.500	1.510
A12	(Atlanta)	3.000	1.515	0.505	0.987
A13	(Atlanta)	7.000	4.140	0.591	0.520
A14	(Atlanta)	2.000	1.000	0.500	1.322
A15	(Atlanta)	3.000	1.494	0.498	1.049
A16	(Atlanta)	13.000	8.501	0.654	0.320
A17	(Atlanta)	6.000	3.076	0.513	0.593
A18	(Roanoke)	1.000	1.000	1.000	1.000
A19	(NYC)	2.000	1.045	0.523	1.188
A20	(Austin)	10.000	7.039	0.704	0.369
A21	(Atlanta)	12.000	7.666	0.639	0.341
A22	(Atlanta)	12.000	8.199	0.683	0.336
A23	(NYC)	3.000	1.513	0.504	1.134

Notes:
EffSize = size of network minus redundancy in network.
Efficiency = effective size / actual size of network.
Constraint = summary measure that taps the extent to which ego's connections are to others who are connected to one another. More in network connection equals higher constraint.

6 The making of transnational urban space: financial professionals in the global city Tokyo

Sakura Yamamura

6.1 INTRODUCTION

Research on global cities, which has focused predominantly on firm- and city-level quantitative data and policy issues (Brenner and Keil, 2006; Derudder et al., 2012), has tended to overlook the agency of human actors in the process of global city making. Oft-cited exceptions include studies of transnational professionals and their business networks spanning the globe (e.g. Beaverstock, 2002, 2005; Faulconbridge, 2008; Morgan, 2001), which adopt qualitative methodologies to study individual actors and their economic practices. Yet, such work still fails to take full account of the role of financial professionals in global city making, since they are primarily considered in terms of their agency and practices within globally operating corporations. Migrant professionals are recognized as crucial agents in global city making but remain situated within the economic framework of the multi- or transnational corporation at which they are employed. Such an approach tends to overlook their impact as *transnational individuals* with specific social practices and who through these practices are involved in urban space-making within particular global cities (Meier, 2015, 2016).

Starting from this point of critique, this chapter discusses the role of transnational professionals as individuals with dual functions in the process of global city making. This duality derives from the fact that these professionals are, on the one hand, decision-makers and business practitioners working in transnational corporations, and on the other hand, individuals whose social and place-making practices characterize them as transnational migrants. The chapter draws on qualitative data collected through semi-structured interviews with 45 transnational professionals in the financial industry. The interviews focused on obtaining information on their social practices, including local and global spatial dimensions, centered on the city of Tokyo, and partly expressed in the drawing of mental maps. Interviews with professionals were complemented by interviews with real estate agencies and group interviews with Tokyoites. Drawing insights from these data, the chapter seeks to provide a complementary view on global city making by presenting a conceptual base and accompanying empirical evidence on space-making processes at the micro-level of transnational migrants who move from one global city to another due to their professional careers.

6.2   CONCEPTUAL FRAMEWORK

Research on global city making has tended to concentrate on the genesis and function of the global cities network within the world economy. Relatively little attention has been paid to the urban spatial dimensions of the making of global cities. Earlier debates on urban transformations focused predominantly on the nature of urban society in global cities (for example, on labour markets and social polarization; Sassen, 1991; Hamnett, 1994), but less on the actual *making* of global city spaces. Although global cities have been identified as the 'most strategic spaces for the formation of transnational identities and communities' (Sassen, 1996, p. 205) within the global economy, and have recently been identified as 'nodal points' which are 'intersections of the global commodity chains and the world city network' and where 'transnationality from above emerges as a distinct physical and social environment' (Parnreiter, 2012, p. 100), the spatial formation processes in these cities in the context of global city making have not yet been sufficiently researched.

In fact, although transnational space has been dealt with extensively (Pries, 2001; Faist, 2000; Jackson et al., 2004), little empirical work has focused on the urban scale. This is especially the case when it comes to taking an actor-based approach that considers transnational professionals as not only actors of the global but also of the local urban through space-making in the context of global cities (Meier, 2015). Research has focused on elitism in daily living rather than on actual involvement in the urban transformation through day-to-day living (e.g. Beaverstock, 2011; Yeoh and Willis, 2005; cf. also the debate on the super-rich by Hay and Beaverstock, 2016, or Webber and Burrows, 2016).

One body of research that has sought to address the issue of urban space-making and global city formation is that on real estate development (Fainstein, 2001; Parnreiter, 2009; Parnreiter et al., 2013; Lizieri, 2009, 2012; Lizieri and Mekic, 2018). This has argued that specific spatial conditions are required by corporations and industries involved in the global economy, such as the finance, real estate and insurance industries as well as other advanced producer services. Yet, in this literature the focus has remained firmly on *corporate* real estate rather than the impact transnational professionals may also have on the private real estate market and the urban economy. Professionals, as individual actors, also have their specific spatial choices and demands, for example residential choices, and an impact on space-making can be anticipated. An actor-based approach enables us to shed light on the impact of these transnational professionals, through their residential and daily locational decisions, on the creation and transformation of transnational urban space in global cities.

Another reason for the lack of actor-based perspectives in studying the urban impacts of global city making is the division between economic–geographical and sociological–anthropological perspectives on transnationalism. In the economic–geographical approach, transnationality is primarily considered in terms of corporate business functions (Dicken, 2007) and focuses on the corporate elite (Sklair, 2001; Beaverstock, 2002, 2005). While such an approach has been labelled as 'world city network from below' (Beaverstock, 2007), it might actually be more accurately thought of as 'transnationality from above' (Parnreiter, 2012, p. 100). In the sociological–anthropological approach, transnationalism is a concept that is situated firmly in the context of underprivileged labour migration 'from below' (Smith and Guarnizo, 1998).

These two diverging approaches, however, do not exist in contradiction to one another. On the one hand, transnational corporations are described as '[having] the power to coordinate and control operations in more than one country, even if [they do] not own them' (Dicken, 2007, p. 106). Spatially they are active 'within transnational production networks' (accompanied by social networks) 'both within and between different countries', and showing 'geographical flexibility' (Dicken, 2007, pp. 106–107). As corporations do not have agency themselves, but rather have agency through decision-makers and actors within these corporate shells, there is a strong assumption that transnational professionals as active corporate actors also share the characteristics attributed above: a specific 'new management mentality' (Bartlett and Ghoshal, 2002, p. 20) of transnational business making as well as personal living. On the other hand, drawing on migration research, transnational migrants can be considered as those who perceive themselves as being different from the local population; they have anchors in specific cultures, especially in their country of origin, but have also developed attachments to the host country or countries; and yet share a specific newly created culture of their own.

Juxtaposing these criteria, it becomes clear that this disciplinary division can be overcome by viewing transnational professionals as part of the transnational migrant population, despite their being highly skilled privileged corporate migrants. Analogously, urban space-making by transnational corporate professionals in global cities can also be understood as part of the making of transnational urban space in the sense associated with transnationalism research. Conceptually bringing together transnationalism in economic geography research with transnationalism in migration research, the aim of this chapter is to examine the dual-natured transnationality of corporate professionals and their impact on space-making in global cities.

6.3   TOKYO AS CASE STUDY

As emphasized above, empirical studies of space-making in global cities are still rather rare, especially those that develop in-depth analyses of actors and their socio-spatial behaviours. Tokyo has often been cited as one of the most established global cities, one of the 'big three' with New York and London (Sassen, 1991), but its status as global city has remained largely empirically unsubstantiated, especially with regard to transnational professionals. This is partly due to the strong shift in general and academic interest to the emergence of other vibrant and economically more dynamic global cities in the Asian region, such as Singapore and Hong Kong, and the long economic downturn in Japan since the early 1990s. However, this shortcoming in empirical work may also be due to the methodological issue that access to the field might be (or might appear to be) more difficult in the Japanese language setting of Tokyo.

During the economic downturn, also known as the Lost Decade(s), scepticism emerged regarding Tokyo's global city status. Reservations regarding Tokyo's status, however, had already been hinted at by Friedmann, who suggested that Tokyo was a 'major atypical case' with regards to 'the concentration and accumulation of international capital', at least in the 1980s (Friedmann, 1986, pp. 75, 73). Yet, literature succeeding the seminal works of Friedmann (1986) and Sassen (1991), based on economic data during a bubble in the economy, unanimously affirmed Tokyo's status as a 'world city' (Rimmer, 1986; Douglass, 1988, 1993; Fujita, 1991; Machimura, 1992).

Subsequently during the economic downturn, however, scholars would again begin to emphasize the specificity of Tokyo among global cities (Machimura, 1994; Kamo, 2000a, 2000b). In addition to Friedmann's (1986) comment on the limited accumulation of international capital, critiques regarding Tokyo's world city status can be summarized roughly into: (1) debates regarding the role of the governmental state, including Tokyo's urban politics and development (White, 1998a; Hill and Fujita, 2000; Douglass, 2000; Kamo, 2000a; Hill and Kim, 2000; Saito, 2003; Saito and

Thornley, 2003); (2) the fact that Tokyo's competitiveness was maintained by manufacturing, whereas the financial industry was characterized as 'immature' compared to New York or London (Fujita, 1991; Kamo, 1988; Johnson, 1982); (3) debates regarding social polarization, including the relatively limited nature of immigration (cf. the exchange in *Urban Affairs Review* 1998 between White (1998b), Sassen and Smith); and (4) the long-lasting post-bubble economic malaise of the Lost Decade(s), which put breaks on urban policy-makers' euphoria and halted the symbolic usage of the vision of a 'world-leading global city' in politics (Machimura, 1998). Despite such doubts, however, data from the Globalization and World Cities (GaWC) research network (Taylor et al., 2011) provide evidence that Tokyo has maintained a Top 10 position amongst the most globally interconnected cities, albeit with some signs of relative connectivity decline in the 2000s (Derudder and Taylor, 2016).

6.4   METHODOLOGY

The novel empirical evidence presented in this chapter is based on 45 semi-structured interviews with professionals of transnational corporations in the financial industry in Tokyo. Interviews were on average 45 to 60 minutes in length; one third were conducted face-to-face and two thirds via telephone. To address the criticism of so-called 'methodological national-ism' (Wimmer and Glick Schiller, 2002) in transnationalism research, the interviewees were not selected according to their ethnicity, but their affiliation to a transnational corporation and their transnational migration background, i.e. only those with extensive short and long-term migration experiences. Such an approach also takes into account the multidirectional and multiethnic nature of this particular form of transnational migration, as well as the interrelation with economic transnationalism. The sample covered a diversity of ethnic and citizenship backgrounds. Citizens of Anglophone countries were the majority, yet with diverse ethnic back-grounds (including Indian, Korean and Slovak).

The research focused on professionals in the financial industry, includ-ing directly related advanced producer service providers. Following the economic definition of transnationalism offered by Dicken (2007), only professionals in higher managerial positions were interviewed, as they are considered to have the most agency in decision-making processes within the transnational corporation, thus have the power to coordinate and control operations transnationally. For the purposes of the case study, all interviewees were required to have worked and resided in Tokyo in the recent past or at the time of study.

The interviews covered biographical backgrounds, with a particular focus on mobility over life and career course; the characteristics of the business culture in the particular transnational corporation and the financial industry in general; and, importantly, questions regarding trans-nationality in their individual lives, i.e. social practices and socio-spatial patterns both in formal, semi-formal and informal or private settings. Face-to-face interviewees were also asked to draw mental maps, and a locational mapping was undertaken of the activity spaces of the professionals based on information gathered in the interviews. Complementary interviews were conducted with other relevant actors in the global city making process, such as real estate agencies specializing in highly skilled foreign customers, and with the municipal authority of Minato ward where this group is spatially concentrated. Findings were triangulated with group interviews with Japanese Tokyoite peers and through ethnographic site surveys.

6.5 MAKING TRANSNATIONAL URBAN SPACE

Focusing on those issues directly relevant to the duality of the contribution of transnational financial professionals to global city making, four main findings can be extricated from the interview data, as outlined in the following sections.

6.5.1 Differentiation of Transnational Migrant Patterns in Urban Space

Socio-spatial patterns resulting from what has been referred to as 'trans-nationalization from below', i.e. transnational migration especially of low-skilled to skilled labour migrants, can be roughly but clearly traced by studying ethnic towns or ethnic enclaves in Tokyo. Places like Little India in Nishi-Kasai, Korean Town in Shin-Okubo, or the Vietnamese quarter in Kamata are such examples. Ethnic shops and restaurants, as well as people of the respective ethnic groups are concentrated in these areas, which are by and large situated in less prestigious districts, often in industrial or residential areas with lower rents (with the exception of the French Town in Kagurazaka). In fact, research on this aspect of transnationalism has been carried out extensively in Japan, focusing specifically on South-American Nikkei and Chinese and Korean Zainichi migrants 'from below' (e.g. Watado et al., 2003; Tajima, 2003; Lesser, 2003; Yamanaka, 2003; Takenoshita et al., 2013). Drawing on extant academic literature and on reports in mass media, these areas of 'transnationalism from below' can be roughly outlined as shown in Figure 6.1 (left), with a spatial concentration to the north and east of central Tokyo.

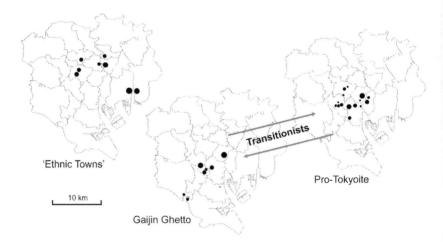

Figure 6.1   Socio-spatial patterns of transnational migrants in Tokyo

In contrast to this map of 'transnationalism from below' are the two maps illustrating the socio-spatial patterns of the transnational financial professionals interviewed as part of this study (Figure 6.1, centre and right). Given the common perception of such highly skilled professionals as very affluent and preferring luxurious lifestyles (giving rise to the label 'transnational elites'; cf. Beaverstock, 2002, 2005; Yeoh and Willis, 2005), it is no surprise that the areas which these transnational professionals popu-late in their daily lives – in formal, semi-formal and informal settings – are different from the transmigrants from below. They concentrate in the more central to southern parts of Tokyo, which are areas with higher rents and prestige. However, there is also a differentiation within the group of trans-national professionals. Compared to the socio-spatial patterns depicted in the central map (Gaijin Ghetto), those on the right (Pro-Tokyoite) are also concentrated in the city centre but show more dispersion and higher diversity. Further, some transnational professionals actively avoid the enclave-like small islands on the outskirts of southwest Tokyo close to the neighbouring prefecture.

The explanation for these two patterns is as follows. The so-called Gaijin Ghetto (centre) can be described as encompassing urban spaces typically adapted to the needs and convenience of affluent foreign residents. These areas house many foreign governmental institutions, such as consulates and embassies, as well as affiliated clubs, for example the Tokyo American Club. In areas such as Roppongi, Azabu, Hiroo or Ebisu, leisure activities are also especially directed at this group of migrants, for example corporate or consulate organized group meetings, English-speaking restaurants and British pubs, international supermarkets with imported gourmet goods, and global chain cafes and fast food chains. Services in these areas, such as mobile phone retail shops or medical and pharmaceutical services, are often provided bi- or even multilingual, and the cityscape is characterized by English language advertisements. Characteristic for these areas is also the location of international schools or the proximity to bus routes to international schools. Housing is not only high-end in terms of cost and amenities, but is also Western-style, in residential areas with a high density of single houses for foreign families.

Such locational choices of transnational professionals are often referred to as a 'bubble' or 'cocoon', as one interviewee described: 'Oh, people call it expat bubble. If you want to, you never have to interact with anybody Japanese.' The name 'Gaijin Ghetto' reflects this, whereby *gaijin* is a slightly pejorative term for foreigner, and 'ghetto' is used ironically as these areas are privileged and highly-esteemed. Yet the use of the term 'ghetto' also clearly indicates the separation of this area from local society. These are areas to which highly mobile transnational migrants can adapt quickly; there is a familiarity with such 'non-spaces' (Augé, 2008), as they are replicated in a similar way in numerous other global cities.

The more novel finding of this study, however, is the pattern which can be described as 'Pro-Tokyoite' (Figure 6.1, right). These socio-spatial patterns partly overlap with the areas of the Gaijin Ghetto. These remain central to the daily life of transnational professionals as places of work where formal and semi-formal business meetings take place and where their families remain attached to institutions, such as the consulate or the international school. However, these 'Pro-Tokyoite' transnational professionals venture out of the 'expat bubble' and seek to build stronger ties with local society and culture. Socio-spatial characteristics of this group include, for example, the choice of international schools with a stronger emphasis on biculturalism in education; or of leisure activities consciously seeking local integration, such as taking children to art classes in the local Japanese neighbourhood or taking yoga classes with Japanese rather than English-speaking clubs.

Furthermore, reflecting a stronger attachment and integration with local society and more direct social contacts with Japanese people, transnational professionals adopting 'Pro-Tokyoite' patterns can also be found in areas such as Ginza or Akasaka, which were described by one interviewee as 'very Japanese'. However, although these Pro-Tokyoite socio-spatial patterns appear to be more strongly localized in Tokyoite urban society, they are still located in quite specific areas of Tokyoite peers, that is to say in areas where mostly upper-class Japanese live and socialize. The transnationalizing urban spaces of the Pro-Tokyoites are located where the original aristocracy and higher caste resided until the nineteenth century (Seidensticker, 1983), and they have remained prestigious areas among the older generation of Tokyoites. Conversely, the Gaijin Ghetto areas are perceived as less prestigious among the old Tokyoites, since areas such as Roppongi are outside the historical city centre and have developed into a red-light district (Cybriwsky, 2011). However, more recently, according to Tokyoite interviewees, these areas have become well established and highly esteemed by younger generations and the *nouveau riche*.

These differentiations in socio-spatial patterns contribute directly to the transformation of urban space because demands of these specific groups of transnational professionals and their families are met by the local supply of goods and services directed towards them. Especially in the case of the Gaijin Ghetto areas, the urban space of Tokyo has been transformed in that multilingual signs and services increasingly prevail amongst the shops and businesses, impacting on the cityscape. At the same time, also in those areas characterized by more Pro-Tokyoite professionals, there has occurred a shift towards a transnationalization of society through social interactions, be it on the personal level or in business.

Of course, socio-spatial patterns are neither rigid nor immutable. Within and beyond the two broad patterns identified above, there is a variety of more complex patterns. For example, a third group of what might be termed 'transitionists' can be identified, which encompasses those professionals who have changed their socio-spatial patterns over time.

6.5.2   Explaining Socio-spatial Patterns

The identification of these distinct socio-spatial geographies requires an exploration of factors influencing the locational decisions that result in the Gaijin Ghetto, Pro-Tokyoite and other patterns. One common feature for all these was the availability of sufficient capital to enable the social practices that are bound up with particular spatial characteristics. Those who lost financial means over the years – as occurred during the global financial crisis – experienced drastic changes in their socio-spatial patterns and faced dislodgement from the central areas of the Gaijin Ghetto and from the upper-class Tokyoite areas.

Factors such as language proficiency in the non-English environment or a Japanese partner appear to be highly influential for the Pro-Tokyoite socio-spatial pattern, leading to increased interaction with local culture and society. However, there are also transnational professionals married to a Japanese partner and with fluency in Japanese, who remain closely attached to the foreign expatriate socio-spatial pattern, preferring the Gaijin Ghetto with its British pubs or the Tokyo American Club. Residential duration was not a conditional factor, nor was the migration experience as such, for example extensive migration experience in childhood or in adulthood.

The following two cases exemplify how very similar backgrounds can result in divergent socio-spatial patterns. Both professionals hold high-level managerial positions in transnational corporations in the financial services, and both relocated from their previous base in New York to Tokyo approximately one year prior to the interviews taking place. Both are American citizens around 40 years of age, married to non-Japanese spouses and accompanied by small children. Being fairly new to the environment, one of the professionals, whose socio-spatial pattern centred on the Gaijin Ghetto, mentioned new technology as a crucial tool for keeping social ties with family and friends: 'So I don't get homesick. Maybe it was different 25 years ago, but now with Skype and Facetime, you just . . . we got to manage the time difference, but it's really easy.' This echoes findings in the literature on transnationalism, where cross-border social ties have been observed to be strongly supported by technological development (Vertovec, 2009).

For the second professional, who has a more Pro-Tokyoite socio-spatial pattern, the usage of such technologies goes beyond this traditional tie-keeping with the home country to include the added dimension of supporting exploration of the local environment and enabling interaction: 'I think a big help is frankly the iPhone and technologies that . . . you can always find a map and sort of show somebody where you want to go in the worst case scenario. We have translation features on the phone that you can speak into and Google translate . . . .'

These cases illustrate how the same technical devices support the transnational character of their everyday lives not only at the global scale, but can also lead to different socio-spatial patterns in the local setting. One can see similar outcomes from bringing up children: some professionals describe their children as the mediators to build stronger attachment with local society, thus resulting in a more Pro-Tokyoite socio-spatial pattern. However, there are also those who perceive the enrolment and involvement of their children in international schools as a reason for being attached more strongly to the Gaijin Ghetto areas.

Affiliation with a specific industry, as well as available financial means, appear to more strongly shape a professional's identity than their ethnic origin, and this is reflected in specific socio-spatial patterns. As an example, one interviewee, an ethnic Korean transnational professional, did not have any ties or patterns in the ethnic Korean Town around Shin-Okubo. Rather, he preferred dining at Jojoen in downtown Tokyo for

Korean food, a Korean restaurant chain with branches in central Tokyo characterized by high prestige and high-end customers. A similar pattern was observed with an ethnic Indian transnational professional, whose social practices were not connected to the area around Nishi-Kasai with a high concentration of Indian population as well as an Indian school, shops and restaurants.

These findings are significant in the context of transnational migration research, which has tended to focus on single ethnic groups in various locations, but which has not addressed the de-nationalizing elements of transnationalism in the sense suggested by Wimmer and Glick Schiller (2002). The results demonstrate that transnational professionals are a group of transmigrants who share comparable migration experiences and demonstrate socio-spatial patterns where ethnic or national origin is less crucial: social interactions and places defined by profession and industrial affiliation significantly shape socio-spatial patterns.

6.5.3 Locational Preferences within the Global City

Affiliation to an occupation within the financial industry appears to be a clear indication of, and reason for, specific urban socio-spatial patterns. On the global level, the locational choice of transnational professionals as to where to migrate to is quite clear and predictable with regard to their occupation in the financial industry: 'Financial services is about money, so most people [in] financial services move to where the money is', that is to say, where business in the global economy is done. On the local level, however, the affiliation to the financial industry is also bound up with specific working practices which again result in particular socio-spatial patterns. The financial industry still requires face-to-face interactions which need adequate locational settings as well as the proximity to business partners. Technological infrastructure allowing access to information and connections to customers and colleagues in other corporate branches is crucial, too.

At the same time, cost and time efficiencies are important features for businesses in the financial industry, which impact socio-spatial patterns in global cities directly. This becomes especially clear when interviewing transnational professionals about their socio-spatial behaviour on business trips or shorter term assignments, which are often followed by prolonged residencies in the same cities. International hotels with standardized equipment and amenities are preferred to allow efficient adaptation to the environment, with hotels or temporary serviced apartments organized by the corporations in arrangements with hotel chains. These 'non-places' (Augé, 2008) within global cities 'are all kind of the same almost, but you need somewhere that is comfortable and quiet and near to the office and good internet access and stuff. That is all you need.' This illustrates what might be termed a socio-spatial 'confinement' for transnational professionals.

Socio-spatial patterns at the local level also depend on the types of business practices in which the professionals are engaged. Amongst those with more contact with local customers, for which intercultural competence and collaboration are required, the tendency to have Pro-Tokyoite socio-spatial patterns is greater. In advanced producer services such as accountancy or corporate law, transnational professionals show stronger tendencies to Pro-Tokyoite patterns as their interactions with the local population are more frequent and semi-formal meetings are also held according to the needs or presumed desires of customers. However, there are also managerial professionals who assign such semi-formal meetings to their Japanese colleagues, and those that maintain their Gaijin Ghetto socio-spatial patterns because they assume that their Japanese customers desire such locations during business contact with transnational corporations.

6.5.4 Impact of the Transnational Corporation on Locational Preferences

The impact of transnational corporations on the locational preferences of professionals in the global city is perhaps most marked with regard to residential choices. The following quotes exemplify the embeddedness of residential choices in a larger picture of transnational corporate strategies on the global scale, and the real estate market as part of the local urban economy. Asked about their decision to reside in the Gaijin Ghetto, one interviewee explained:

> I used to stay in the Imperial Hotel. And then they moved [me] from the Imperial Hotel into a serviced apartment. And the serviced apartment . . . was in the middle of Azabujuban. So when my wife came over, obviously, there are more Westerners round there . . . there are a couple of international supermarkets. Restaurants tend to be a little bit more foreigner-friendly. They have pictures or they will have English menus tucked away somewhere.

This quote indicates the services provided in these Gaijin Ghetto areas and the preferences the interviewee and his spouse have regarding the more Western environment. Yet it is the transnational corporation that had originally dispatched this professional to Tokyo on a short-term basis, first placing their employee in a (five star) hotel, then relocating him to a serviced apartment already in the middle of the Gaijin Ghetto. It is then perhaps no surprise that the transnational professional, after becoming accustomed to the area, remained there when the corporation assigned him for a longer stay. The residential choice of the transnational professional and, thus, his subsequent socio-spatial patterns, are bound up in the corporate policies and strategies in which the professional is embedded.

Furthermore, the following quote from a transnational professional with a stronger Pro-Tokyoite pattern illustrates the role that mediating real estate and relocation agencies – which often collaborate with transnational corporations – play in the selection of the socio-spatial patterning:

> It was funny when I was looking for apartments, I kept asking the brokers, I do not want to be limited to just this thing, 35 choices here [Gaijin Ghetto] and no choices outside. I said, "What about Aoyama and Meguro and all these places I have heard great things about? We would like to look a little bit more than just here", and I did not know the residential areas and I haven't been in them very much. So I always felt like he kept driving in circles that I could not figure out where we were. And then I said: "Wait, that building looks familiar", and we make a ride and come back and then he showed me another apartment. I said: "You are only showing me a part, like even if I ask you to go somewhere else."

This example illustrates clearly that even transnational professionals who are interested in going beyond the Gaijin Ghetto may be confined in their choice. As noted above, transnational corporations often collaborate with real estate agencies specialized in foreign corporate professionals, as this process is more time and cost efficient on the corporate side. It has been reported by real estate agencies that the trend to commission relocation companies even increased after the global financial crisis.

Corporate strategies are therefore one of the crucial elements for the emergence of the observed socio-spatial patterns. Not only are transnational professionals influenced in their social practices by the formal and semi-formal meetings which take place in corporate settings, and by the location of the corporations in the central business districts. It is also the global corporate strategy in relocating and dispatching professionals, which influences the socio-spatial patterns of transnational professionals and thus urban space-making in these global cities. Due to the high level of flexibility and adaptability to work and living conditions that is expected from transnational professionals, the need of transmigrants for an efficient adaptation to the environment is higher than if they were given more time for the planning of relocation. Transnational professionals, for example, tend to send their children to an international school as such schools can be found in other major cities worldwide and allow a smoother integration than local schools. Also, given constraints in terms of language ability and limitation in leisure time, many transmigrants have little capacity to engage with others outside their own families. Thus the demands of working in the industry impact directly and indirectly on the locational socio-spatial patterns of transnational professionals. This, in turn, demonstrates the complex interconnectedness of the global economy and transnational corporations and the urban socio-spatial patterns of transnational migrant professionals who contribute to the transformation of urban space within global cities.

6.6 CONCLUSION

Findings from this study demonstrate how the process of global city making cannot only be studied at the macro-level of the transnational corporation. Global city making is also a phenomenon affecting the transformation of urban space at the local level through the creation of transnational urban spaces in global cities. In this context, transnational professionals as corporate actors, but also as individuals with specific social practices and socio-spatial geographies, play a dual role in global city making: as managerial elites of transnational corporations they are involved in strategic decision-making that shapes the global economy and the position and role of particular cities within it. At the same time, through their business and private socio-spatial patterns, they are also directly involved in the transformation of global city spaces within a particular city. This chapter points not only to the dual nature of the role of transnational professionals in global city making, but draws attention to the importance of conceptually differentiating these roles, whilst at the same time highlighting their interconnection. Recognizing transnational professionals as the binding link between decisions and practices at the transnational corporate level, and spatial outcomes and impacts at the local level, can contribute to a better understanding of the complex economic and spatial dynamics of the making of global cities.

The use of Tokyo as a case study may appear problematic at first glance because the city has shown divergent characteristics to other global cities like New York or London. Yet, the focus on Tokyo provides a significant contribution to our understanding of processes of global city making outside these key English-speaking global cities. Transnational professional migrants face potentially more significant difficulties settling in Tokyo, for example due to language barriers as well as the visibility of their foreign status, than in more diverse and multilingual cities in Asia such as Hong Kong or Singapore. Thus the drive to cultivate socio-spatial patterns that are distinct from the local population could be exacerbated in the case of Tokyo. Yet, the findings of this research suggest there are a substantial number of transnational professionals who overcome such constraints.

The study further suggests that the socio-spatial patterns of transnational professionals observed in Tokyo are not necessarily limited to this context, but are also – and sometimes even more strongly – expressed during stays in other global cities. Interviews with those who had already moved away from Tokyo to other global cities, such as Singapore or Hong Kong, indicate that their socio-spatial patterns remained similar to those in Tokyo.

This chapter has argued that transnational urban spaces are a phenomenon locally anchored in specific global cities, yet simultaneously embedded in transnational corporate strategies. Since transnational corporations remain concentrated in a specific set of global cities, these transnational spaces spread on the global scale according to the logic of the world city network but require contextualized analysis as they concretize in specific places.

REFERENCES

Augé, M. (2008), *Non-Places: An Introduction to Supermodernity*, London: Verso.

Bartlett, C.A. and S. Ghoshal (2002), *Managing Across Borders: The Transnational Solution*, Boston, MA: Harvard Business School Press.

Beaverstock, J.V. (2002), 'Transnational elites in global cities: British expatriates in Singapore's financial district', *Geoforum*, **33** (4), 525–538.

Beaverstock, J.V. (2005), 'Transnational elites in the city: British highly-skilled inter-company transferees in New York City's financial district', *Journal of Ethnic and Migration Studies*, **31** (2), 245–268.

Beaverstock, J.V. (2007), 'World city networks "from below": International mobility and inter-city relations in the global investment banking industry', in P.J. Taylor, B. Derudder, P. Saey and F. Witlox (eds), *Cities in Globalization: Practices, Policies and Theories*, London: Routledge, pp. 52–71.

Beaverstock, J.V. (2011), 'Servicing British expatriate "talent" in Singapore: Exploring ordinary transnationalism and the role of the "expatriate" club', *Journal of Ethnic and Migration Studies*, **37** (5), 709–728.

Brenner, N. and R. Keil (eds) (2006), *The Global Cities Reader*, London: Routledge.

Cybriwsky, R.A. (2011), *Roppongi Crossing: The Demise of a Tokyo Nightclub District and the Reshaping of a Global City*, Athens, GA: University of Georgia Press.

Derudder, B. and P. Taylor (2016), 'Change in the world city network, 2000–2012', *The Professional Geographer*, **68** (4), 624–637.

Derudder, B., M. Hoyler, P.J. Taylor and F. Witlox (eds) (2012), *International Handbook of Globalization and World Cities*, Cheltenham, UK, Northampton, MA, USA: Edward Elgar Publishing.

Dicken, P. (2007), *Global Shift: Mapping the Changing Contours of the World Economy* (5th edition), New York: Guilford Press.

Douglass, M. (1988), 'The transnationalization of urbanization in Japan', *International Journal of Urban and Regional Research*, **12** (3), 425–454.

Douglass, M. (1993), 'The "new" Tokyo story: Restructuring space and the struggle for place in a world city', in K. Fujita and R.C. Hill (eds), *Japanese Cities in the World Economy*, Philadelphia, PA: Temple University Press, pp. 83–119.

Douglass, M. (2000), 'Mega-urban regions and world city formation: Globalization, the economic crisis and urban policy issues in Pacific Asia', *Urban Studies*, **37** (12), 2315–2335.

Fainstein, S.S. (2001), *The City Builders: Property Development in New York and London, 1980–2000* (2nd edition), Lawrence, KS: University Press of Kansas.

Faist, T. (2000), *The Volume and Dynamics of International Migration and Transnational Social Spaces*, Oxford: Oxford University Press.

Faulconbridge, J.R. (2008), 'Managing the transnational law firm: A relational analysis of professional systems, embedded actors, and time-space-sensitive governance', *Economic Geography*, **84** (2), 185–210.

Friedmann, J. (1986), 'The world city hypothesis', *Development and Change*, **17** (1), 69–83.

Fujita, K. (1991), 'A world city and flexible specialization: Restructuring of the Tokyo metropolis', *International Journal of Urban and Regional Research*, **15** (2), 269–284.

Hamnett, C. (1994), 'Social polarisation in global cities: Theory and evidence', *Urban Studies*, **31** (3), 401–424.

Hay, I. and J.V. Beaverstock (eds) (2016), *Handbook on Wealth and the Super-Rich*, Cheltenham, UK, Northampton, MA, USA: Edward Elgar Publishing.

Hill, R.C. and K. Fujita (2000), 'State restructuring and local power in Japan', *Urban Studies*, **37** (4), 673–690.

Hill, R.C. and J.W. Kim (2000), 'Global cities and developmental states: New York, Tokyo and Seoul', *Urban Studies*, **37** (12), 2167–2195.

Jackson, P., P. Crang and C. Dwyer (eds) (2004), *Transnational Spaces*, London: Routledge.

Johnson, C. (1982), *MITI and the Japanese Miracle: The Growth of Industrial Policy, 1925–1975*, Stanford, CA: Stanford University Press.

Kamo. T. (1988), *Toshi no Seijigaku* [Politics of the City], Tokyo: Jichitai Kenkyusha.

Kamo, T. (2000a), 'An aftermath of globalisation? East Asian economic turmoil and Japanese cities adrift', *Urban Studies,* **37** (12), 2145–2165.

Kamo. T. (2000b), 'Examining Japanese city-regions in the light of the Asian economic crisis', *Asian Geographer*, **19** (1–2), 21–36.

Lesser, J. (ed.) (2003), *Searching from Home Abroad: Japanese Brazilians and Transnationalism*, Durham, NC: Duke University Press.

Lizieri, C. (2009), *Towers of Capital: Office Markets & International Financial Services*, Oxford: Wiley-Blackwell.

Lizieri, C. (2012), 'Global cities, office markets and capital flows', in B. Derudder, M. Hoyler, P.J. Taylor and F. Witlox (eds), *International Handbook of Globalization and World Cities*, Cheltenham, UK, Northampton, MA, USA: Edward Elgar Publishing, pp. 162–176.

Lizieri, C. and D. Mekic (2018), 'Real estate and global capital networks: Drilling into the City of London', in M. Hoyler, C. Parnreiter and A. Watson (eds), *Global City Makers: Economic Actors and Practices in the World City Network*, Cheltenham, UK and Northampton, MA, USA: Edward Elgar Publishing, pp. 60–82.

Machimura, T. (1992), 'The urban restructuring process in Tokyo in the 1980s: Transforming Tokyo into a world city', *International Journal of Urban and Regional Research*, **16** (1), 114–128.

Machimura, T. (1994), '*"Sekai toshi" Tōkyō no kōzō tenkan. Toshi risutorakuchuaringu no shakaigaku*' ['World City' Tokyo's Structural Revolution: The Sociology of Urban Restructuring], Tōkyō: Tōkyō Daigaku Shuppankai (Shakaigaku shirīzu).

Machimura, T. (1998), 'Symbolic use of globalization in urban politics in Tokyo', *International Journal of Urban and Regional Research*, **22** (2), 183–194.

Meier, L. (ed.) (2015), *Migrant Professionals in the City: Local Encounters, Identities and Inequalities*, New York: Routledge.

Meier, L. (2016), 'Dwelling in different localities: Identity performances of a white transnational professional elite in the City of London and the Central Business District of Singapore', *Cultural Studies*, **30** (3), 483–505.

Morgan, G. (2001), 'Transnational communities and business systems', *Global Networks*, **1** (2), 113–130.

Parnreiter, C. (2009), 'Global-City-Formation, Immobilienwirtschaft und Transnationalisierung: Das Beispiel Mexico City', *Zeitschrift für Wirtschaftsgeographie*, **53** (1–2), 138–155.

Parnreiter, C. (2012), 'Conceptualizing transnational urban spaces: Multicentered agency, placeless organizational logics, and the built environment', in S. Krätke, K. Wildner and S. Lanz (eds), *Transnationalism and Urbanism*, London: Routledge, pp. 91–111.

Parnreiter, C., J. Oßenbrügge and C. Haferburg (2013), 'Shifting corporate geographies in global cities of the South: Mexico City and Johannesburg as case studies', *Die Erde*, **144** (1), 1–16.

Pries, L. (ed.) (2001), *New Transnational Social Spaces: International Migration and Transnational Companies in the Early Twenty-First Century*, London: Routledge.

Rimmer, P. (1986), 'Japan's world cities: Tokyo, Osaka, Nagoya or Tokaido Megalopolis?', *Development and Change*, **17** (1), 121–157.

Saito, A. (2003), 'Global city formation in a capitalist developmental state: Tokyo and the waterfront sub-center project', *Urban Studies*, **40** (2), 283–308.

Saito, A. and A. Thornley (2003), 'Shifts in Tokyo's world city status and the urban planning response', *Urban Studies*, **40** (4), 665–685.

Sassen, S. (1991), *The Global City: New York, London, Tokyo*, Princeton, NJ: Princeton University Press.

Sassen, S. (1996), 'Whose city is it? Globalization and the formation of new claims', *Public Culture*, **8** (2), 205–223.

Sassen, S. (1998), 'Swirling that old wine around in the wrong bottle: A comment on White', *Urban Affairs Review* **33** (4), 478–481.

Seidensticker, E. (1983), *Low City, High City: Tokyo from Edo to Earthquake*, New York: Knopf.

Sklair, L. (2001), *The Transnational Capitalist Class*, Oxford: Blackwell.

Smith, M.P. (1998), 'The global city – whose social construct is it anyway? A comment on White', *Urban Affairs Review*, **33** (4), 482–488.

Smith, M.P. and L.E. Guarnizo (eds) (1998), *Transnationalism from Below*, New Brunswick, NJ: Transaction Publishers.

Tajima, J. (2003), 'Chinese newcomers in the global city Tokyo: Social networks and settlement tendencies', *International Journal of Japanese Sociology*, **12** (1), 68–78.

Takenoshita, H., Y. Chitose, S. Ikegami and E.A. Ishikawa (2013), 'Segmented assimilation, transnationalism, and educational attainment of Brazilian migrant children in Japan', *International Migration*, **52** (2), 84–99.

Taylor, P.J., P. Ni, B. Derudder, M. Hoyler, J. Huang and F. Witlox (eds) (2011), *Global Urban Analysis: A Survey of Cities in Globalization*, London: Earthscan.

Vertovec, S. (2009), *Transnationalism*, London: Routledge.

Watado, I., Y. Hirota and J. Tajima (eds) (2003), *Toshiteki sekai/community/ethnicity. Postmetropolis-ki no toshi ethnography-shusei* [Urbanized Society/Community/

Ethnicity. Compilation of Urban Ethnography in the Postmetropolis Era], Tokyo: Akashi Shoten.

Webber, R. and R. Burrows (2016), 'Life in an Alpha Territory: Discontinuity and conflict in an elite London "village"', *Urban Studies,* **53** (15), 3139–3154.

White, J.W. (1998a), 'Old wine, cracked bottle? Tokyo, Paris, and the global city hypothesis', *Urban Affairs Review*, **33** (4), 451–477.

White, J.W. (1998b), 'Half-empty bottle or no bottle at all? A rejoinder to Sassen and Smith', *Urban Affairs Review*, **33** (4), 489–491.

Wimmer, A. and N. Glick Schiller (2002), 'Methodological nationalism and beyond: Nation-state building, migration and the social sciences', *Global Networks*, **2** (4), 301–334.

Yamanaka, K. (2003), 'Feminized migration, community activism and grassroots transnationalization in Japan', *Asian and Pacific Migration Journal*, **12** (1–2), 155–187.

Yeoh, B.S.A. and K. Willis (2005), 'Singaporean and British transmigrants in China and the cultural politics of "contact zones"', *Journal of Ethnic and Migration Studies*, **31** (2), 269–285.

7 The making of Mumbai as a global city: investigating the role of the offshore services sector

Bart Lambregts, Jana Kleibert and Niels Beerepoot*

7.1 INTRODUCTION

Global cities are conceived as critical nodes in the organization and administration of the global economy – nodes, in other words, from where command and control functions are wielded and world-wide capitalist production is organized. The main actors identified to fulfil this function in the global economy are advanced producer service (APS) firms. The financial services industry is accredited a particularly important role in the process of global city making. It is through financial service firms' agglomeration in relatively few major cities and through the firms' enabling, intermediating, deal making and controlling practices that these cities become command points in the global economy and the world city network (Sassen, 2001; Taylor, 2004). The industry is in a constant state of flux: it expands, contracts, reorganizes and relocates at vigorous rates. Among the industry's more notable recent 'turns' is its large-scale expansion into many parts of the Global South. This expansion has been two-pronged. One wave has been driven by the emergence of new markets for (advanced) financial services in such countries as China, India, Brazil, Mexico and Indonesia (World Bank, 2011). This has fuelled the rise of a new generation of financial centres (e.g. Shanghai, Mumbai, São Paulo, Dubai) where local and global financial and other APS firms conglomerate, attempt to generate revenue and contribute to these cities' commanding capacities in the global economy (see e.g. Lai, 2012; Meyer, 2009; Sassen, 2006). A second, parallel wave has been driven by

* The authors would like to thank Marcel Heemskerk of the Amsterdam Institute for Social Science Research for his GIS support and the editors of this volume for their constructive comments on an earlier version of this chapter.

the industry's desire to reduce its production costs. Since the 1990s, the financial services industry, along with other industries, has engaged in the relocation of a large and still increasing array of what are essentially support activities from the Global North to a variety of places mainly (but not exclusively) in the Global South. This process, also known as business process outsourcing (BPO) or services offshoring, has resulted in several millions of workers in places such as Manila, Mumbai, Cebu City, Delhi, Chennai and Pune producing electronically transmittable support services for global financial and other services industries (Dicken, 2011; Gereffi and Fernandez-Stark, 2010; Kleibert, 2016; Lambregts et al., 2016). Like finance firms' revenue-generating activities, offshored support services favour urban environments since this is where the key inputs (skilled labour and reliable information and communication technology (ICT) services) are found. However, since these support services, in comparison to the revenue-generating activities, rely much less on having optimal access to clients, peers, intelligence and top talent, and since their relocation is usually part of cost-saving strategies, they are not necessarily attracted to (more costly) financial centres and disperse more easily to second- or even third-tier cities (Kleibert, 2014).

The two developments in combination work to create a globally more polycentric and functionally segregated financial services production landscape and hence widen the collection of 'global cities in the making'. This trend has not gone unnoticed in global city research. Recent years have seen an increase in studies exploring how and in what role(s) cities in the Global South become part of global networks of economic production and exchange (see e.g. Nijman, 2012; Parnreiter, 2010). So far, however, few have specifically looked into the role played by offshored services in the making of global cities. One exception is Kleibert who, in a qualitative study of Manila's offshore services industry, argues that while the local presence of the industry does help to further insert the city into global production networks and thus the global economy, it does not directly translate into the accumulation of command and control capacities but rather fixes such cities in what is essentially a dependent relationship with the faraway places from where the offshored activities are directed (Kleibert, 2017). This insight, however, does not render the offshore services industry irrelevant to global city research and, in particular, the study of global city making processes in the Global South. The presence of a sizable sector comprised of offshored support services arguably carries a much different weight for cities in the Global South than for cities in the Global North. In the latter, support services in terms of value creation, prestige, local wealth effects and human capital formation are by all means welcome but often also an unremarkable part of the urban economy. They are not generally considered an important contributor to a city's integration in the global economy or a catalyst for change. In contrast, in the Global South offshored support services are a clear expression of global integration and sit firmly at the higher end of cities' economies. The offshore services industries of cities like Bangalore, Mumbai and Manila are overwhelmingly export-oriented, recruit from the better educated segments of the urban labour force, and pay wages that are at the higher end of local wage ranges (Krishnan, 2016; Marasigan and Lambregts, 2017). Recent studies indicate that the industry, especially in cities where it achieves size relative to the urban economy, has the capacity to propel substantial change (Lambregts et al., 2016), with impacts felt in, amongst others, the domains of consumption, human capital formation, education, infrastructure provision and auxiliary services production. Even though the industry may accumulate little in the sense of global command and control capacities by itself, where such impacts help to advance other industries that are more central to global city making, it is arguably possible to envisage the industry as a 'backstage global city maker'.

The presence of such industries more central to global city making ('lead actors', one could say), is a precondition for this hypothetical backstage role of the offshore services industry to materialize. A study aimed at exploring the merits of the premise should therefore look at cities where a sizable offshore services sector evolves in tandem with a sizable 'onshore' financial and APS industry. Mumbai, India, is one of the very few places in the world meeting this condition (Delhi and Shanghai would be other candidates). In recent years, the city has gained relevance as the financial capital of and gateway to the vast and increasingly lucrative South Asian market and, as such, has become home to an increasingly versatile complex of home-grown and international financial service firms providing many of the high value-added corporate and consumer-oriented financial services commonly found in international financial centres and global cities (referred to as Mumbai's onshore financial services sector or industry from here). Simultaneously, and rather uniquely for an emergent financial centre and global city, Mumbai has also developed into one of the world's prime destinations for outsourced and/or offshored support services. Tens of thousands, if not more, college and university graduates in Mumbai, employed by both Indian and foreign service providers, deliver electronically transmittable support services to the global financial services industry.

Mumbai as such plays a dual role in the global financial services production landscape. While its growing onshore financial services industry, as it has done and still does for cities like New York, London, Tokyo, Hong Kong, Singapore, Dubai and Shanghai, furthers Mumbai's articulation in the global economy and its significance as a global city, the contribution of Mumbai's offshore services sector to this process is much less clear. Does the production of support services for global finance and other industries generate assets, trigger processes or create synergistic effects that contribute to the making of Mumbai as a global city? Or does this sector rather operate in isolation from the city's onshore financial services industry and are its impacts too modest to make a difference? We investigate these questions drawing largely upon qualitative data obtained from in-depth interviews with people who are part of Mumbai's offshore services industry. Our broader aim is to draw attention to the – in our view – real possibility that certain categories of actors who are generally not conceived as 'global city makers' in the Global North can assume a 'global city making role' in cities of the Global South. Moreover, by presenting a qualitative, place- and actor-oriented case study situated in the Global South we offer complementary value to the quantitative and network-oriented studies that have dominated world city research during the past 15 years, so heeding calls for diversification in research focus, methodology and geographical accents (Derudder and Parnreiter, 2014; Parnreiter, 2014; Watson and Beaverstock, 2014). The outcomes of our study implicate that global city research should indeed be sensitive to the notion that the local context co-defines which actors are or are not instrumental to processes of global city making.

The chapter from here is broken down into six parts. We first take a closer look at recent dynamics in financial services production with special attention to the trend towards outsourcing and offshoring of tradeable support functions. Next, after having briefly explained our research methodology, we turn to Mumbai. We portray the city's economic significance and its financial industry, give a more detailed account of its offshore services industry and assess how the latter contributes to the accumulation of assets that strengthen Mumbai's global city status. The chapter ends with a discussion of the study's broader implications.

7.2   GLOBAL CITY FORMATION AND DYNAMICS IN FINANCIAL SERVICES PRODUCTION

Global cities combine centrality in international production networks with high levels of local capital accumulation (Sassen, 2001; Taylor, 2004). The financial services industry plays an important role in the creation of both: first, by enabling other economic actors to accumulate capital and expand production networks (Coe et al., 2014); and, second, by the processes of capital accumulation and network formation that take place within the industry itself. The industry has exhibited spectacular growth, especially during the decades leading up the 2008 global financial crisis when it expanded beyond its traditional intermediary function and engaged with a wide array of non-banking activities (Greenwood and Scharfstein, 2013). The financial crisis and its aftermath have dampened that growth and have led many finance firms to reconsider their (global) strategies. However, the tendency for high value-added, revenue-generating financial activities to agglomerate in the world's leading cities has remained unchanged. Much economic production continues to be organized in the shape of complex global production networks and these continue to be controlled and managed from a relatively small number of central offices (Sassen, 2001; Coe et al., 2014). For financial service firms, being able to easily relate to key clients is crucially important, as is being able to associate with adjacent advanced producer services (e.g. law, accountancy, consulting), and having access to talent and the latest information about business opportunities and market moving events (Coe et al., 2013). Trust-based relationships, face-to-face interaction, and thus spatial proximity, underlie these dependencies and constitute the rationale for the concentration of higher-end financial service activities in global cities.

The global financial crisis has also not diminished (global) finance firms' pre-occupation with reducing production costs – on the contrary. Automation and relocation to lower-cost production environments of business processes have been and still are the main methods of choice. Relocation first took the shape of back-office functions being moved from city centres to nearby urban peripheries. However, from the 1990s on, rapid advances in ICT, lowering of trade barriers and narrowing of the skills gap between the Global North and South have enabled firms to shift business processes also overseas and thus take advantage of wage differences at a global scale. What started as a trickle of customer care and IT-related tasks being offshored from the US above all to India has evolved into the large-scale migration of an ever wider array of electronically transmittable tasks from various countries in the Global North to multiple destinations in the Global South. It mainly concerns support activities: activities that are necessary to maintain finance firms' basic operations (e.g. payroll processing, client data management) or provide inputs for the firms' revenue-generating activities (e.g. data collection and analysis in preparation for deal-making or product development, IT infrastructure support for trading). This sets them apart from the less easily tradeable and revenue-generating activities that tend to take place in finance firms' headquarters and regular business offices (e.g. command and control, deal-making, trading, asset and client relations management).

While services outsourcing and offshoring is practised by most if not all industries, financial services firms have been the driving force and forerunner of the development. Its 32 per cent share in the global offshore services market makes the financial service sector by far the largest sector engaging in offshoring (Gereffi and Fernandez-Stark, 2010, p. 28) and in India, arguably the world's main destination for services offshoring, the banking, financial services and insurance (BFSI) sector accounts for more than half of the offshore services sector (NASSCOM, 2011). Outsourcing and offshoring in the financial services industry takes place virtually across the board and pertains to low-value and routine business processes such as customer services and data processing, a range of mid-value IT-related processes, and, increasingly, more knowledge-intensive and high value tasks such as market research, financial analysis and modelling, and the development of complex (trading) software (Currie et al., 2008; Deloitte, 2005; Dossani and Kenney, 2009). In services outsourcing jargon these are respectively known as business process outsourcing (BPO), information technology outsourcing (ITO) and knowledge process outsourcing (KPO) (Gereffi and Fernandez-Stark, 2010, p. 28). The trend has increased the complexity of finance firms' production networks and led to the establishment of offshore services centres, mostly in developing countries, where cost–benefits (notably in the domain of labour), economies of scale (accrued from centralized or shared service provision), and access to specific kinds of talent are secured. With the workforce in established offshore services destinations becoming increasingly capable and with more finance business processes becoming suitable for digitization, there is considerable scope for offshorable tasks to further increase in number and advance along the financial services value chain.

With offshorable services advancing along the value chain, simple dichotomies such as back- versus front-office, low versus high value-added, or low versus highly skilled are decreasingly adequate to describe the difference between offshored and onshore financial service activities. As discussed above and summarized in Table 7.1, the two differ in many respects and notably in terms of the logics guiding their development (market-seeking versus cost-saving), the type of work involved (revenue-generating versus support activities) and the main mode of exchange (face-to-face versus electronic). However, the value, skills and knowledge gap between them is diminishing as the activities offshored, especially those delivering inputs to firms' revenue-generating activities, become increasingly sophisticated. This, in combination with our earlier remarks about the sector's catalytic potential in a Southern context, renders the question if and how the sector contributes to processes of global city making an increasingly interesting one.

Table 7.1   Distinguishing 'onshore' and 'offshored' financial services activities

	'Onshore' financial services	'Offshored' financial services
Main logic	Market-seeking	Cost-saving
Type of work	Core, revenue-generating business such as financial intermediation, trading, capitalization, securitization, wealth management, retail banking	Support services such as customer care, administration, IT support, data processing and analysis, market research, trade support
Main mode of exchange	Face-to-face	Electronic
Market orientation	Mostly domestic, some international; corporate, retail, wealth sectors	Export-oriented, but intra-firm or direct to outsourcing client
Organizational entities involved	Investment and retail banks, institutional investors, brokers, fund managers, regulators, trade facilitators	Subsidiaries or shared service centres of financial firms; local and global providers of outsourced services
Level of added value	Medium to high	Low to medium
Skill-level of work	Mostly medium to very high: in-depth domain knowledge, judgement skills and creativity required	Mostly low to medium with some higher-skilled; often scripted routine functions
Front-/back-office	Mainly front-office, limited back-office	Mainly back-office, some front-office
Employment perception	Prestigious, providing status	Decent income but less prestigious
Location preference	Cities, business hubs, offering proximity to clients, peers, other APS providers	Cities, not necessarily business hubs, offering access to sufficiently skilled labour and reliable ICT services at low costs

7.3   DATA COLLECTION AND METHODOLOGY

This case study of Mumbai's offshore services sector investigates how the sector contributes, whether or not in a symbiotic relationship with the city's 'onshore' financial services sector, to the accumulation of assets that support Mumbai's profile as a global city. The study is based on fieldwork in Mumbai and on relevant literature in the form of academic studies, business reports and newspaper articles. Interviews were conducted during an initial visit to Mumbai in 2011 and during a three-month stay from January to March 2012. Challenges met were the difficulty of accessing information in the highly secretive offshore financial service sector of Mumbai. Most respondents requested anonymity, referring to the sensitivity of information in their line of business, and less than half of all interviewees granted voice-recording of interviews. In all other cases, notes were taken during the interview.

The data collected are based on a total of 20 interviews. These were conducted with current and former chief executive officers (CEOs), managing directors, vice presidents, heads of human resources and mid-level managers of companies that are engaged in offshore financial service delivery in Mumbai (with company size varying from 35 to 20 000+ employees) as well as with representatives from relevant business associations and public sector representatives. We commence the analysis with introductions to Mumbai's global city qualities and its onshore and offshore financial services sectors.

7.4   MUMBAI AS A GLOBAL CITY AND FINANCIAL CENTRE

There exists little doubt about Mumbai today being India's most globalized city. The city of 12.4 million (2011 population census data) embodies a multifaceted accumulation of capital and connectivity unmatched by any other city in the region.

7.4.1   The City as a Reservoir of Capital . . .

Mumbai is India's leading economic powerhouse. Over the past 25 years its economy, which used to rely heavily on trade and (textiles) manufacturing, has successfully diversified, notably into modern services. Financial services, entertainment (Bollywood) and IT and ITES (i.e. the export of IT-heavy business support services) have emerged as the city's new economic pillars (Municipal Corporation of Greater Mumbai, 2015).

Mumbai currently generates close to 3 per cent of India's gross domestic product (GDP) (Government of Maharashtra, 2015) and about one third of India's corporate and income tax revenues (*The Indian Express*, 2015). The city is home to the headquarters of 35 per cent of India's 500 largest corporations measured by revenues, ahead of Delhi, which houses 22 per cent (*Fortune India*, 2011). The city's economic clout endows its inhabitants with per capita income at about 2.3 times India's national average (Government of Maharashtra, 2015). While Mumbai accounts for less than 2 per cent of India's population, the city's banks hold close to 17.5 per cent of India's deposits (Reserve Bank of India (RBI), 2015a). Within the Indian context Mumbai also constitutes a large reservoir of human capital. The enrolment rate in higher education in Maharashtra state (of which Mumbai is the capital) is almost twice the national average (25.9 versus 13.8 in 2011) (Deloitte, 2013). With Mumbai accounting for a – relative to its population – disproportionally large share of the state's universities, colleges, and management and engineering institutes, the city's enrolment rate is likely to be higher still. Mumbai's success in growing and attracting business, wealth and talent is reflected in its steady advance – from 49th in 2008 to 41st in 2014 – in the *Global City Index* (AT Kearney, 2014).

7.4.2 . . . And a Source of Connectivity

Mumbai's traditional gateway function is still very much alive. Its two ports together handle over 20 per cent of India's sea-borne trade (Mumbai Port Trust, 2015) and its airport is the busiest in the region after Delhi's (Airport Council International (n.d.), data for 2014). Indicative as well is that ten out of 20 of India's most globally active firms are headquartered in Mumbai, with runner-up Bangalore accounting for only two (Siliconindia, 2012). Further confirmation comes from work carried out by the Globalization and World Cities (GaWC) research network. In the global, inter-city network spun by advanced producer services firms Mumbai stands out as one of the developing world's best connected cities. In the 2012 version of *The World According to GaWC* (GaWC, 2018), Mumbai ranks 12th for global network connectivity. From the developing world only Shanghai (6th), Beijing (8th) and Dubai (10th) rank higher. Between 2000 and 2012, Mumbai consistently consolidated its position in the world city network (rising from 21st to 12th), also relative to India's capital Delhi (Taylor and Derudder, 2014). Disaggregated data show that Mumbai's banking and financial sector contributes substantially to the city's global network connectivity (Taylor, 2004, p. 99).

7.4.3 Mumbai's Finance Industry

Mumbai is also India's primary financial centre and basically has been so since Calcutta lost its capital city status to Delhi in 1911 (Pacione, 2006). It hosts the country's two most important stock exchanges, the Bombay Stock Exchange (BSE) and the National Stock Exchange (NSE), the RBI, the headquarters of most of India's several dozens of private and state-owned banks, a large variety of investment banks, brokerage houses, and insurance and asset management companies (including 80 per cent of the country's mutual funds and 75 per cent of foreign institutional investors), India's key regulatory and supervisory agencies for the financial industry, and a significant pool of legal and accountancy experts providing ancillary services (Clark and Moonen, 2014; Municipal Corporation of Greater Mumbai, 2015; Pacione, 2006). The city's financial services complex is estimated to employ some 240 000 people, which compares to about 380 000 in London (Sutherland, 2014). Spatially, most of it is concentrated in Nariman Point, Worli, and in the Bandra-Kurla Complex a little up north (Figure 7.1). The economic liberalization and banking reforms implemented from the early 1990s on have helped the industry to further internationalize. This has resulted in, among other things, growing numbers of foreign banks operating in India and outbound expansion by Indian banks. In 2015, 46 foreign banks had operations in India (up from 31 in 1996). Of these, nearly 80 per cent maintained a presence in Mumbai, with the Mumbai office often being the corporation's main office for India (PricewaterhouseCoopers, 2013). Foreign financial institutions in India engage in a wide variety of – meticulously regulated – financial activities. They cater to the financial service needs of multinationals operating in India, provide access to global capital and debt markets for Indian corporations, and engage in trade financing, investment banking, treasury activities, wealth management and retail banking (the latter on a limited scale and aimed at high-end clients). They moreover provide non-banking financial services such as stock broking and merchant banking, operate multiple back-office service centres in the city and its environs, and are seen to have played an important role in bringing innovations to the industry, in developing human capital, and in raising specific industry standards (PricewaterhouseCoopers, 2013). Indian banks, meanwhile, compete with their foreign peers in most of the domains mentioned above and dominate the rapidly growing retail market for financial services. They too, over the past decade or so, have actively expanded overseas, primarily to service the flourishing Indian diaspora but also to support the outbound expansions of other Indian firms (*Livemint*, 2008; PricewaterhouseCoopers, 2013). The number of Indian banks with overseas activities has increased from nine in 2003 to 27 in 2015 (RBI, 2015b), with Dubai, Singapore, Hong Kong and London attracting most of the investments.

The above suggests that Mumbai in recent years and decades has been successful in (further) establishing itself as a global city, a development confirmed by the advance of the city in various rankings measuring 'global cityness'. Whether the city will be able to further advance on this path is seen to be contingent on how it manages to address important challenges in, amongst others, the domains of finance and market-related regulations, human capital, political uncertainty, and physical infrastructure and liveability (Ministry of Finance, Government of India, 2007; PricewaterhouseCoopers, 2013; Research Republic, 2008).

7.5   MUMBAI'S OFFSHORE SERVICES SECTOR – ACTORS, ACTIVITIES AND DYNAMICS

In a 2016 ranking of global services offshoring and outsourcing destinations Mumbai ranked third, only surpassed by the 'IT capital' of Bangalore and the 'call centre hub' of Manila (Tholons, 2016). Mumbai is India's starting point for the software industry and the origin of one of the largest Indian offshore service firms, Tata Consultancy Services (TCS). In 2006, the city's offshore services sector reportedly employed close to 279 000 people (Chatterji, 2013), a figure that may well be higher today. Remarkably, Mumbai attained this position despite its labour and real estate costs being higher than in all other Indian cities (PricewaterhouseCoopers, 2005, p. 12). Mumbai, being the financial hub of the country, has especially attracted offshored services catering to the global financial industry (Ministry of Finance, 2007).

To comprehend Mumbai's offshore services actor landscape, it is important to realize that services offshoring is generally organized in two different ways: either within the boundaries of the firm (i.e. by the establishment of overseas services production centres) or by outsourcing to third-party providers with overseas production units. In case of the former, the offshore production units are usually referred to as 'captives', which provide services to the mother company, often via global or regional headquarters. Outsourced operations can take on various forms. Many services are delivered through global outsourcing firms offering a range of services, the so-called 'integrated players'. In addition, there are many smaller, usually locally owned third-party suppliers that engage in low- as well as high-end service activities.

Almost all major global banks operate in-house, captive units in Mumbai. Examples include Bank of America's BA Continuum India,

Deutsche Bank's Deutsche Knowledge Services, and Citibank's Citigroup Global Services. They support consumer and investment banking activities such as transaction processing and research. The majority of the services conducted in Mumbai for financial institutions' global operations are in the field of IT. At one American investment bank subsidiary some 80 per cent of the 2000 full-time employees deliver IT services (Interview with IT Manager, 26 February 2012). Although these companies are the most integrated and visual parts of the global production networks of financial corporations in Mumbai, the majority of their staff do not engage in high-end, knowledge intensive functions. A European bank's 3500 employee strong subsidiary in Mumbai has only 200 staff engaging in what can be termed financial KPO, whereas the rest work in the operations section of the firm. Other financial service providers have offshored their customer services and helpdesk operations to Mumbai, employing large numbers of customer service representatives who advise American retail banking clients over the phone.

Apart from these captive entities, Mumbai is also home to several large, all-round, integrated players offering a wide range of outsourced IT, BPO and KPO services. These include the well-known global corporations such as IBM and Accenture, and the Indian giants such as Infosys, Wipro and TCS. These are enormous corporations (some employ 200 000 staff or more) that maintain production sites in multiple locations around the world and have the resources to meet the advanced IT infrastructure requirements by modern (investment) banking. They have obtained a large share of the market for financial services outsourcing and offshoring.

Next, there are the more specialized outsourced services providers, many of which focus entirely on BPO. These may be foreign or locally owned and offer back-office processing or call centre activities. They too tend to be very large and operate on the basis of economics of scale. Another category consists of specialized software or IT providers that cater to the specific IT infrastructure needs of financial service corporations. A Mumbai-based IT firm developed software products specifically for the financial service industry, creating a very successful product that is now used by all major banks (Interview with former CEO, Indian-owned IT firm for financial services, 19 March 2012).

Lastly, there are specialized KPO firms that provide specific financial research and analysis, for example to hedge funds and investment banks. These niche players are often founded and managed by Indian returnee migrants or former managers of captives or large integrated players. The CEO of one such firm, a 200–250 staff strong KPO firm for financial services research, started his firm when a contact at an investment bank approached him with the request to deliver some outsourced work (Interview with CEO of Indian-owned KPO, 15 March 2012). He estimates that his segment of the KPO sector is relatively small (comprised of firms such as Evalueserve, Copal Amba, Irevna, SG Analytics and eClerx) with a total of only about 10 000 employees in the whole of India.

The offshore services sector is very dynamic and the actors themselves subject to frequent change. Ownership patterns, for instance, change rapidly as the result of mergers, acquisitions and divestments between and among global banks. Also, firms reconsidering whether to keep activities in-house or to outsource them to third-party providers add to frequent changes in Mumbai's offshore services production landscape. The global financial crisis of 2008 has certainly not put an end to this – quite the contrary. The crisis, for instance, in 2008 prompted Citigroup to outsource its 17 000-employee foreign subsidiary Citigroup Global Services to Indian provider TCS in order to increase liquidity (Lakshman, 2008) – a good illustration also of the fact that it is not only cost reduction and other management considerations that determine whether work is outsourced or kept within the company.

7.6   THE OFFSHORE SERVICES SECTOR AS A GLOBAL CITY MAKER?

Earlier in this chapter we argued that while the presence of an offshore services sector does not directly add to a city's command and control capacities, there are reasons to believe the sector is capable of helping other industries that are more central to global city making to advance and, as such, to envisage the sector as a 'backstage global city maker'. In this section we empirically investigate this claim. We seek to answer the question of how the production in Mumbai of support services for global finance and other industries generates assets, triggers processes or creates synergistic effects that directly or via the city's onshore financial services sector contribute to the making of Mumbai as a global city. We subsequently analyse interactions between the onshore and offshore financial services sectors; the offshore services sector's contribution to the development of inputs and resources relevant to the onshore finance industry; the offshore services sector's contribution to local demand for financial services; and the offshore services sector's contribution to Mumbai's image as a global city.

7.6.1 Interactions between the Offshore and Onshore Financial Services Sectors

It appears that limited interaction takes place between the revenue seeking onshore finance industry and the cost-cutting offshore service operations in Mumbai. For instance, a Japanese investment bank conducts mainly IT-related work from its office in Powai, a suburban area in northeast Mumbai. It directly reports to offices in New York, London and Tokyo. The firm's Indian front-office, simultaneously, is managed through a separate regional (Asian) office located 30 kilometres away in South Mumbai and there reportedly is virtually no interaction between the two (Interview with Assistant Vice President, 22 January 2012). Quite similarly, the 'Centre of Excellence' captive back-office division of a large US bank services mainly its headquarters in New York, the Asian Pacific market through Hong Kong and the European and Middle East market through London. Although limited, they do have some interactions and occasionally meet in person with clients from the Indian branch office in Nariman Point, to whom they deliver services as well. This contact, however, would first be arranged through the US headquarters (Interview with IT Manager, captive financial service provider, 26 February 2012). The examples highlight also the physical separation of the two different industry segments in Mumbai. Most of the major onshore finance operations are located in Nariman Point, the financial district of old in the southernmost tip of Mumbai, while most of the offshore services firms are concentrated in enclaves to the north and west (Figure 7.1).

These newly constructed office hubs have mainly been built for the offshore services sector (e.g. Technopolis Knowledge Park, Mindspace, Hiranandani Business Park) and function as 'islands of globalisation', offering tax incentives for services-exports, similar to developments in the Philippines (Kleibert, 2015). The spatial distance, in combination with Mumbai's notorious traffic conditions, limits the opportunities for (chance) face-to-face meetings between employees from either segment and hence the creation of bonds and the sharing of 'buzz' (Bathelt et al., 2004). Conditions in this respect may, however, improve with the completion of a new financial hub, the Bandra-Kurla Complex (BKC). This business complex, located just south of the airport, initially attracted many offshore service providers, but companies such as Standard Chartered, Deutsche Bank, JP Morgan and Royal Bank of Scotland are moving their front-offices from Nariman Point to BKC, too (*The Indian Express*, 2012; *Mumbai Mirror*, 2012). This may pave the way for more intense exchange between onshore and offshore functions and employees in the future.

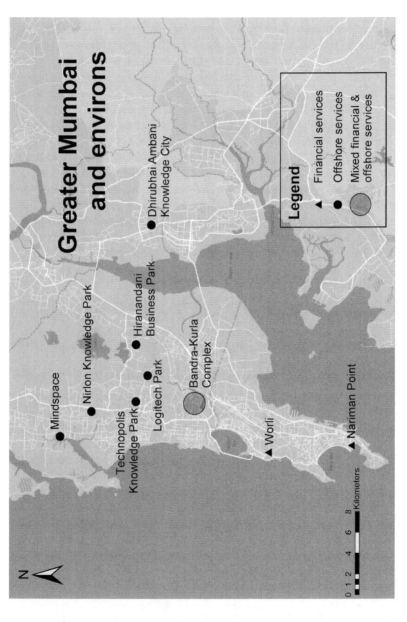

Source: Esri, HERE, DeLorme, MapmyIndia, © OpenStreetMap contributors, and the GIS user community.

Figure 7.1 Key concentrations of offshore and onshore financial services firms in Mumbai

Mumbai's onshore and offshore financial services sectors also appear to tap from two different labour pools. The jobs in the more prestigious and higher-rewarded financial services sectors are generally filled with engineering and MBA graduates from the top-level schools, such as the Indian Institutes of Management. The upper end of this segment (there is a large layer of lower-end roles as well), requires intensive interaction with clients and peers, cutting-edge knowledge, sound judgement qualities and creativity to get deals done and solve problems. Candidates with such qualities are considered over-qualified for and usually not hired by offshore operations. This segment, even the KPO part of it, instead draws largely on what are considered 'B-grade' schools graduates with bachelor degrees in business or commerce, who are then intensively trained on the job for back-office work (Interview with Executive Director, financial services shared service centre, 25 January 2012).

Moreover, the share of actual finance jobs within the offshore services sector tends to be low. In an investment bank's shared service centre, it is estimated that less than 20 per cent of all roles are related to finance, another 25 per cent to operations, and more than 55 per cent to technology (Interview with Executive Director, financial services shared service centre, 25 January 2012). The distinction between the skills, roles and type of work and level of interaction with clients between both segments limits job mobility between the two (Interview with CEO of consultancy firm and former manager of BPO firm, 15 March 2012). According to one respondent this even holds for the most knowledge-intensive part of the offshore segment, the KPO:

> Some of them [the workers] are attracted to the front-office, but for that you need a different. . . . It is not everyone that is attracted can be good enough for that. The top premier MBA schools in India, those guys don't join KPO – they join front-office. Or they'll directly join Morgan Stanley and others, the high-ends. We don't recruit from the high-ends; we don't need high-ends. They are too expensive, arrogant and too ambitious. So I honestly don't hire. But those are also just a very tiny percentage of management graduates in India. Those guys go to the front-office or London or New York, that's where they go. They are not even going anywhere but Mumbai, London, New York . . . We hire B-grade or C-grade, mainly B-grade. A-grade we don't even touch, they are too expensive and high maintenance. The quality of these [B/C] candidates is a problem, so you have to work a lot on that. (Interview with CEO of Indian KPO, 15 March 2012.)

This confirms the picture also painted by, for instance, Sen (2015) that in the domain of offshore services competition for skills mainly takes place at the national level, with Mumbai attracting skilled labour from virtually all over India, while the onshore finance sector joins the global competition for talent (see also Beaverstock and Hall, 2012; Beaverstock and Smith, 1996) with Mumbai facing the challenge of retaining locally grown top talent vis-à-vis competing global cities such as London and New York.

Slightly better opportunities to move from the offshore to the onshore sector exist for employees in captive operations, as they enjoy easier access to company-internal information about job openings elsewhere in the firm. Studies tracking the career paths of former call centre agents in India have revealed that banking, insurance and finance are sectors which take up the largest share of workers exiting the offshore service sector (Vira and James, 2012, p. 465). Given the above, however, this is more likely to facilitate mobility between the offshore services sector and the lower layers of the onshore finance industry than to ease access to the latter's higher ranks.

7.6.2   The Offshore Services Sector's Contribution to the Development of Inputs Relevant to the Onshore Finance Industry

The limited labour mobility between Mumbai's onshore finance and offshore services sectors does not mean that relevant human capital is not being developed. Processes of skills formation and knowledge accumulation naturally occur in both segments and contribute to the creation of a thick labour pool most members of which possess domain knowledge in financial services and experience in working in an international environment. While much of the knowledge and skills employed in the offshore services sector are comparatively basic and narrow, enhancement does take place. Other studies have shown how BPO and ITO employees further develop existing and acquire new skills while working in the industry, both by formal learning in the workplace and by learning by doing (Bird and Ernst, 2009; Fernandez-Stark et al., 2011; Marasigan and Lambregts, 2017; Wadhwa et al., 2008). Employees usually first receive basic induction sessions preparing them for the tasks they will perform. These may be followed up with more advanced training programmes aimed at acquiring more advanced technical or managerial skills or domain knowledge. Furthermore, employees may receive help in skill certification and be given access to advanced formal degree programmes such as MBAs or other master's programmes (Fernandez-Stark et al., 2011; Wadhwa et al., 2008). Skill development initiatives for workers differ depending on the firm's position in the value chain and on whether the firm engages with BPO, ITO or KPO. Employee training in ITO firms (Mumbai's main category) tends to be heavy on technical (IT) skill development and, if the firm operates in a higher value-added segment of the market, on the acquisition of up-to-date certifications and training that enhances analytical and problem-solving skills and innovative thinking (Fernandez-Stark et al., 2011).

While the learning processes described above in combination with Mumbai's offshore services gradually moving up the (financial) services value chain do enhance the city's capacity to further develop its financial functions, the skills gap between ordinary offshore services and higher-end financial services remains large and hard to bridge (Ministry of Finance, Government of India, 2007). The most promising route to narrowing the gap most probably runs via further development of those offshore services activities requiring greater domain knowledge in financial services.

Mumbai's offshore services sector also triggers processes of upgrading in supporting facilities and services. First, there has been upgrading in the domain of urban infrastructure, which has been identified as a barrier to Mumbai's development as an international financial centre (Ministry of Finance, Government of India, 2007). The arrival of the offshore services sector has been accompanied by substantial investments in modern, high-quality urban infrastructure. One example is the newly created BKC financial services business hub, which provides office space, high-end residential housing and other amenities for high-income professionals in the financial service industry.

In addition to this, the city's offshore services sector has also been found to lead to upgrading and corporatization in basic supplier industries such as security services, facility management and private transport services (Beerepoot and Kumar, 2015; Kumar, 2016). Local firms that (wish to) supply such services to firms involved in the production of offshore services for global clients have to meet high (international) quality standards and are therefore forced to improve their service levels. The sheer volume of the city's offshore services sector in combination with the business opportunities generated by the finance industry and adjacent APS also mean that Mumbai has developed into an attractive market for global suppliers of such basic services such as G4S, ISS-SDB, Jones Lang LaSalle and CB Richard Ellis. Their presence adds to global business connectivity and ensures that (global) firms wishing to run operations in Mumbai are able to source basic services from trusted global brands. The global brands, however, provide tough competition for local firms. So far, few of the latter have managed to gain market share as 'first-line' providers. Local firms are more commonly found in the role of subcontractors to the global players or, if they cannot meet requirements, confined to servicing the local market. While this segmentation of the market for auxiliary services creates opportunities for upward mobility for the more capable and ambitious workers (Kumar, 2016), at the corporate level it means that much of the value created is captured by global firms.

7.6.3 The Offshore Services Sector's Contribution to Local Demand for Financial Services

Compared to local standards, the several hundreds of thousands of workers in offshore services receive very decent salaries, catapulting them income-wise right into the city's middle class or even into the upper ranges thereof (Krishnan, 2016; Nijman, 2012). Their numbers are yet too small to have a real impact on middle class formation at the national level (Hatekar and More, 2016), but the effects in the industry's focal points such as Bangalore, Delhi, Mumbai and Chennai are tangible indeed (Fuller and Narasimhan, 2007; Murphy, 2011). While a substantial part of the money earned is spent on consumer goods and services (Krishnan, 2016), as a group, the offshore services workers are also likely to soon become a reservoir of business opportunities for Mumbai's onshore financial services providers (Asian Development Bank, 2010) – initially for retail bankers and in a later stage possibly also for vendors of more advanced financial products. The merger and acquisition desks of investment banks meanwhile are likely to benefit from the frequent mergers, acquisitions and divestments affecting the offshore services sector, and the larger and more successful offshore services firms (such as TCS) expanding across the country and abroad present business opportunities for investment banks as well. While it is hard to quantify such effects, they surely add to Mumbai's market for financial services and thus support the city's onshore financial industry.

7.6.4 The Offshore Services Sector's Contribution to Mumbai's Image as a Global City

Arguably the most immediate contribution of the offshore service sector to Mumbai's global city status is in image building, in terms of both raising the visibility of the financial services sector in the city itself and in supporting the city's position in international rankings. Image creation and representation, also because of their performative effects, are of vital importance in the competition between emerging international financial centres (Engelen and Glasmacher, 2013). By having multiple large, branded financial office spaces dotting the skyline of Mumbai, epitomizing a financial district, reputational capital is created and the image-making of a financial centre is conjured, notwithstanding the fact that it is 'only' offshore services activities taking place behind many of these shiny glass and steel walls. Similarly, with popular global city and financial centre rankings usually just taking into account the presence of firms but not considering the type of functions they perform, Mumbai's offshore services sector, notably the captive part of it, contributes to Mumbai's standing in such rankings, even though the sector, as in Manila (Kleibert, 2017), is not likely to directly yield command and control capacities. The offshore services sector's reputational value may be short-lived if the actual work on the ground remains focused on lower-end back-office processing, ICT-transmitted customer service and IT support, which are generally not associated with the fast-paced front-office investment banking activities that shape global financial centres around the world. In this sense, Mumbai runs the risk of becoming a financial hub 'just in name', accruing its attractiveness from imagined status but not from the actual work processes occurring on the ground (Interview with Operations Manager, Indian financial service provider, 9 March 2012).

In a similar vein, the aforementioned discretionary spending power of Mumbai's many offshore services workers also provides additional fuel for the transformative processes taking place in the city's retail and hospitality sectors. As revealed by Krishnan (2016) and others, and comparable to what happens in places like Manila, Bangalore and Delhi, the mostly young and unfettered workers enjoy spending money on fashion, luxury items, exotic food, trendy coffee varieties, and more. As such they contribute their bit to the modernization and internationalization of Mumbai's retail and hospitality landscape (Cushman & Wakefield, 2014), which in turn contribute to creating the 'images and myths that support global-city status' (Jansson and Power, 2010, p. 889).

7.7   CONCLUSIONS

This chapter has sought to elucidate how Mumbai's offshore services industry contributes to processes of global city making in India's financial capital. More specifically it looked for synergies between the city's offshore services sector and its onshore financial services sector, nursing the idea that the latter, as argued by much of the global city literature, should be regarded as Mumbai's main 'global city maker', and exploring the hypothesis that the offshore services sector contributes to global city making mainly by supporting the functioning of the city's onshore finance sector. Our analysis shows that while direct, operational interactions between Mumbai's offshore and onshore financial services sectors are limited and while the offshore services activities themselves should not be associated with the accumulation of commanding powers in global production networks, the offshore services industry in various ways does lend support to the city's onshore finance sector and thus to the making of Mumbai as a global city. The sector triggers processes of upgrading in various types of auxiliary services, fosters local demand for financial services, and helps to bolster the city's image and reputation as a financial centre and global city. The sector's arguably most important contribution, however, is in human capital formation. The offshore services industry has enabled hundreds of thousands of Mumbai's better educated to gain working experience in an international, modern, 'white-collar' working environment. Some of these workers will acquire financial domain knowledge in the process and as such move closer to becoming also employable in the onshore finance industry.

With an eye on the future, it is also here where the greatest potential for further synergies between the offshore and onshore sectors lies. Mumbai, with its costly real estate and high cost of living (which translates into relatively high remuneration for workers) has already become a comparatively expensive place to produce offshore services. Lower value-added financial back-office work is seen leaving Mumbai for more affordable Indian cities such as Pune, Gurgaon (close to New Delhi) and Chennai. Some work also moves abroad, for instance to the Philippines where Manila has recently overtaken Mumbai as the call centre capital of the world (*Financial Times*, 2015). Competition is fierce and the sector, by definition, virtually footloose. Mumbai's higher operating costs require that work performed here should be higher value-added (as compared to work performed in lower-cost destinations) in order to remain profitable. This means that Mumbai's offshore services sector must continue to pursue upward movement along the value chain and thus that the sector and its associated institutions must continue to invest in the productive capabilities of its (prospective) employees. Obviously, this would help to further narrow the skills and knowledge gap between the offshore services and onshore finance sectors, and increase the potential for synergistic feedback loops to evolve between them.

The chapter on a different level has demonstrated that there is value in looking beyond the role of high-end financial and other APS in global city research. While the latter may be the most central to processes of global city making, they neither operate in a vacuum nor act alone. Their potential to thrive and thus to add to cities' clout in a global context not only depends on the richness of the business environment, but is also affected by the quality of backward linkages and, in addition, may benefit from symbiotic relationships with other economic actors. To deepen our understanding of the performance of APS as global city makers not only requires attention for the global networks they weave, but also for the ways in which their functioning is affected – for better or worse – by other actors operating in their (local) environment. Such locally defined, inter-actor interdependencies are not easily exposed by quantitative research but require qualitative approaches and a focus on the processes taking place within globalizing cities themselves instead. Such research, moreover, should be open to the possibility that the answer to the question of which actors matter and what roles they play in global city making is context dependent. As this chapter has demonstrated, an actor like the offshore services sector is likely to play a different and arguably more important role in global city making processes in the Global South than in the Global North.

An interesting question for further study is how the offshore services industry contributes to processes of labour market polarization often found in global cities (Sassen, 2001). As detailed above, the sector creates employment opportunities at the higher end of Mumbai's labour market. Entry barriers are lower than in the high-end segments of the city's onshore finance industry. Yet, they are high enough to effectively limit access to already relatively privileged segments of the city's labour force (Krishnan, 2016). Further research into (a) who has (no) access to work in the offshore services sector, who has (no) access to the educational and skills formation trajectories that provide access to work in the sector, and (b) the degree to which the sector – by providing relatively well-paid jobs at the higher end of the spectrum – leads to a more efficient allocation of labour and trickle-down effects, may provide answers to the question of whether the sector helps to either reinforce or moderate processes of polarization in Mumbai's labour market.

Additionally, further research is needed to understand Mumbai's experience in comparison with other offshore service locations. Shanghai has been mentioned as a possible similar case and would be interesting as a comparative case study, but also Manila has recently emerged as a recipient of investments from the financial offshore service sector. In contrast to Mumbai, Manila does not have a history as a regional financial hub, which makes it interesting to see if and how synergistic dynamics between the offshore and onshore financial services sectors here differ from those occurring in Mumbai. Lastly, with the current study having conceived of the offshore services sector as a collective actor in the global city making practice, additional research into the actions of individuals working in or for the industry could be revealing as to the role played by, for instance, education, migration, and broader socio-cultural and socio-political factors.

REFERENCES

Airport Council International (n.d.), *Worldwide Airport Traffic Report – Calendar Year 2013*, accessed 6 December 2015 at https://en.wikipedia.org/wiki/List_of_the_world's_busiest_airports_by_passenger_traffic.
Asian Development Bank (2010), *Key Indicators for Asia and the Pacific 2010*, Mandaluyong City, Philippines: Asian Development Bank.

AT Kearney (2014), *2014 Global City Index and Emerging Cities Outlook*, Chicago, IL: AT Kearney.

Bathelt, H., A. Malmberg and P. Maskell (2004), 'Clusters and knowledge: Local buzz, global pipelines and the process of knowledge creation', *Progress in Human Geography*, **28** (1), 31–56.

Beaverstock, J.V. and S. Hall (2012), 'Competing for talent: Global mobility, immigration and the City of London's labour market', *Cambridge Journal of Regions, Economy and Society*, **5** (2), 271–288.

Beaverstock, J.V. and J. Smith (1996), 'Lending jobs to global cities: Skilled international labour migration, investment banking and the City of London', *Urban Studies*, **33** (8), 1377–1394.

Beerepoot, N. and R. Kumar (2015), 'Upgrading service delivery and employment conditions through indirect insertion in global value chains', *Competition & Change*, **19** (5), 374–389.

Bird, M. and C. Ernst (2009), *Offshoring and Employment in the Developing World: Business Process Outsourcing in the Philippines*, Geneva: International Labour Organization.

Chatterji, T. (2013), 'Localizing production of the globalized knowledge enclaves: The role of the sub-national states in development of the IT-ITES clusters in India', in P. Cooke, G. Searle and K. O'Connor (eds), *The Economic Geography of the IT Industry in the Asia Pacific Region*, London and New York: Routledge, pp. 243–263.

Clark, G. and T. Moonen (2014), *Mumbai: India's Global City. A Case Study for the Global Cities Initiative: A Joint Project of Brookings and JPMorgan Chase*, accessed 23 October 2016 at www.jpmorganchase.com/corporate/Corporate-Responsibility/document/gci_mumbai_02.pdf.

Coe, N.M., P.F. Kelly and H.W.C. Yeung (2013), *Economic Geography: A Contemporary Introduction* (2nd edition), Hoboken, NJ: Wiley.

Coe, N.M., K.P.Y. Lai and D. Wójcik (2014), 'Integrating finance into global production networks', *Regional Studies*, **48** (5), 761–777.

Currie, W.L., V. Michell and O. Abanishe (2008), 'Knowledge process outsourcing in financial services: The vendor perspective', *European Management Journal*, **26** (2), 94–104.

Cushman & Wakefield, (2014), *New Retail Frontiers: Emerging Main Streets in India*, accessed 20 November 2015 at www.cushmanwakefield.com/~/media/reports/india/New%20Retail%20Frontiers%20Report.pdf.

Deloitte (2005), *Global Financial Service Offshoring: Scaling the Heights*, London: Deloitte Touche Tohmatsu.

Deloitte (2013), *Perspectives on Skill Development in Maharashtra – Matching Aspirations to Opportunities*, accessed 4 December 2015 at www2.deloitte.com/content/dam/Deloitte/in/Documents/IMO/in-imo-skill-development-in-india-noexp.pdf.

Derudder, B. and C. Parnreiter (2014), 'Introduction: The interlocking network model for studying urban networks: Outline, potential, critiques, and ways forward', *Tijdschrift voor Economische en Sociale Geografie*, **105** (4), 373–386.

Dicken, P. (2011), *Global Shift: Mapping the Changing Contours of the World Economy* (6th edition), London: Sage.

Dossani, R. and M. Kenney (2009), 'Service provision for the global economy: The evolving Indian experience', *Review of Policy Research*, **26** (1–2), 77–104.

Engelen, E. and A. Glasmacher (2013), 'Multiple financial modernities: International financial centres, urban boosters and the internet as the site of negotiations', *Regional Studies*, **47** (6), 850–867.

Fernandez-Stark, K., P. Bamber and G. Gereffi (2011), *The Offshore Services Global Value Chain: Economic Upgrading and Workforce Development*, Durham, NC: Center on Globalization, Governance & Competitiveness (CGGC), Duke University.

Financial Times (2015), 'Manila eclipses Mumbai as services outsourcing magnet', *Financial Times*, 5 May, accessed 20 November 2015 at www.ft.com/cms/s/0/1658 baac-f30a-11e4-a979-00144feab7de.html.

Fortune India (2011), 'Fortune India 500', special issue, December, summary accessed 7 December 2015 at www.mxmindia.com/2011/12/fortune-india-brings-out-its-top-500-ranking/.

Fuller, C. and H. Narasimhan (2007), 'Information technology professionals and the new-rich middle class in Chennai (Madras)', *Modern Asian Studies*, **41** (1), 121–150.

GaWC (2018), *The World According to GaWC*, accessed 11 May 2018 at http://www.lboro.ac.uk/gawc/gawcworlds.html.

Gereffi, G. and K. Fernandez-Stark (2010), *The Offshore Services Global Value Chain*, CORFO Report, Durham, NC: Center on Globalization, Governance & Competitiveness (CGGC), Duke University.

Government of Maharashtra (2015), *Economic Survey of Maharashtra 2014–15*, Mumbai: Directorate of Economics and Statistics, Planning Department, Government of Maharashtra.

Greenwood, R. and D. Scharfstein (2013), 'The growth of finance', *The Journal of Economic Perspectives*, **27** (2), 3–28.

Hatekar, N. and K. More (2016), 'The rise of the new middle class and the role of offshoring of services', in B. Lambregts, N. Beerepoot and R.C. Kloosterman (eds), *The Local Impact of Globalization in South and Southeast Asia: Offshore Business Processes in Services Industries*, London and New York: Routledge, pp. 169–182.

Jansson, J. and D. Power (2010), 'Fashioning a global city: Global city brand channels in the fashion and design industries', *Regional Studies*, **44** (7), 889–904.

Kleibert, J.M. (2014), 'Strategic coupling in "next wave cities": Local institutional actors and the offshore service sector in the Philippines', *Singapore Journal of Tropical Geography*, **35** (2), 245–260.

Kleibert, J.M. (2015), 'Islands of globalisation: Offshore services and the changing spatial division of labour', *Environment and Planning A*, **47** (4), 884–902.

Kleibert, J.M. (2016), 'Services-led economic development: Comparing the emergence of the offshore service sector in India and the Philippines', in B. Lambregts, N. Beerepoot and R.C. Kloosterman (eds), *The Local Impact of Globalization in South and Southeast Asia: Offshore Business Processes in Services Industries*, London and New York: Routledge, pp. 29–45.

Kleibert, J.M. (2017), 'On the global city map, but not in command? Probing Manila's position in the world city network', *Environment and Planning A*, **49** (12), 2897–2915.

Krishnan, S. (2016), 'How the BPO industry contributes to the formation of a consumerist new middle class in Mumbai', in B. Lambregts, N. Beerepoot and R.C. Kloosterman (eds), *The Local Impact of Globalization in South and Southeast Asia: Offshore Business Processes in Services Industries*, London and New York: Routledge, pp. 183–194.

Kumar, R. (2016), 'Corporatisation and standardisation of the security services industry catering to ITES-BPO firms in Mumbai', in B. Lambregts, N. Beerepoot and R.C. Kloosterman (eds), *The Local Impact of Globalization in South and Southeast Asia: Offshore Business Processes in Services Industries*, London and New York: Routledge, pp. 153–166.

Lai, K. (2012), 'Differentiated markets: Shanghai, Beijing and Hong Kong in China's financial centre network', *Urban Studies*, **49** (6), 1275–1296.

Lakshman (2008), 'India's Tata wins big Citi outsourcing deal', *Business Week*, 10 October 2008, accessed 5 July 2013 at www.businessweek.com/stories/2008-10-10/indias-tata-wins-big-citi-outsourcing-dealbusinessweek-business-news-stock-market-and-financial-advice.

Lambregts, B., N. Beerepoot and R.C. Kloosterman (eds) (2016), *The Local Impact of Globalization in South and Southeast Asia: Offshore Business Processes in Services Industries*, London and New York: Routledge.

Livemint (2008), 'Overseas plans: Indian banks undeterred by financial turmoil', *Livemint*, 3 December 2008, accessed on 12 December 2015 at www.livemint.com/Money/3yomFsOuJy9FomeEi5gwsL/Overseas-plans-Indian-banks-undeterred-by-financial-turmoil.html.

Marasigan M.L. and B. Lambregts (2017), 'Services offshoring and skill development in emerging economies: Evidence from Metro Manila, Philippines', in N. Beerepoot, B. Lambregts and J. Kleibert (eds), *Globalisation and Services-driven Economic Growth: Perspectives from the Global North and South*, London and New York: Routledge, pp. 185–206.

Meyer, D.R. (2009), 'International financial centers', in R. Kitchin and N. Thrift (eds), *International Encyclopaedia of Human Geography*, Oxford: Elsevier, pp. 146–152.

Ministry of Finance, Government of India (2007), *Report of the High Powered Expert Committee on Making Mumbai an International Financial Centre*, New Delhi: Sage India.

Mumbai Mirror (2012), 'Why Nariman Point is running on empty', *Mumbai Mirror*, 17 December, accessed 2 July 2013 at www.mumbaimirror.com/mumbai/others/Why-Nariman-Point-is-running-on-empty/articleshow/17863545.cms.

Mumbai Port Trust (2015), 'Traffic handled at major ports during last 5 years', accessed on 7 December 2015 at www.mumbaiport.gov.in/writereaddata/nmainlinkFile/File956.pdf.

Municipal Corporation of Greater Mumbai (2015), *Draft Development Plan – 2034 Greater Mumbai*, accessed 4 December 2015 at www.mcgm.gov.in/irj/portal/anonymous/qlddevplan.

Murphy, J. (2011), 'Indian call centre workers: Vanguard of a global middle class?', *Work, Employment and Society*, **25** (3), 417–433.

NASSCOM (2011), *Strategic Review 2011: The IT-BPO sector in India*, New Delhi: NASSCOM.

Nijman, J. (2012), 'Mumbai as a global city: A theoretical essay', in B. Derudder, M. Hoyler, P.J. Taylor and F. Witlox (eds), *International Handbook of Globalization and World Cities*, Cheltenham, UK and Northampton, MA: Edward Elgar Publishing, pp. 447–454.

Pacione, M. (2006), 'Mumbai', *Cities*, **23** (3), 229–238.

Parnreiter, C. (2010), 'Global cities in global commodity chains: Exploring the role of Mexico City in the geography of global economic governance', *Global Networks*, **10** (1), 35–53.

Parnreiter, C. (2014), 'Network or hierarchical relations? A plea for redirecting attention to the control functions of global cities', *Tijdschrift voor Economische en Sociale Geografie*, **105** (4), 398–411.

PricewaterhouseCoopers (2005), *The Evolution of BPO in India*, accessed 12 June 2013 at www.pwc.in/en_IN/in/assets/pdfs/evolution-of-bpo-in-india.pdf.

PricewaterhouseCoopers (2013), *Foreign Banks in India: At an Inflection*, accessed 27 November 2015 at www.pwc.in/assets/pdfs/publications/2013/foreign-banks-in-india.pdf.

RBI (2015a), *Quarterly Statistics on Deposits and Credit of Scheduled Commercial Banks, 2015 Q2*, accessed 4 December 2015 at https://rbi.org.in/Scripts/QuarterlyPublications.aspx?head=Quarterly%20Statistics%20on%20Deposits%20and%20Credit%20of%20Scheduled%20Commercial%20Banks.

RBI (2015b), *Country-wise Branches of Indian Banks at Overseas Centres as on October 31, 2015*, accessed 4 December 2015 at https://rbidocs.rbi.org.in/rdocs/Content/pdfs/71206.pdf.

Research Republic (2008), *The Future of Asian Financial Centres: Challenges and Opportunities for the City of London*, London: City of London.

Sassen, S. (2001), *The Global City: New York, London, Tokyo* (2nd edition), Princeton, NJ: Princeton University Press.

Sassen, S. (2006), *Cities in a World Economy* (3rd edition), Thousand Oaks, CA: Pine Forge Press.

Sen, S. (2015), *Calling India: How India Became the Offshoring Capital of the World*, New Delhi: Bloomsbury India.

Siliconindia (2012), '20 Indian companies that are most global', *Siliconindia*, 13 May 2012, accessed 5 December 2015 at www.siliconindia.com/news/business/20-Indian-Companies-that-are-Most-Global-nid-115527-cid-3.html.

Sutherland, G. (2014), *Performance and Potential: Toronto's Financial Services Sector, 2014*, Ottawa: The Conference Board of Canada.

Taylor, P.J. (2004), *World City Network: A Global Urban Analysis*, London and New York: Routledge.

Taylor, P.J. and B. Derudder (2014), 'Tales of two cities: Political capitals and economic centres in the world city network', *Glocalism: Journal of Culture, Politics and Innovation*, (3), 1–16.

The Indian Express (2012), 'BKC beats Nariman Point to become country's most expensive office space', *The Indian Express*, 6 April, accessed 2 July 2013 at www.indianexpress.com/news/bkc-beats-nariman-point-to-become-country-s-most-expensive-office-space/933162/.

The Indian Express (2015), 'Direct tax mop-up likely to miss revised target by R19K cr', *The Indian Express*, 7 April, accessed 10 December 2015 at www.indianexpress.com/article/business/banking-and-finance/direct-tax-mop-up-likely-to-miss-revised-target-by-r19k-cr/.

Tholons (2016), *Tholons 2016 Top 100 Outsourcing Destinations: Rankings & Executive Summary*, accessed 7 September 2016 at www.tholons.com/TholonsTop100/pdf/Tholons_Top_100_2016_Executive_Summary_and_Rankings.pdf.

Vira, B. and A. James (2012), 'Building cross-sector careers in India's new service economy? Tracking former call centre agents in the National Capital Region', *Development and Change*, **43** (2), 449–479.

Wadhwa, V., U.K. De Vitton, and G. Gereffi (2008), *How the Disciple Became the Guru: Is it Time for the U.S. to Learn Workforce Development from Former Disciple India?* Durham, NC: Duke University and the Kauffman Foundation.

Watson, A., and J.V. Beaverstock (2014), 'World city network research at a theoretical impasse: On the need to re-establish qualitative approaches to understanding agency in world city networks', *Tijdschrift voor Economische en Sociale Geografie*, **105** (4), 412–426.

World Bank (2011), *Multipolarity: The New Global Economy. Global Development Horizons 2011*, Washington, DC: The World Bank.

8 Focal firms, grand coalitions or global city makers? Globalization vs. new localism in Hamburg's maritime network

Markus Hesse

8.1 INTRODUCTION

Maritime industries are highly important enablers of global trade. Indeed, ports have been termed 'frontline soldiers of globalisation' (Ducruet and Lee, 2006), and global cities are often port cities. As such, port institutions and port-city officials can be viewed as ideal global city makers, in that they target global flows to serve local interests. However, contemporary port-city relationships are characterized by increasing tensions resulting from competitive pressures in the maritime business, which tends to be a virtually global industry. The maritime sector has undergone significant technological and institutional changes recently: most notably in the increasing degree of containerization; the shifting dynamics of world trade; and the trend towards a specialization of service providers within the maritime economy alongside supply chains. At local and regional levels, the expansion of the maritime industry has contributed to regional growth and employment, and the promise of becoming a 'hub' tempts engagement from many local governments. However, maritime activities are also placing an increasing burden on the port-city interface, on port-urban neighbourhoods and on the natural environment, which seems prevalent in most of the leading maritime cities worldwide.

   In this context, this chapter critically analyses the interplay of a range of public and private economic actors in the making of a global (port) city. Hamburg's city government has a long-standing, critical liaison with the port, seeking to maintain its competitive position, while at the same time mitigating related concerns and conflicts. In response to recent challenges, port and city representatives are developing a renewed port-city policy, including: an emphasis on more efficient land use strategies in core port areas; a stronger

policy of opening up the port for the public and the city, based on an urban
product portfolio associated with the cruise ship industry; the construction
of a 157 hectare large flagship *Hafencity* redevelopment project on former
port and warehousing land; and the organization of the 2013 International
Building Exhibition (IBA) in the Southern Elbe area, dedicated to the
upgrading of deprived port neighbourhoods (Merk and Hesse, 2012).

With the city pursuing such ambitious policy and planning goals, the
case of Hamburg illustrates the complexity of related governance patterns. The conflict between the different interests of port and city is often
perceived as a clash between the global (goods flow) and the local (urban).
In this case, Hamburg provides a complex and contradictory case study of
the dynamics of localism and globalization. Indeed, hegemonic discourses
of the port community claim that politics need to adapt to an increased
global competition. However, local business networks attempt to prevent
foreign capital from gaining shares in Hamburg maritime firms, such as the
terminal operator HHLA or the Hapag-Lloyd (HL) shipping line, based
in Hamburg since the foundation of its predecessor Hapag in 1847. Here,
ironically, local government officials often tend to act in a rather global
way, eager to host a world-class port, while the business milieux exert a
strong sense of localism.

Given the increasing globalization of the maritime industries, this chapter discusses both the local embeddedness of services and their current
de-coupling from the traditional mainport. It explores public discourses on
how best to respond to the rising competition among ports and port cities,
and showcases, most notably, the extent and legitimacy of state intervention in order to support local networks. As Hamburg's city makers have
a strong sense for local interests, the research reveals the not so common
case of a somehow reluctant global (port) city evolving from the particular
interplay of the various actors. In order to elucidate this claim further, the
chapter will first provide a brief account of globalization and globalizing
maritime cities (Section 8.2), an overview of the research concept and
methodology, and will introduce the port-city setting of Hamburg (Section
8.3). The remainder of the chapter will then describe the key findings of
the research and related interpretations (Section 8.4). Some conclusions,
both specific and more general, will be presented (Section 8.5).

8.2   SEA PORTS, MARITIME LOGISTICS CHANGES AND THE MAKING OF GLOBAL CITIES

Port-city practices can be associated quite strongly with the emergence of
the global city region as such (Scott, 2002), and also with ongoing processes

of globalizing the urban (Marcuse and van Kempen, 2000). One reason is obvious in that the historical trajectory of port cities is particularly linked to flows and connectivities of all kinds, as global cities have quite often been, and still are, also coastal cities (Boschken, 2013). The other reason is related to the observation that major sea ports are still urban, as their economic performance is strongly linked to local labour markets in general and to the variegated maritime services offered by localized networks in particular (Hall and Jacobs, 2012).

Overall, there is striking evidence that seaports deserve to be considered the 'frontline soldiers' of globalization (Ducruet and Lee, 2006). However, in the course of massive geo-political, socio-economic and technological transformations, they have changed significantly. The trend towards integrated supply chain-management (McKinnon, 2001; Robinson, 2002) and the emergence of complex logistics networks (Christopher, 2005), both effectively driven by the introduction of new information and communication technologies and the deregulation of markets, have substantially transformed ports and port cities. The same applies to the related flows and the associated geographies (McCalla et al., 2004). A highly competitive regime has evolved in the maritime trade and transport industries, which is reflected by institutional issues such as the globalization and 'terminalization' of seaports (Slack and Frémont, 2005).

These developments have not only decoupled the flow of goods and the associated handling operations from their ties to particular places and specific settings, thus mobilizing the maritime economy; they have also transformed the arena of policy-making and related discourses. Shipping lines or global terminal-operator conglomerates have gained new freedom in selecting ports and locations for their operations (Slack, 1993; Olivier and Slack, 2006), which has resulted in a certain footloose-ness of core maritime activities. As a consequence of the re-structuring of maritime logistics chains, ports have lost their natural advantages based on water access, proximity to services, agglomeration and related economies of scale; in many cases, the conversion of derelict port areas into glossy waterfronts has already provided opportunities for compensation, placing a city on the global investment map (e.g. for promoting office real estate). Others, however, try to adapt to the imperatives of maritime competition, which includes the development of a strong business portfolio and also the adjustment of port areas and nautical conditions to the ever-increasing size of container ships, which brings particular tensions to both port and city.

While not neglecting the role of structural determinants and path dependencies in port and port-city development, there is no doubt that actors and institutions play a central role in this respect. The related governance and policy practices reveal a broad range of actors and institutions involved in the associated steering processes, negotiations, communication and conflict. Key players included here are most notably host cities and port authorities, and also shipping lines, goods handling firms and other services providers. Doig (2001) emphasized the role of the public port authority in his historical account of the New York Port Authority, which provided a great deal of infrastructure policy and connectivity in the New York City of the New Deal era. More recently, private stakes have become rather influential in the maritime business and in port operations and planning for two different reasons. First, the role of the port authority has changed from a traditionally public entity primarily owned and steered by the city, to a corporate or semi-corporate body with only loose connections to the municipal council (Notteboom and Winkelmans, 2001; Verhoeven, 2010). Second, the rise of the global logistics corporation and related alliances (Frémont, 2007; Bowen, 2012) has changed the playing field substantially by providing significant power gains to corporate actors. As a result of these shifts in power relations and the increasing mobility of assets (through routing decisions, satellite terminals, foreign investments and portfolio strategies), large corporations were able to play off ports and cities, in order to optimize their operating conditions. This change occurred in the context of privatization and neoliberalization – ideological frameworks that became hegemonic in trade politics, maritime industries and port management as well. Nevertheless, it is clear that these corporate interests could only materialize in a setting where public bodies provide the appropriate institutional environment, for example regarding ownership, land regulation or governance issues such as the overall claim for port 'reform' (see Ng et al., 2013; Notteboom et al., 2013). Moreover, in the context of the cluster-based policy model, establishing maritime and logistics networks also became a popular concept pursued by port city and industry communities to support local linkages and spill-overs between sites and agents.

8.3   INVESTIGATING GLOBAL CITY MAKING – THE CASE OF THE PORT CITY OF HAMBURG, GERMANY

8.3.1   Research Context and Methods

The main interest of the research presented here is to explore the implications of globalization and the role of assumed *global city makers* in the case of a major port city, by reconstructing the political frames and narratives that have evolved around certain fields of development, policy and conflict. Thus, this research aims to contribute to the debate on how far a 'global city' is necessarily considered 'global' based on obvious and 'objective' criteria – often expressed by numerical indicators and rankings (see the Globalization and World Cities (GaWC) databases at www.lboro. ac.uk/gawc as a useful tool in this respect) or whether the classification of a city as 'global' can also be understood as a particular outcome of the deliberate practices and discourses of policy and politics. Here the global is viewed as a product of scalar construction, not only communicatively but also with material policies (for example, by governance arrangements, financial subsidies) at centre stage. These policies are legitimized by the claim that the mainport as a global gateway needs local support and backing, in order to remain sustainable in the light of changing framework conditions and increased global competition.

In methodological terms, this chapter draws upon fieldwork carried out between 2011 and 2014, particularly a series of interviews with representatives of maritime firms, port authorities and public officials (a total of 38), which were conducted in the course of the OECD's Port-Cities project (cf. Merk and Hesse, 2012). Following the main field research, which took place in 2011, a small set of additional selected interviews were undertaken, focusing on a local alliance in support of the city's maritime economy (see the following section).

In addition, a document analysis was carried out, with secondary data and materials, parliamentary documents and newspaper articles being the core of the corpus.[1] The findings were obtained by applying a discourse analysis, as well as techniques following Clarke's (2005) situational analysis. Situational analysis has been developed as a hybrid of grounded theory and interpretative approaches (most notably Foucauldian concepts on the sociology of knowledge), whose major promise is to overcome the somehow narrow focus of qualitative research on the microcosm of individual actors, and to include broader meso- and macro-scale analyses, by adding discourse-theoretical and -analytical elements to grounded theory. Its major ambition is to explore and give meaning to certain discourses, through the particular sorting and mapping of different social worlds and also of leading narratives (discursive, virtual, historical). In this context, 'situation' claims that analyses need to open up to discourse formation and structuration, and also be sensitive to the structuring role of power. This may provide a fuller account of a given subject matter, compared to secondary data analysis or simply interviewing people.

8.3.2   City making and Port-urban Development in Hamburg, Germany

City making in the case of the port city of Hamburg is embedded in a particular practice- and discourse-arena of city officials, industry representatives and the public. The relevance of the port for the city, both in economic terms and regarding its identity, is historically rich and can hardly be underestimated. It certainly goes far beyond the mere numbers that indicate current performance, such as the amount of container handlings, which is often perceived as the clinical thermometer that tracks the port cities' well-being. Situated as a city port close to core urban areas, objects such as ocean ships, container bridges, other maritime facilities and, of course, the River Elbe are visibly present as major parts of the urban landscape, most notably in core urban areas. The city's flagship expansion area *Hafencity* at the eastern part of the central waterfront can be read as an attempt to capture the gain of port and water for ambitious urban development. An area adjacent to the *Hafencity* (the *Kleiner Graasbrook*) was intended to become the centre of the Olympic Village for the 2024 Olympic Games, for which the city together with major sports associations and the National Olympic Committee (DOSB) wanted to apply. This application was part of an envisaged push for urban development that the city aimed for, another grand alliance of the political establishment with the business community and parts of civil society. It failed in a referendum in November 2015, as citizens disagreed about where the funds for this supposedly costly endeavour could come from. However, the maritime communities are among the leading political bodies of the city, well represented in Hamburg's chamber of commerce, and the *Überseeclub* still provides an important, discreet stage for politicians to connect with business people. The maritime sense of the city also materializes in the port's anniversary, an event that is publicly celebrated each year on 7 May, bringing more than 1.5 million visitors to the city on a single weekend. The year 2016 was dedicated to commemorate the 827th anniversary of the port.

In economic terms, based upon GaWC analysis of networks of advanced producer services (APS) firms Hamburg is not considered an Alpha-level world city, and it ranks 25th in terms of the connectivity of European cities (Taylor et al., 2013, p. 291), significantly behind other German cities such as Frankfurt (see also Parnreiter, 2018). Notwithstanding the results of this analysis, Hamburg has been identified as one of the most globalized port cities worldwide (Verhetsel and Sel, 2009). The port of Hamburg is a traditional gateway and mainport situated at the Atlantic North Range, and is by far the biggest seaport of Germany as well as the core of the country's most advanced maritime and logistics network (Die Bundesregierung, 2015). This network can be understood as a cluster, including a variety of supplier and customer relationships.[2] Today, these are mostly comprised of APS firms (Parnreiter, 2015, 2018), and to a much lesser extent industrial activities such as shipbuilding or food-processing as was the case in the 1970s and 1980s. The cluster is thought of as locally embedded, while the linkages are effectively quite dispersed (Brandt et al., 2010; Wiese and Thierstein, 2014). In maritime terms, the port of Hamburg has always been a comprehensive port, while containerization has been the major growth trend in recent times. Based upon the number of standard containers (TEUs) handled, it has ranked 2nd or 3rd in Europe for some time now, behind Rotterdam and close to its rival Antwerp.[3] The competitive advantages of the port are its strategic location (reaching about 120 kilometres from the coast upstream along the river Elbe), a traditionally large hinterland with excellent rail access, and, since 1989/90, the re-opening of Central and Eastern European markets served by feeding lines connected to Hamburg. However, as the Elbe faces certain constraints in terms of river gauge and tide, the nautical conditions may no longer allow the most recent class of 19/20k TEU or even bigger container ships to pass through. This is turning the physical advantage of the river port into a competitive detriment, compared to the rivals named above.

Reflecting the contested nature of city-making processes, the recent history of the city is characterized by political battles that were focused on the cost and benefits of port expansion (Hesse, 2006). These debates actually trace back to the late 1980s, when the *Altenwerder* container terminal was starting to be developed, for which eventually a number of smaller settlements in the western port area had to be given up. The strong growth of the maritime business since the 1990s was accompanied by rising concerns as to whether the local efforts that are taken by public budgets, primarily of state and city, would be sufficiently balanced by local economic benefits such as jobs creation and tax generation. Particularly, the need to dredge the Elbe appears rather costly and yet of limited benefit, given the trend to even bigger container vessels that is dominating the maritime industries, exerting an increasing pressure on ports and cities to adapt to the changing shipping industry (see OECD/ITF, 2015). Also, it is increasingly unclear whether such efforts and associated costs can be politically justified further as there is an important mismatch between initiatives, responsibilities and risks, which are often local, and potential returns, which are usually distributed more broadly (Merk, 2013). While it would be an exaggeration to say that the public mindset in Hamburg is divided over the port, there are pressing concerns about the competitiveness of the port and city in the future. This is the particular setting within which (global) city making takes place in Hamburg.

8.4   FOCAL FIRMS, GRAND COALITIONS OR GLOBAL CITY MAKERS? THE *ALBERT BALLIN KONSORTIUM*

8.4.1   The Storyline in a Nutshell

The strong local setting of port city, maritime industries and related communities and networks is often considered to be a competitive advantage
of Hamburg. However, it is also noticeable that such a setting can lead to
adverse effects such as institutional lock-ins, and thus create vulnerability
with regard to the predatory attitude deployed by global players in the shipping and terminal operator businesses. By evoking the weaknesses of strong
ties, the problem addressed here calls for careful balancing of the pros and
cons of ties and networks. This is exactly the challenge that sets the scene for
a current dispute – a situational case which is analysed here in more depth.
It illustrates the peculiarities and controversies of local–global governance
by addressing the *Albert Ballin Konsortium* (ABK). The ABK, named after
a former Director General of the Hapag-Lloyd (HL) shipping line, was
founded in 2008, as an investors' alliance whose goal was to ensure local
stakes in the shipping line and to avoid its possible takeover by a global competitor, the Singaporean Neptun Orient Line (NOL). HL is Germany's most
important shipping line, seventh on the list of the world's biggest container
lines (judging from transport volume in TEUs). After the 2013 merger with
the Chile-based *Compañía Sud Americana de Vapores* (CSAV; see below), it
now ranks fourth. Before the merger HL employed an overall staff of almost
7000 people worldwide, of which about 1700 were based at its Hamburg
headquarters, in the prestigious Albert Ballin building on *Ballindamm*.

In the late 2000s HL was controlled by TUI, a conglomerate of tourism
and cruise industry businesses that was engaged in ocean shipping for
historical reasons, but wanted to sell its shares and leave this sector behind.
Given the concrete interest of NOL to take over a majority of shares in
HL, it was expected that consolidation would follow the takeover, thus
closing down the local headquarters of HL and leading to the loss of
many well-paid jobs in the city. In contrast, it was argued that the shipping
line would be essential for Hamburg's maritime cluster, as an apparently
focal firm or backbone of the cluster, given the strategic role of the line
as it brings concrete demand for container transhipment to the port.
Consequently, a handful of people got together with the city government
and developed a strategy for keeping HL under Hamburg control.[4] This
was meant to avoid the takeover and to ensure the local stake in the shipping line, save its headquarters for the city, and help Hamburg retain its
strong position as a maritime hub.

Backed by a two-stage political decision-making process undertaken by different government coalitions between 2008 and 2012, the city invested about €1.14 billion of public funds, in order to obtain 26 per cent of the HL-shares in 2008, a proportion that increased to 36 per cent in 2012. Effectively, the shares were owned by the *Hamburgische Gesellschaft für Vermögensbeteiligungen* (HGV), a public body controlled by the city that also bundles other public shares. While the initial decision in 2008 to engage in the ABK was made unanimously by the then ruling coalition of Conservatives and Greens, the Greens turned to opposition after the 2011 elections and remained sceptic, together with Liberals and the Left. The Social Democrats, who came to power with an absolute majority in 2011, were rather supportive given their claims regarding the economic importance of the port in general, and of blue-collar workers in particular, which was also decisive for the support provided by the labour unions, which are usually strong in the maritime industries.

Without any public notice or political debate taking place before, the ABK was disbanded in 2013, which effectively gave the control of shares back to individual investors. Any returns on the enormous financial spending of the city were expected to flow back by the planned initial public offering (IPO) of HL, an event that had already been announced to take place as early as 2011. However, it had to be delayed for another four years, due to the ongoing crisis in the shipping market. This IPO eventually took place in November 2015, releasing HL shares for around €20 each (about half of what the city had to pay in 2008 and 2012). While the financial loss is obvious, it remains to be seen whether the ABK helped to maintain Hamburg's role as a mainport and stabilized its maritime cluster. The next two sections will give further indication as to the leading narratives used by representatives from various social worlds, in order to clarify why and to what end the city engages in saving the local stake in a global shipping line, and the extent to which this represents a case of global city making (or not).

8.4.2 The Practice of Global City Making: Social Worlds and Leading Narratives

The social world that made up ABK seems easy to understand, as the actors and responsibilities were clearly defined, but in fact comprised a complex and fuzzy constellation of actors with various overlaps (Figure 8.1). The core is represented by the business community (the shipping line's corporate supporters) on the one hand, and the city as the main public body on the other. 'The city' is, as always, a construct built upon different functions and interests, including the city government with the First Mayor, the Senate

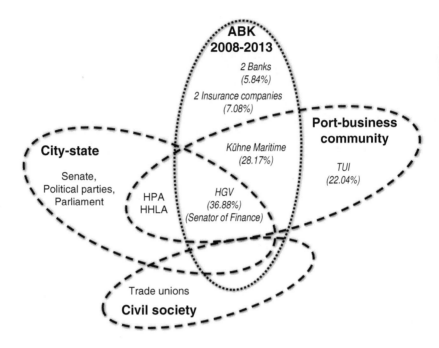

Note: Percentages: Shares in Hapag-Lloyd as of 2012.

Source: Author.

Figure 8.1   The social worlds of the Albert Ballin Konsortium (ABK)

administration (the city-state's government), the city's executing body in charge (the HGV), and, last but not least, the port authority as major supporters. The parties in the parliament are almost naturally divided on the issue in ideological terms, but this also varies over time (see above).

Fragmentation applies to the HL shareholders as well, who were divided on the issue of whether to sell (mostly TUI) or to keep the shares. Single shareholders such as Klaus M. Kühne, probably the driver of the consortium, were playing different roles, as he is both co-owner and an important customer of HL, a major carrier for Kühne & Nagel sea freight. The corporate port community as such is too big and too heterogeneous to be simply added here (the Association of Port Corporations having 100 firms alone). Some of the bigger players gave their backing to ABK, while many small and medium sized firms were rather critical of the city engaging here.

Finally, civil society actors were involved at different ends as well, such as trade unions (in this case the services union *Verdi*) and the Chamber of

Commerce, who were both strongly in favour of the deal. The unions were particularly important for fostering the sense of localness in Hamburg, not least due to the triple role carried out in person by the head of the services union *Verdi*, who is also a member of Hamburg's Parliament for the Social Democrats and sits on the governing board of HL simultaneously. Relevant civil society actors opposed to the deal were not known, while the local media, most notably the daily newspaper *Hamburger Abendblatt* has had some sympathy for the ABK.

The leading narratives of the ABK discourse can be divided into the following five themes: (i) strong support for local jobs for local people (politics); (ii) the shipping line as a focal firm of the cluster (the maritime network's claim); (iii) a political view on subvention and risk (opposition); (iv) and (v): two different experts' positions taken on the ABK, one from within the Hamburg community, and the other from outside. The city is core to the 'Hamburg position' that claims to secure local jobs for local people, which applies to the maritime network overall, but also to the qualified services jobs in the HL headquarters. This claim has evolved against the background of a massive change in the economic profile, whereby services alone are perceived as being insufficient for generating jobs and growth. A city would also need the material process, based on the association between corporate headquarter functions and shipping flows. According to this perspective, scale-effects and competitive advantages bring freight volumes and turnover to Hamburg, and partly also contribute to local tax-generation. The link between infrastructure and modern services frames HL as an 'anchor corporation'.

In governance terms, a distinction is to be made between the position of the city and that of the business community. 'The city is territorially distinct. For centuries, this city has been a port city and it aims to remain so, thus ownership in major port assets is key for the city to ensure this' (Interview with city official). The idea of global connectivity in logistics has been discussed rather actively for quite some time now, but still lacks evidence that its application is already paying off for local places. As one city official said: 'What should be our interest as a city to invest somewhere around the world? We are in charge to provide local jobs for local people' (Interview with city official). The claims of the economic importance of the port, and presumably for blue-collar workers as well, were also quite decisive for the strong support for public engagement provided by the labour unions.

When the 2012 decision was made, the city was confident that it was limiting its financial risk, arguing that, given the presumed economic development of Hapag-Lloyd, the financial burden carried by HGV would be compensated for by returns for the city based on dividends starting no later than 2013 (Senatskanzlei, 2012, press release of the city of Hamburg, 21 February). However, while global market conditions are hard to predict (which presents a constant challenge to global city making), the city took over its central role not deliberately, but only due to the lack of sufficient private capital. The decision of 2008, which in retrospect was said to have been made rather 'shirt-sleeved' (Interview city official), turned out to be unsatisfactory in terms of keeping the majority of shares locally. As a consequence of this development path, the city felt obliged to stay on board. 'The Senate now in charge has to continue the decision made by its predecessor, in order to ensure that the city's engagement makes further sense' (First Mayor Olaf Scholz, *Regierungserklärung*, 29 February 2012 – Bürgerschaft der Freien und Hansestadt Hamburg, 2012, p. 2011). Thus the city assumed this role almost accidentally, although the involvement of the mayor appeared to be unquestioned when he claimed that 'Yes, we do want our money back' (First Mayor Olaf Scholz, *Regierungserklärung* of 29 February 2012, p. 2013). This statement also evolved from experiences of two comparable earlier instances of bailing out industrial firms (Beiersdorf and Aurubis), where the city 'moderated' ownership changes by providing temporary financial backing, in order to prevent a takeover and the associated loss of headquarter functions. The outcome of these efforts is still considered to be beneficial for Hamburg.

However, while acknowledging the general importance of the port for the city, a strong point against state intervention was made by the political opposition (Interview with a member of Parliament). The competitive gesture that considers the port as a growth machine and thus as a legitimate subject for significant state support (such as that offered in the case of the HL bailout) is viewed here as reminiscent of the past, leading back to the early twentieth century, when the Port of Hamburg was the largest port in the world and HL was the world's largest shipping line. At that time, a particular attitude emerged by which Hamburg separated itself, at least ideologically, from the rest of the world. It is argued that the perception of this sort of historical divide is still applicable today when key port institutions try to keep the port under local control and not open the port's assets to third parties from outside.

Another part of the local narrative within the frame of the global maritime industries has viewed HL as a *focal* firm or backbone of Hamburg's maritime cluster. This point was particularly made by core port businesses, given the strategic role of the line, as it brings about 40 per cent of the demand for container transhipment to the port, and also as there are local shares in the company. Whether or not this would require a firm to be locally based with its headquarters (thus deserving the government's backing) remains unanswered here. A particular point in support of the

ABK came from the port as such, the Hamburg Port Authority (HPA), a 100 per cent subsidiary of the city. The HPA claimed that port growth and expansion was necessary but should be achieved under local control. This position applies also to the largest terminal operator (HHLA), characterized by a strong commitment to doing business primarily, if not exclusively, for Hamburg and in Hamburg. While the politico-industrial alliance in favour of supporting the shipping line gained hegemony, the perspective of the political opposition (most notably liberal and left) remained critical, for different reasons. While Liberals were critical of the public spending towards a private corporation, the Left saw an enormous risk faced by the public budget, for which there would be only poor justification.

Finally, a rather critical claim can be made on the basis of positions taken by external experts. First, findings of the OECD Port-Cities study revealed that on average about 90 per cent of the benefits generated by major sea ports are distributed across a much larger territory, whereas the negative impacts tend to be concentrated mostly within port cities (Merk, 2013, p. 7, p. 29ff.). This is a dilemma for which dedicated local politics of interest are no longer effective. Not unlike cities, ports are increasingly thought of in the context of wider processes that have exceeded their traditional form and format.

Second, in this context, local experts critically commented on the obsession of Hamburg actors and strategies with the city's territory and institutions, which was less justified than it might have been decades ago. Today it might be more effective to establish a regional network of services, infrastructure and access provision, and to develop associated sharing mechanisms between the different territorial units involved. Regional nodes that serve the maritime and logistics industries have already been evolving, particularly at the southern leg of the Hamburg Metropolitan Region and also along the Unterelbe, offering further potential for much more integrative, collaborative strategies. As long as the port focuses exclusively on expansion under the city's control, backed by an urban policy that is almost entirely oriented to its own territory, things might be difficult to improve.

8.5   THE DILEMMAS AND CONTRADICTIONS OF GLOBAL CITY MAKING

The exploration of the social worlds from which the above mentioned frames evolved, or were created, follows the assumption that global city making is not necessarily, and not exclusively, the business of single actors. It also needs a certain setting – a community of practice (Hughes et al., 2007), based on shared beliefs among key actors which leads to such a project coming into being. The case of the ABK not only reveals the ideological frame within which global, urban – and sometimes also imminently local – politics are justified, but also illustrates the risks, contradictions and limitations of such a policy. Different from usual cases of globalization discourses and rhetoric, a new localism can be identified here, which is interpreted as a certain reluctance to become fully globalized, and signals a tricky attempt to make the best out of combining the local and the global.

First of all, market interventions by public bodies are confronting different sorts of risk, which includes both the city (that is, the public) and the shipping line. The city of Hamburg has invested a significant amount of money in an unstable market area, representing a big risk, also leaving behind any concerns about its own role as a public body backing a private firm. However, it remains unclear whether, first, this opens the door for other cases to follow, and, second, whether there will be a reliable payback to the city's budget. Effectively, the city could only receive a sufficient return on its investment if Hapag-Lloyd was put on the stock exchange – which eventually occurred at the end of 2015, also placing a huge loss on the city's budget. And since then the company has no longer been under local control, but is instead subject to the decision-making of various kinds of players (even though local players retained a majority).

The risk is there also for HL: it has indeed successfully managed the IPO, yet the cash liquidity that the owners were able to mobilize turned out to be smaller than was initially expected. Also, as the money acquired is supposed to be used for purchasing more container vessels, this may add to the overcapacity that is already prevalent (in terms of ships, load capacity and terminal capacity). This makes the entire issue an admittedly risky endeavour for the line as well. However, relying on a politics of scale seems to be strategized by HL. As early as 2013, merger talks were initiated by HL in order to achieve a competitive overall size of the firm and its businesses. In December 2014, a merger of HL with the Chilean shipping company CSAV and the integration of their primarily South America-oriented container shipping business was decided, creating the fourth-largest liner shipping firm in the world.[5]

Second, there is a significant dilemma resulting from what could be called the illusion of localness in an increasingly globalized world. The belief that a firm – even a big one – can somehow be considered *focal* for a network or cluster, and the backbone for many others, thus providing an island of stability in an ocean of volatility, is difficult to follow. This idea is probably more a result of received wisdom rather than based on robust knowledge and empirical evidence. The location of the headquarters of a shipping line in Hamburg does not actually result in any more ships calling into the port.

The location choice of maritime services firms can either follow the flow of goods and maritime economic activities, or the overall rationale of service firms seeking critical mass and qualified personnel, thus choosing their market presence in metropolitan areas (Hall and Jacobs, 2012).

However, things are also increasingly dynamic today in the highly embedded ship financing and insurances sectors. The 2013 takeover of *Germanischer Lloyd* (GL) by its Norwegian competitor, *De Norske Veritas* (DNV), provides a striking example. GL had existed as a ship register body since 1864 and can be considered as prestigious and economically crucial for Hamburg's maritime cluster as Hapag-Lloyd was, or still is. Even the employment figures (globally then 6900, locally 1400 for GL) are comparable. In 2006 GL was subject to an unfriendly takeover attempt, but it was kept independent by an injection of about €575 million from a wealthy local industrialist. However, when DNV sought to take over GL in 2012, there was no white knight around to take the majority shares of the firm in order for it to remain a Hamburg-based body. The headquarters of DNV-GL were established in Oslo, Norway, and this new firm ranks third among ship register firms worldwide. This takeover points to the dynamics of inter-firm relations that develop across various regions and territories, making individual places vulnerable to market forces and also to power issues of any kind. Clusters are no recipe against instability, particularly at local and regional scales, and in practice this questions the engagement of public agents in securing local economic structures (Hassink, 2005). This interpretation reflects recent discourses on evolution, volatility and temporalities of regional development in economic geography, emphasizing the process rather than network-based perspective (Ibert et al., 2015).

Third, there is a certain sentiment of new localism, an emotional component in these Hamburg-related policies that seems to contrast with the overall rhetoric of globalization that is usually applied by city leaders. 'Local patriotism brings local capital' (Interview with city official). However, this perspective might not be supported by empirical evidence. This criticism is not to be interpreted as a suggestion that only economic facts (apparently 'hard' facts) should be seriously considered relevant and thus trusted. We are by now quite aware of the obscure, hidden side of competition, globalization rhetoric and the like, often driven by rationales other than solid economic foundations (Hesse, 2013, p. 39). But how far can or should such localism go, if economic activities tend to be no longer territorially bounded? Would there still be good reason to take on massive financial risks just for sentimental reasons?

In this respect, the claim for localness that was made within the Hamburg port-city nexus bears some similarities to a debate in the US a few years earlier: the Dubai ports controversy. In 2005, the United Arab Emirates (UAE) government-owned ports and terminal operator Dubai Ports World (DP World) was about to acquire rights to run the terminal operations at six US ports, effectively through the takeover of the British company P&O, which was then holding these dues. This planned foreign investment became subject to critical debates in politics and in the broader public, especially in the aftermath of 9/11 when there was an increasing awareness of the role of critical infrastructures, such as ports, for national security. Thus the public sentiments can be distilled in the question whether the US should 'let them in' or 'keep them out': 'the thought of a Middle Eastern government running U.S. port operations struck many as putting the fox in charge of the henhouse' (Mostaghel, 2007, p. 610). As a consequence of the review process and the contested debate, DP World decided to sell its port operations to a US-based company. While national security issues obviously did not play a role in Hamburg's port issues discussed above, the similarities are striking in that such sentiments play a role for the actors and their decision-making.

To conclude this chapter, and taking into account the very broad range of practices of global city making, Hamburg seems to represent an unusual case of localness, if not reluctance to go for the 'global'. On one hand, the port appears as the iconic gateway and link to the world 'out there', particularly given its long tradition as a trading place with countries as remote as China or Japan. Also, in terms of concrete practice, the city aims at global visibility, as it wanted to become an Olympic city (bidding twice at the national level, for the 2012 and – later cancelled – for the 2024 Olympic Games), and hosted the G20 meeting in 2017. On the other hand, the reservations against foreign shares in core port firms and activities and the interest in keeping flagship companies under apparently local control mark a significant contrast. It remains to be seen whether this attitude is difficult to retain under increasingly globalized and volatile market conditions, or whether the Hamburg sense of localness prepares the city for a possible (re)turn of the economic order back to national interests and protectionism (which seems less unrealistic now than only a few years ago).

Practically speaking, there is no formula as to how best respond to such changing environments. City makers might be best advised to follow international debates and developments, to prepare their institutional environment for dealing with such issues successfully, and integrate the global scale into their strategies for urban development, without either neglecting or overstating the local level.

NOTES

1. Most of the relevant parliamentary documents, such as press releases, official announcements of the Senate, minutes of the *Bürgerschaft* (state parliament) and commission meetings and government responses to official queries from parliamentary groups were obtained from Hamburg's parliamentary database *Parlamentsdatenbank*.
2. The overall employment 'generated' by port- and maritime-related activities in the Hamburg area is estimated to be around 150000 jobs (according to Planco Consulting GmbH, 2015), which can be almost equally divided into direct and indirect employment effects. These numbers are also spreading across the entire metropolitan region and beyond.
3. The handling of containers almost doubled between 2000 and 2005 to about 8 million TEUs and reached an all-time peak of 9.7 million TEUs in 2008. As a consequence of the economic crisis, numbers dropped down to 7 million TEUs in 2009 (minus 28 per cent). Since that time, the shipping and logistics sectors have become rather volatile: while the number of transhipments reached a level of almost 9.3 million TEUs by 2013, most recent developments stagnate below 9 million TEUs (8.8 million by 2015; data: Port of Hamburg).
4. The ABK was established by the co-owner of Kühne & Nagel logistics and freight forwarding, Klaus-M. Kühne, institutions such as the ship-financing firm HSH Nordbank, the M.M. Warburg bank, insurance companies such as the Hamburg based Hanse-Merkur and Signal Iduna and the city.
5. Talks were initially held between HL and Hamburg-Süd, Germany's second largest shipping line (also located in Hamburg) that would have been complementary to the HL's portfolio. This merger did not materialize though, reportedly due to a lack of trust and understanding among the owners on both sides. As a result of the merger with CSAV, the Chileans took a 34 per cent stake in HL. TUI is still holding a minority share of 13.9 per cent, the former ABK-allies are also still on board, such as the city (HGV, 23.2 per cent), Kühne Maritime (20.8 per cent) and the banks and insurance companies (minor shares between 1.1 and 3.3 per cent).

REFERENCES

Boschken, H.L. (2013), 'Global cities are coastal cities too: Paradox in sustainability?', *Urban Studies*, **50** (9), 1760–1778.

Bowen, J.T. (2012), 'A spatial analysis of FedEx and UPS: Hubs, spokes, and network structure', *Journal of Transport Geography*, **24**, 419–431.

Brandt, A., M.C. Dickow and C. Drangmeister (2010), 'Entwicklungspotenziale und Netzwerkbeziehungen maritimer Cluster in Deutschland', *Zeitschrift für Wirtschaftsgeographie*, **54** (1), 238–253.

Bürgerschaft der Freien und Hansestadt Hamburg (2012), Plenarprotokoll 20/27, 29 February, accessed 11 May 2018 at http://www.buergerschaft-hh.de/ParlDok/dokument/36542/plenarprotokoll-20-27.pdf.

Christopher, M. (2005), *Logistics and Supply Chain Management: Creating Value-Adding Networks* (3rd edition), London: Prentice Hall.

Clarke, A.E. (2005), *Situational Analysis: Grounded Theory after the Postmodern Turn*, London: Sage.

Die Bundesregierung (2015), *Nationales Hafenkonzept für die See- und Binnenhäfen 2015*, accessed 6 July 2016 at www.bmvi.de/SharedDocs/DE/Artikel/WS/nationales-hafenkonzept.html.

168   *Global city makers*

Doig, J.W. (2001), *Empire on the Hudson: Entrepreneurial Vision and Political Power at the Port of New York Authority*, New York: Columbia University Press.
Ducruet, C. and S.W. Lee (2006), 'Frontline soldiers of globalisation: Port-city evolution and regional competition', *GeoJournal*, **67** (2), 107–122.
Frémont, A. (2007), 'Global maritime networks: The case of Maersk', *Journal of Transport Geography*, **15** (6), 431–442.
Hall, P.V. and W. Jacobs (2012), 'Why are maritime ports (still) urban, and why should policy-makers care?' *Maritime Policy & Management*, **39** (2), 189–206.
Hassink, R. (2005), 'How to unlock regional economies from path dependency? From learning region to learning cluster', *European Planning Studies*, **13** (4), 521–535.
Hesse, M. (2006), 'Global chain, local pain: Regional implications of global distribution networks in the German North Range', *Growth and Change*, **37** (4), 570–596.
Hesse, M. (2013), 'Cities and flows: Re-asserting a relationship as fundamental as it is delicate', *Journal of Transport Geography*, **29**, 33–42.
Hughes, J., N. Jewson and L. Unwin (eds) (2007), *Communities of Practice: Critical Perspectives*, London: Routledge.
Ibert, O., J. Hautala and J.S. Jauhiainen (2015), 'From cluster to process: New economic geographic perspectives on practices of knowledge creation', *Geoforum*, **65**, 323–327.
Marcuse, P. and R. van Kempen (eds) (2000), *Globalizing Cities: A New Spatial Order?* Oxford: Blackwell.
McCalla, R.J., B. Slack and C. Comtois (2004), 'Dealing with globalisation at the regional and local level: The case of contemporary containerization', *The Canadian Geographer/Le Géographe canadien*, **48** (4), 473–487.
McKinnon, A. (2001), 'Integrated logistics strategies', in A. Brewer, K. Button and D. Hensher (eds), *Handbook of Logistics and Supply Chain Management*, London: Elsevier, pp. 157–170.
Merk, O. (ed.) (2013), *The Competitiveness of Global Port-Cities: Synthesis Report*, Paris: OECD.
Merk, O. and M. Hesse (2012), 'The competitiveness of global port-cities: The case of Hamburg', *OECD Regional Development Working Papers*, 2012/06. Paris: OECD Publishing, accessed 6 July 2016 at dx.doi.org/10.1787/5k97g3hm1gvk-en.
Mostaghel, D.M. (2007), 'Dubai Ports World under Exon-Florio: A threat to national security or a tempest in a seaport?', *Albany Law Review*, **70**, 583–623.
Ng, A.K.Y., P.V. Hall and A.A. Pallis (2013). 'Guest editors' introduction: Institutions and the transformation of transport nodes', *Journal of Transport Geography*, **27**, 1–3.
Notteboom, T., P. De Langen and W. Jacobs (2013), 'Institutional plasticity and path dependence in seaports: Interactions between institutions, port governance reforms and port authority routines', *Journal of Transport Geography*, **27**, 26–35.
Notteboom, T.E. and W. Winkelmans (2001), 'Structural changes in logistics: How will port authorities face the challenge?', *Maritime Policy & Management*, **28** (1), 71–89.
OECD/ITF (2015), *The Impact of Mega-Ships*, Paris: OECD.
Olivier, D. and B. Slack (2006), 'Rethinking the port', *Environment and Planning A*, **38** (8), 1409–1427.
Parnreiter, C. (2015), 'Managing and governing commodity chains: The role of producer service firms in the secondary global city of Hamburg', *Die Erde*, **146** (1), 1–15.
Parnreiter, C. (2018), 'Producer service firms as global city makers: The cases of

Mexico City and Hamburg', in M. Hoyler, C. Parnreiter and A. Watson (eds), *Global City Makers: Economic Actors and Practices in the World City Network*, Cheltenham, UK and Northampton, MA, USA: Edward Elgar Publishing, pp. 23–40.

Planco Consulting GmbH (2015), *Prognose des Umschlagpotenzials und des Modal Splits des Hamburger Hafens für die Jahre 2020, 2025 und 2030*, Essen: Planco.

Robinson, R. (2002), 'Ports as elements in value-driven chain systems: The new paradigm', *Maritime Policy & Management*, **29** (3), 241–255.

Scott, A.J. (ed.) (2002), *Global City-Regions: Trends, Theory, Policy*, Oxford: Oxford University Press.

Senatskanzlei (2012), 'Senat beschließt Drucksache zur Übernahme weiterer Anteile an Hapag-Lloyd', press release, 21 February, accessed 31 October 2012 at http://www.hamburg.de/pressearchiv-fhh/3302820/2012-02-21-hapag-lloyd/.

Slack, B. (1993), 'Pawns in the game: Ports in a global transportation system', *Growth and Change*, **24** (4), 579–588.

Slack, B. and A. Frémont (2005), 'Transformation of port terminal operations: From the local to the global', *Transport Reviews*, **25** (1), 117–130.

Taylor, P.J., M. Hoyler and S. Sanchez-Moral (2013), 'European cities in globalization: A comparative analysis based on the location strategies of advanced producer services', in J.R. Cuadrado-Roura (ed.), *Service Industries and Regions: Growth, Location and Regional Effects*, Heidelberg: Springer, pp. 285–304.

Verhetsel, A. and S. Sel (2009), 'World maritime cities: From which cities do container shipping companies make decisions?', *Transport Policy*, **16** (5), 240–250.

Verhoeven, P. (2010), 'A review of port authority functions: Towards a renaissance?', *Maritime Policy & Management*, **37** (3), 247–270.

Wiese, A. and A. Thierstein (2014), 'European port cities: Embodiment of interaction – knowledge and freight flow as catalysts of spatial development', in S. Conventz, B. Derudder, A. Thierstein and F. Witlox (eds), *Hub Cities in the Knowledge Economy: Seaports, Airports, Brainports*, Farnham: Ashgate, pp. 95–119.

9 Chasing the phantom of a 'global endgame': the role of management consultancy in the narratives of pre-failure ABN AMRO

Michiel van Meeteren and David Bassens

9.1 INTRODUCTION

On 10 October 2007, even before the smouldering North Atlantic financial crisis erupted in earnest, the curtain fell for the Dutch bank ABN AMRO. After a protracted hedge fund-initiated takeover battle, the bank was split up and sold to Banco Santander, Fortis and the Royal Bank of Scotland at a record high of 72 billion euros. Less than a year later, on 3 October 2008, the financial crisis fully hit continental Europe and the Dutch government bailed out the part of ABN AMRO that was sold to Fortis. In the aftermath of the takeover a broad consensus emerged that this was the inevitable fate of an underperforming company in a financialized global economy (*Het Financieele Dagblad*, 2007): ABN AMRO had played 'the global endgame' and had lost (Smit, 2008). This chapter sets out to explain how and why procyclical corporate mechanisms associated with 'global endgame discourse', such as the radical reorganization of the bank to the purpose of shareholder value creation that sealed ABN AMRO's fate, took root at the bank. More specifically, the chapter enquires into the scope of the agency of ABN AMRO's management as it was leading a 'second tier' bank from a 'second tier' global city in decline – i.e. Amsterdam – during the late-1990s and early-2000s (Engelen, 2007; Faulconbridge et al., 2007; Fernandez, 2011; Larson et al., 2011).

From a world and global cities research perspective, reconstructing the influence of advanced producer services (APS) firms on strategic and tactical management practices at multinational organizations is central (Bassens and van Meeteren, 2015; Watson and Beaverstock, 2014). The case of ABN AMRO is instructive, due to the visible role of management consultancy firms shaping key strategic decisions and procyclical corporate mechanisms that ultimately led to the bank's tragic demise in 2007. Drawing on ABN AMRO's account, the chapter intends to contribute to political-economy debates within world and global cities research on the relationship between APS and their large globally active clients while appreciating the changes herein under financialization (Bassens and van Meeteren, 2015).

During the 1990s and 2000s, world and global cities research often focused on the ability of APS to provide seamless service to their global clients (e.g. Beaverstock, 2007) by bridging institutional barriers and offering specialized 'outsourced' corporate functions. Recent research has increasingly emphasized the contribution of APS in enabling regulatory arbitrage and tax optimization for their clients (Wójcik, 2013; van Meeteren and Bassens, 2016). In the abstract, the role of APS in the world-economy is hypothesized as follows: APS constitute obligatory passage points in corporate networks that allow APS clients to obtain 'normal' profits as clients feel the gaze and expectations of financial markets (Bassens and van Meeteren, 2015). Some of the advanced services offered by APS consultants – such as balance sheet or organizational restructurings – directly work on the financial numbers of the corporation. Yet, as will become evident below, consultancy firms also provide off the shelf narratives on globalization, consolidation and shareholder value that help identify the financial geographies of risk and opportunity (Froud et al., 2000).

From the onset, we should make clear the Amsterdam-based bank ABN AMRO was operating in a rapidly shifting banking landscape where it was often uncertain to what degree a bank operating from a second-tier global city like Amsterdam had a future among the emerging global players. First, European banking reregulation during the 1980s and 1990s stimulated the start of a consolidation wave which led to a growing concentration of means in a limited number of very large banks (Leyshon and Thrift, 1992). Second, a shift to market-based banking in continental Europe (Hardie and Howarth, 2013) implied that operational geographies of banking became increasingly dependent on a spikier geography of global cities – with London increasingly dominating – where in normal times deep and liquid wholesale markets could be accessed. And, third, under market-based banking the large dependence of Dutch banks on international wholesale market-finance (Chang and Jones, 2013) raised the structural importance of producing performance narratives and numbers to reassure institutional investors (Froud et al., 2006). Nevertheless, there remained a clear political-economic interest to keep Amsterdam in place as a global city. Important global city makers gathered throughout the 1980s and 1990s in the Amsterdam Financial Centre initiative. This initiative was organized around the Amsterdam Stock Exchange, the derivative market, the Dutch Central Bank, the Ministry of Finance, the Municipality of Amsterdam, a number of large Dutch banks, the bankers' organization, insurance companies, and investment funds under the strategic advice of management consultancies such as McKinsey and others (Fernandez, 2011, p. 123).

Embedded in this context, the history of ABN AMRO reveals how the bank increasingly acted upon interpretations of a worldwide merger and acquisition craze that global consultancy firms labelled as 'the global endgame' in banking. This teleological narrative was internalized by the bank's management, but was also implemented through 'innovative' organizational and managerial control technologies and metrics geared to enhancing value creation within the bank – a strategy that eventually contributed to the bank's failing in 2008. This chapter provides a picture of how, in large and complex multinational corporations prone to share-holder pressure, strategic management consultancy narratives enable a managerial 'leap of faith' in order to convince employees, customers and shareholders about the validity of what remains ad-hoc manoeuvring. It also illustrates the limits of agency of both the client and the APS firm, as the performativity of the invoked narratives equally depends on their reception by financial market actors, who can ultimately discipline the firm. The implication of the argument for global cities research is that APS in general, and management consultancy firms in particular, act as important vectors to tie firms operating from semi-peripheral nodes of the world city network into financial markets centred on core global cities. As will become clear, the status of Amsterdam as a global city was propped up for quite a while, a situation that fits the frame of influential growth coalitions in the city. Yet, when international investors reshuffled their bets, the city was ultimately put in its second-tier place when its banking sector had to deleverage.

9.2   CORPORATE AGENCY DURING FINANCIALIZED GLOBALIZATION

As fallible human beings with bounded rationalities, the agency of bank managers and their consultants reflects the paradoxical notion that 'history makes people, but people make history' (Ortner, 2006, p. 2). Although actors are guided by the structures in which they are socialized, they nevertheless shape their own trajectory through their practices (Ortner, 2006; Yeung, 2003). People act on their definition of the situation, shaped by the cognitive understanding – their knowledge – of that situation (Berger and Luckmann, 1966; Denzin, 1970). As these situational definitions are continuously reproduced in everyday life, they become common sense, institutionalize, and tend to increasingly be perceived as the naturalized frames within which social life unfolds (Berger and Luckmann, 1966, p. 20; Goffman, 1974; Douglas, 1986). When the pace of social change is relatively slow, institutionalization produces distinct 'social fields'. A social field is an arena for action that defines specific roles, collective actors and cognitive and cultural frames that guide interactions between these actors (Fligstein, 2002, p. 15). According to Fligstein (2002), social fields are crucial if we want to sociologically understand how varieties in markets are produced and change. A social field, for instance as defined by a corporation, is never a closed system as fields overlap and share boundaries with regulators, competitors, and other socially proximate actors (Fligstein, 2002). Actors continuously navigate different fields, and experience transitions and shocks when navigating lesser-known ones (Berger and Luckmann, 1966). Moreover, within stable and shared fields, organizations will start to become more alike through, for instance, shared practices, mimicry, socialization of new members and legal obligations (DiMaggio and Powell, 1983). Through drawing on the field-specific cognitive frames, actors engage in 'bricolage' (Douglas, 1986, pp. 63–67) when making decisions: fragments of knowledge are put together in an assessment of the situation, which might be regarded as 'rational', or 'practically adequate' (Sayer, 1992) according to those involved (cf. Engelen et al., 2011).

This bricolage is done with varying degrees of consciousness (Emirbayer and Mische, 1998). Part of bricolage is habitual, informed on how things are 'routinely' done, but other dimensions are more reflexive. Agency can also be projectively oriented to imagine alternative possibilities, and toward the present – as a '"practical-evaluative" capacity to contextualize past habits and future projects within the contingencies of the moment' (Emirbayer and Mische, 1998, p. 963). In these reflexive types of agency, strategic thinking plays a larger role. As corporations engage in the serious game of capitalism (Ortner, 2006, p. 148), boardroom members harness their practical-evaluative and projective skills to outsmart other participants in the field. Nevertheless, even boardrooms have their creative limits and rely on common sense so that blind spots can occur where there is difference between locally specific fields across time and place. Schoenberger (1997) vividly describes how, despite being ruthless capitalists, American companies simply could not comprehend how to compete with Japanese firms in the 1980s. Japanese firms had strategies which gave higher profits, but which did not fit the American way of running a firm, hence not playing the game seriously according to well-established rules. Although American firms could define competitive strategies within their own frame, the cognitive distance (Nooteboom, 2008; van Meeteren, 2015) with the frame of Japanese competitors was too big.

Therefore, in order to remain competitive in a game with changing rules, much of what happens in 'corporate command and control' is navigating these differences: 'learn the changing rules of the game', 'span boundaries', but also try to internalize the bridge between contexts in the knowledge resources embedded in the firm (Faulconbridge et al., 2012; van Meeteren, 2015). It is here where the APS traditionally come into play as part of a cultural circuit of capital (Thrift, 2005) where knowledge about how to navigate economies worldwide is stored, recombined and evaluated. The seamless service component of APS allows for boundary spanning between institutional contexts (Nooteboom, 2008; Faulconbridge et al., 2012). As frames and fields between the firm and APS overlap, but are not coterminous, the 'global culture' fostered within the APS firm can bridge the cognitive and institutional distance that allows the focal firm to learn new practices (Nooteboom, 2008). Therefore, much of the influence of APS is based on soft power (Wójcik, 2013): they teach corporations new tricks to navigate different social fields and be competitive in new markets.

Moreover, the narratives and knowledge provided by APS also have a second function. Frames slowly evolve as processes associated with globalization generate overlaps between social fields. Each social field has a particular conception of control: the rules of the game that determine which stakeholders have to be taken into account and to what degree (Fligstein, 2002). Many authors make the case that, from the 1980s onwards, a conception of control based on 'shareholder value' has become dominant (Fligstein, 2002; Froud et al., 2006; O'Neill, 2001), first in the US, but increasingly so in other contexts where dependence on capital markets has increased (Engelen et al., 2011). Corporate financialization means that the corporation also has to align with the definition of the situation of the shareholder and hence provide a narrative of the firm for outside consumption (Froud et al., 2006). If deemed plausible by the stock market, the share price of the firm will go up, if implausible, it will go down and the management of the firm will be scrutinized. On the strategic level, consultants will be ready to provide suggestions on which strategies will be to the liking of this invisible stock market leviathan. In order to make corporations comparable for analysts and shareholders, corporations are made legible through crude aggregated (often ratio-based) measures based on 'total return on equity' (ROE) or 'total return to shareholder' (TRS) (Froud et al., 2000, 2006; O'Neill, 2001). The implementation of these measures often necessitates corporate reorganizations to make visible where exactly profits are made and to assess whether companies are not 'too big' (O'Neill, 2001). If the latter is the case they become, like ABN AMRO, susceptible to private equity and hedge fund takeovers (Engelen et al., 2011). For this implementation, there are 'tactical' consultancy packages available that can help the executive of the firm to identify where 'value is created' and 'money is wasted' to prevent a hostile takeover fate (Froud et al., 2000, 2006).

9.3   METHODS AND METHODOLOGY

Our main method is to gauge the agency of ABN AMRO, its consultancies, and the role of narratives therein through historical reconstruction. The analysis intends to uncover how strategic and tactical decisions were made within ABN AMRO and which cognitive frames informed them, the role of APS in informing these decisions, and how these decisions were received in ABN AMRO's environment (cf. Yeung, 2003). Moreover, by comparing the resulting internal and external narratives to the subsequently occurring actual events, it is possible to appraise whether ABN AMRO's bricolage had the desired effects in the social fields that the bank navigated (Froud et al., 2006). There are many different perspectives and audiences possible – the bank itself, stockbrokers, consultants, regulators – that will reflect differences in narratives about the demise of ABN AMRO. Hence, data triangulation of different sources is paramount (Denzin, 1970). Regarding the narratives of ABN AMRO a file of historical primary and secondary sources was assembled in the period 2010–2016[1] that is used to reconstruct the influence of APS on the bank. Apart from the secondary academic literature cited throughout, our file contains extensive documentation in the Dutch and English language financial press during the period 1990–2008 (*The Banker, The Economist, Het Financieele Dagblad*, the *Financial Times*), the annual reports of the bank (1990–2006), the archive of the ABN AMRO employee magazines (*Bankwereld, Bankers World, Connections*, 1990–2003),[2] journalistic reconstructions of ABN AMRO's demise (e.g. Smit, 2008), consultancy books and reports narrating products and strategies that were implemented at ABN AMRO (Hamoir et al., 2002; James et al., 1997; McTaggart et al., 1994), parliamentary hearings, and some miscellaneous sources such as old advertising campaigns (supplied by ABN AMRO's archive) and old executive PowerPoint presentations, internal documents, and old versions of ABN AMRO websites (retrieved through the Internet Wayback archive). Together they make it possible to tentatively reconstruct some of the narratives that informed the definition of the situation for the executive board of ABN AMRO in the period 1990–2006 and to understand how these narratives were translated to, and received by, the rest of the field in which ABN AMRO was strategically navigating.

9.4 ABN AMRO IN CONTEXT: FRAMES AND CONJUNCTURES

When discussing agency, it is useful to distinguish between the notions of 'frame' and 'conjuncture' (Engelen et al., 2011). The frame is the common-sense backdrop in front of which firms manoeuvre. History is refracted through the frame and, as changes within its associated social field unfold, actors position themselves strategically within the field. However, the field's most advantageous position will differ from episode to episode in the frame. These episodes within the financial sector are termed conjunctures by Engelen et al. (2011, p. 50): fragile periods of stability, lasting between four to seven years, in which a particular financial strategy and its narrative seems to be successful in the market. We will see below that APS often seduce the executive boardroom into a particular conjunctural strategy while aligning the conjunctural strategy with a frame shared by the boardroom and the APS. In order to appreciate that dynamic, we have to briefly sketch the frame in which ABN-AMRO considered itself and the major conjunctures through which it navigated.

An important reason why a frame seems like natural history to the actors involved is because it is understood as continuity with the past. The major theme in the frame of the Dutch banking sector in the 1990s was that of sectorial consolidation and inevitable globalization. As the Dutch banking sector had been consolidating for 200 years (Boschma and Hartog, 2014), further mergers and sectorial consolidation were a logical expectation. Moreover, it was commonly understood that banking consolidation had been accelerating from the crisis of the 1970s onwards (Engelen et al., 2011). Simultaneously, the information and communication technology (ICT) revolution was under way, which necessitated large-scale investment to provide economies of scale for banks. In turn, the ICT revolution was assumed to drive 'disintermediation' where banks would supposedly become obsolete unless they reinvented themselves (Engelen et al., 2011). In Europe, this general narrative was compounded by the expectations of Europeanization: the disappearance of institutional and currency barriers in the EU was assumed to accelerate consolidation even more (Leyshon and Thrift, 1992; Larson et al., 2011). Thus, the narrative of a 'global endgame' in banking emerged: the imminent moment of inevitable final consolidation of the global banking sector. Conjunctural narratives and strategies that resonated with this wider endgame frame were seductive.

For ABN AMRO, located in the historically important but nevertheless second-tier financial centre of Amsterdam, these developments incited the feeling of being a large fish in a small and shrinking pond. Globalization and Europeanization were quickly making the traditional stock market and currency exchange functions of Amsterdam obsolete (Faulconbridge et al., 2007; Fernandez, 2011). Moreover, the clientele of ABN AMRO, the large Dutch corporate clients and pension funds, were increasingly glo-balizing themselves and demanded ever-more sophisticated services for the privilege of being their preferred banker (van Zanden and Uittenbogaard, 1999; Westerhuis, 2008), compounding the need for ICT investments and investment bank services that drives the need for upscaling. The 'large fish, small pond' frame was institutionalized throughout the field of the Dutch financial sector. Already in 1976, the Managing Board of ABN Bank had concluded that survival of the bank was contingent on the bank becoming one of the world's largest (Westerhuis, 2008, p. 38). Moreover, the frame of inevitable consolidation was an important reason for the Dutch Central Bank to be a strong supporter of the merger of ABN and AMRO bank in the 1990s. In one transaction, an economic actor was created that had sufficient scale and scope to engage in the coming onslaught of the 1990s and to give Amsterdam as a financial centre a chance to have a significant future (Larson et al., 2011).

Within this frame, ABN AMRO and its legal predecessors had acted upon the previous conjunctures. In the 1960s and 1970s, when times for corporate banking were rough, the most profitable strategy had been retail banking resulting in costly branch networks for both the ABN and AMRO banks (van Zanden and Uittenbogaard, 1999). In the 1980s, the conjuncture had shifted toward merchant and investment banking, where AMRO had specialized in investment banking – particularly Initial Public Offerings (IPOs) and wholesale credit – while ABN, with its historically dense international network, excelled at merchant banking and service to Dutch multinationals abroad (Westerhuis, 2008). After the ABN AMRO merger, this heritage, given the bank's top-heavy sunk costs in both retail and corporate banking, made a strategy to develop a universal bank – that combined off-balance and on-balance banking in commercial and retail sections – nearly self-evident in the 1990s (van den Brink, 2003). However, in order to achieve sufficient scale to profitably offer capital-intensive services such as 'global transactions services' – which concerns the techni-cal infrastructure for seamless global payments – the bank had to grow significantly. As one can only acquire so many banks with cash before the war chest is empty, a listing on the New York stock exchange eventually became inevitable in order to do more mergers (Berendsen, 1999).

During the 1990s, ABN AMRO and the entrepreneurial strategy of the Amsterdam financial centre initially seemed to flourish. ABN AMRO was successful in the IPO business that defined this conjuncture. However, due to its heritage and large retail network, the bank retained a top-heavy cost structure (Jonker, 2008). Especially when investment banking experienced setbacks with the bursting of the dotcom-bubble, these retail-related cost structures were increasingly scrutinized by the stock market. When traditional financial centre activities failed to recover in Amsterdam after the dotcom crisis (Faulconbridge et al., 2007), the Dutch political economy increasingly became dependent on tax planning and avoidance services, pension fund activities, and mortgage securitization markets (Aalbers et al., 2011; Engelen and Konings, 2010; Palan et al., 2010), making a national champion universal bank less instrumental to the wider political economy. This ultimately helped sealing ABN AMRO's fate as its cost structure became exposed to the gaze of large institutional investors in the mid-2000s (Engelen et al., 2008).

9.5   STRATEGIC AND TACTICAL CONSULTANCY AT ABN AMRO DURING THE MILLENARIAN CONJUNCTURE

9.5.1   Strategic Consultancy: 'Playing the Global Endgame'

A view from the management consultant office

In the 1990s conjuncture, management consultancy and investment banking were buzzing with the global endgame leitmotiv, culminating in a series of industry reports by leading APS firms. AT Kearney, Morgan Stanley and McKinsey all produced their version of this strategic consultancy narrative, but the discourse codified a more widely shared belief within the APS complex. McKinsey, who had a long-lasting consultancy relationship with ABN AMRO (Dankers and Arnoldus, 2000), published 'Playing to the endgame in financial services' (James et al., 1997), which predicted a 'nascent and unprecedented consolidation' (James et al., 1997, p. 171). Witnessing the growing relaxation of geographical constraints on banking activity, McKinsey's projection was that the near future (the 2000s) would come to revolve around a handful of very large, globally active banks. Such a consolidation fitted the above-sketched frame held by ABN AMRO, but it also projected a sense of urgency to the situation, as banks needed to act in this particular conjuncture in order to 'win the endgame' in the next. It was expected that prior consolidation in the US would be mirrored in a 'pan-European endgame' marked by a 'domino effect' in mergers and acquisitions (M&As) (see Hamoir et al., 2002, pp. 121–122), a hypothesis that was also steering academic projections in that period (Abraham and Van Dijcke, 2002).

Furthermore, consultancy narratives shaped the rules of the game at the firm level. McKinsey stated that 'any serious player must adopt an explicit growth strategy that incorporates both expertise in mergers and acquisitions and options-based valuation' (James et al., 1997, p. 172). The most effective way to grow and to 'stake out territory in the new landscape' was through M&As, which would generate economies of scale. Large corporations would be better placed to take on the 'colossal advertising and promotion efforts' (James et al., 1997, p. 175), to build a 'truly national brand' (p. 175) and, lastly, to maintain investments in technology. There was, in other words, a shared idea that the sheer size of corporate assets was a key component to efficiency – or at least survival – in the banking sector (Larson et al., 2011). But there were other elements of so-called 'rational economics', besides striving for economies of scale, to engage in M&As: 'Unlike past merger booms, this consolidation wave is less about empire building than about raising revenue, cutting costs, and locking in continuous productivity gains to boost shareholder value' (James et al., 1997, p. 175). The McKinsey article, interestingly enough, is silent about the ample examples of unsuccessful M&As. As the case of ABN AMRO itself illustrates, cost–benefit ratios after mergers do not necessarily improve (see Froud et al., 2006, p. 115; Leyshon and Thrift, 1992): the bank was continuously confronted with high costs and, as a corollary, low efficiency ratios (Jonker, 2008).

However, these kinds of inconveniences tended to be skated over in consultancy narratives through circular reasoning. Ultimately, 'highly skilled, productive players . . . and players with unique brands, distribution systems, and management talent will succeed in M&A' (James et al., 1997, p. 178). Therefore, consultants advised banks to use M&As to acquire more profitable business, like investment banking, embedded in a strategy of 'ensuring a virtuous acquisition cycle' (James et al., 1997, p. 182). High stock prices were considered a necessary condition to enter the M&A game, but, once you were successfully in and had acquired others, this would almost naturally boost stock valuation. *Winning the Merger Endgame* (Deans et al., 2003), a management consultancy book by AT Kearney, spelled out the argument in more detail, but the ingredients are basically the same: deregulation, globalization, consolidation, the need to grow to compete, and therefore realizing the shareholder value to venture into M&A markets. In the eyes of consultants (and increasingly in the eyes of bankers) the endgame was about 'controlling your own destiny', meaning that

for would-be winners with national and global aspirations, market capitalization is the metric to watch. It is the best indicator we have of how well managers are performing; indeed, recognizing this, many companies have now linked senior management compensation to shareholder value creation. As regulation falls away and competition intensifies, management talent and insight will become scarce commodities. (James et al., 1997, p. 197)

The insights of these books are presented as a natural history, with inevitable properties, unmediated by human action, and of prophetic value.[3]

A view from the ABN AMRO cockpit

When we investigate how the global endgame narrative was consumed by the financial industry, we start to observe how this natural history is the outcome of human agency embedded in social fields. Bankers became more susceptible to consultancy narratives in framing and acting upon the world while the Dutch financial sector was rapidly changing under outside influence. The motivation for ABN AMRO's ambitious merger decisions in the 1990s were often backed by alluding to the global endgame. For instance, when ABN AMRO acquired Banco Real (1998) the narrative had clearly entered the mindset of ABN AMRO's then Foreign Division director, Michael Drabbe. When interviewed for the company magazine, he explicitly stated that 'the whole world should be considered ABN AMRO's "playing field"', while the front cover depicts him pondering over his next move at the chessboard in front of him (*Bankwereld*, 1998; see Figure 9.1). Probably not totally coincidentally, the same imagery of a chessboard features prominently in McKinsey's global endgame report (James et al., 1997) at a moment when McKinsey was heavily involved in a strategic consultancy trajectory with the bank's senior management.

Gradually, the company magazines indicate elements of corporate financialization, as the 1990s internal discourse of the bank starts to connect strategic decisions to the imperatives of creating shareholder value. The continuous struggle to cut costs was troubling the then CFO Tom de Swaan, as the efficiency ratios that also figured centrally in various consultancy reports at the time were problematic. Witnessing that costs were constantly outgrowing revenues, de Swaan was firm in his statement: 'The outside world – I am thinking about our shareholders, analysts, and rating agencies – will rightfully question the fact that we are apparently not able to control costs. Especially when one looks at other banks in the so-called peer group, a category of collegial banks to which we belong' (*Bankwereld*, 1999, pp. 4–5). In his view the 'outside guard' would raise serious questions about ABN AMRO's capacity to manage the bank properly. Simultaneously, the pressure to enhance shareholder value through M&As was relativized by parts of the higher management. Jan Kalff, Chairman of the Executive Board until the turn of the millennium, made no direct connection between the relatively low value of ABN AMRO stocks and the potential danger of (hostile) takeovers, indicating that the latter was simply non-existent (*Bankwereld*, 1999). Kalff was repeatedly criticized for his prudent old-fashioned style of banking, which

Source: Cover reproduced from Bankwereld (1998, p. 63). Reproduced by kind permission
of 'Collectie ABN AMRO Kunst & Historie, Amsterdam'.

*Figure 9.1   'ABN AMRO, increasingly prominent on the world map', with
Board member Michael Drabbe playing the global endgame*

for a while was the preferred angle of the press to explain ABN AMRO's
alleged underperformance (Smit, 2008, pp. 89, 172). Nevertheless, it was
under Kalff's leadership, through listing the bank on the New York Stock
Exchange (1997) and early experiments with shareholder value metrics,
that the shareholder value conception of control first entered the bank
(Smit, 2008). Both actions had become necessary to obtain sufficient

capital to keep the M&A machine rolling (Berendsen, 1999; Larson et al., 2011).

It was only in 2000, when Kalff was succeeded by Rijkman Groenink, that shareholder value really moved centre stage in the strategic narratives of the bank, again backed by explicit references to the ongoing global endgame. Although Groenink was widely considered a more bullish banker than his predecessor, he nevertheless made his career in the more traditional segments of the AMRO bank (Smit, 2008). As such he was as much a product of the previous era as he would become an agent of change. Prior to his accession as chairman, Groenink initiated 'Project Arrow', an internal working group that was to build a new strategy for the bank (Smit, 2008, p. 145). In a keynote delivered by Groenink just before his appointment, in January 2000, the first results became public. On a slide titled 'the endgame, a US example' explicit reference was made to the consolidation waves in the US, to project the potentially dystopian view that globally in a few years the top 10 banks would each have a market capitalization of US$ 200 billion. Groenink made a plea for radical change, arguing that the ultimate motivation for (higher) management lies in a constant fear of hostile takeover (Smit, 2008, p. 149). At that time, Groenink saw quite a lot of 'unused potential' for that within the bank (Smit, 2008, p. 149). Immediately after taking up the position as chairman, following the advice of the house consultants McKinsey, Groenink replaced the old geographically based structure of the bank with one focused on business and product segments, thereby creating three global and largely autonomous 'strategic business units' based on client profiles (Van den Brink, 2003; Claes, 2008, p. 91).

Interestingly, a McKinsey report (Hamoir et al., 2002) discussed a fictionalized example of a bank with a strong retail component like ABN AMRO, which they called 'Eurofin'. One of the elements that was emphasized is that 'Eurofin' should organize itself in a 'modularized way' after it expanded in different types of activities:

> Universal cross-border giants that go on trying to be all things to all customers will ultimately deliver less shareholder value than the emerging, more competitive large-scale specialists. Banks that make their earliest cross-border deals with their potential specialties in mind are likely to do better in the long term than those that rush into the first available deal. (Hamoir et al., 2002, p. 125)

It is unclear whether the hypothetical Eurofin example was inspired by ABN AMRO, but the modularized approach became the main tactic at the bank after Groenink's appointment in May 2000, while uttering the term 'universal bank' was forbidden inside the walls of ABN AMRO over the subsequent seven years (Smit, 2008, p. 364). The bottom line was that the management of the bank would from then on focus on strategy, while the various business units took care of their own business, i.e. they had their own human resources, information technology, and communication departments (Broersen and Verdonck, 2002) and had to charge one another for their business at commercial rates. Together, these organizational changes were geared towards a maximization of shareholder value, which was deemed necessary to win the global endgame. In fact, both elements were considered inseparable under these circumstances (*Bankwereld*, 2000; Claes, 2008, p. 94; Larson et al., 2011, p. 50).

9.5.2   Tactical Consultancy: 'Managing for Value'

As M&As fuelled by rising stock prices were considered inevitable strategic moves during the global endgame, the adoption of shareholder value logic – where firms are incentivized and disciplined to optimize the short-term profits for their shareholders (Froud et al., 2006) – became a necessary tactic. Groenink chose Marakon Associates over McKinsey to implement shareholder value principles throughout the ABN AMRO reorganization (Cramb, 2000; Smit, 2008). Through shared personal connections between the Arrow team and Marakon at INSEAD Business School, Marakon had been introduced in the social networks of the managing board and Groenink had become impressed by Marakon's devotion to their own management principles (Smit, 2008, p. 173). As a result, 25 management consultants from Marakon – priced at 5000–7500 euros a day according to Smit (2008, p. 173) – were hired to put a number on the value added of each separate ABN AMRO business unit. Implementing Marakon's 'managing for value' measure was hoped to allow management to exert strategic control at a distance while making the organization legible for shareholders.

A view from the management consultant office

As with the global endgame narrative, managing for value tactics and metrics had been part and parcel of the management consultancy repertoire ever since the shareholder value conception of control emerged (Froud et al., 2000, 2006). Marakon's version is spelled out in their 'magnum opus' *The Value Imperative* (McTaggart et al., 1994), a business management book carefully composed by Marakon's then chairman, president and vice-president. The book explores how to realign corporate organization with the imperative of shareholder value creation, which is argued to be the only sustainable approach for corporate success. Marakon's solution of 'value based management' is 'a combination of beliefs, principles, and processes that effectively arm the company to succeed in its battle against competition from the outside and the institutional imperative from the inside'

(McTaggart et al., 1994, p. 42). The latter was on par with the former, as in their view large organizations tended to move toward mediocre 'suboptimal' performance – 'to drift in the direction of what seems safe and easy rather than to make hard decisions and challenge performance standards. Whatever the reason, the consequences are the same – there is extensive use of the shareholder's money to subsidize activities, practices and business strategies that do not create wealth' (McTaggart et al., 1994, p. 45).

The Marakon approach, which they were applying at Bank of America, Boeing, Coca Cola, Disney, Barclays, Lloyds, and others, was predicated on the 'strategic business unit' structure that at ABN AMRO emerged from Project Arrow. Marakon claimed that 'effective control' of the firm was expected to emerge from the implementation of metrics such as Total Return to Shareholders (TRS), Economic Profit (EP), and Economic Value (EV) to (i) assess the contribution of wealth creation within the bank's different (sub)units; (ii) to use these to (re)allocate funds within the firm; and (iii) to provide carrots and sticks to the lower management through the linking of remunerations to performance of the unit.[4] Importantly, TRS was not only to be defined in absolute terms, but also served to compare the performance of firms within the market. As stated by McTaggart et al. (1994, pp. 267–268): 'We think that, on balance, the best single measure is the company's total return to shareholders relative to the return of similar, peer, companies.'

A view from the ABN AMRO cockpit

The TRS goal at the enterprise level was translated into EP as a short-term benchmark for different business units, while EV allowed choosing between various alternative resource allocation scenarios in terms of whether an activity would generate value in the long term. Besides these inward-looking metrics, there had been a longer tradition of outward-looking benchmarks such as the use of a 'peer group' of banks with whom ABN AMRO was comparing itself. The company magazines indicate that it became salient to do so following the bank's listing on the New York Stock Exchange, after which the bank entered a global playing field and became sensitive to the lists circulating in the financial media (e.g. those produced by *The Banker*, see *Bankwereld*, 1996). Most of the peers at that time were universal banks with a similar type of cost structure (e.g. Deutsche Bank). Gradually, and in line with the 'managing for value' philosophy, which deems that profitability is to be preferred over specialization (McTaggart et al., 1994: pp. 10–11), it became common practice within the bank to seek comparison with banks operating in the Anglo-Saxon tradition, including large UK and US banks, with New York- or London-based activities in investment banking niches (e.g. Barclays, Citicorp, JP Morgan Chase, Merrill Lynch).

The peer group, however, took on a new performative character under the command of Groenink when it was explicitly linked to the goal of achieving shareholder value. As a part of the strategic business unit reorganization in 2000, the bank's senior management composed a peer group of 20 banks with the explicitly communicated aim of ending up within the top five in terms of TRS in the near future. The peer group, according to Groenink and CFO de Swaan, was evenly balanced to avoid distortions such as selecting too many US bulge bracket investment banks, because 'a string of bad years in Wall Street would make it too easy for ABN AMRO to achieve its TRS goal or, conversely, a string of good years making our TRS goal unattainable'. The selection of peer banks was also based on similarities in customers, geography and product offering, and, interestingly, also the presence of a 'formidable management team' (*Bankers World*, 2000, pp. 26–27), which ABN AMRO intended to beat. Although geographical differences between banks were seemingly avoided, one can argue that peer group thinking remained in fact insensitive to the geographies underpinning markets. What became internalized in the management's worldview was a very aspatial, neoclassical way of looking at markets, as if markets were taking place at a pin's head (cf. Lee, 2002). Such views were reinforced by the global endgame narrative that projected a future in which geography lost its relevance altogether.

This argument, in turn, legitimized divestment from the costly international merchant bank network that had evolved from ABN's tradition to provide 'seamless service' to Dutch capital in foreign contexts and where cross-subsidizing was allowed for strategic reasons. In the philosophy of Marakon's McTaggart et al. (1994, p. 16) such 'strategies [cannot] be justified on [the] grounds that any resulting increase in customer satisfaction will be worth it in the long run . . . Whenever shareholders subsidize customers in a significant way, the financial health of the company is diminished, ultimately to the detriment of all stakeholders'. This illustrates how the peer group allowed the bank to translate its capital market ambitions into internal performance targets. On the basis of projective comparisons with these peers the bank's senior management concluded it had to double TRS every four years to enter the top five. By linking the remuneration of (senior) management to those results, the crucial link between external market pressure and internal corporate control was at last firmly established; a link which was assumed to be a crucial step in unlocking the virtuous acquisition circle, but which in the end would lead to the failure of the bank when challenged by the bank's shareholders.

Global city makers

9.6 EPILOGUE AND CONCLUSIONS

The early 2000s were a rough time for wholesale banking, and it turned out pretty quickly that ABN AMRO had made a wrong move in their self-induced global endgame. Not only was the reorganization from a matrix to a business unit organization complicated and costly to implement, within two years it became clear that retail banking was much more important to the bank's revenue than its investment banking arm, particularly when considering the TRS, EP and EV measures. By that time, the bank had already spent an enormous amount of money in strengthening the wholesale strategic business unit (Smit, 2008; Larson et al., 2011). It is this perception of mismanagement that 'stuck' with the financial press and eventually contributed to ABN AMRO's hostile takeover in 2007 (Engelen et al., 2008). However, the bank had meanwhile become a pioneer in the securitization of Dutch mortgages (Aalbers et al., 2011) and, therefore, below the radar, ABN AMRO had developed the capabilities crucial to the conjuncture of the mid-2000s, nevertheless without sufficiently convincing stockholders. It was these capabilities which would incite the financial crisis of 2008 and which keep the financial system vulnerable today (Engelen et al., 2011). ABN AMRO's inheritance would later help sink the Royal Bank of Scotland, which acquired the assets following the takeover (Financial Services Authority Board (FSA), 2011). This underscores that having the right strategy in a conjuncture is not a sufficient condition for being the winner of the endgame, as convincing others with the narrative is crucial too. Further, and crucially, it indicates that the winning strategy in each conjuncture may turn out to be far from the most socially desirable one in hindsight.

Abstracting from the ABN AMRO case, this chapter has illustrated how APS firms have been instrumental in the production of changing conceptions of corporate control and processes of corporate financialization that have profoundly reshaped the European banking landscape and wider European political economy in the last decades (Wójcik, 2013; Bassens and van Meeteren, 2015). Quantitative models of the world city network (Taylor and Derudder, 2016) provide a system-wide estimation of the geography of this interaction between APS and the firms they service. However, mere co-presence in a city does not necessarily equate to power and influence, and qualitative in-depth studies can provide important qualification and corroboration in world cities research (Krijnen et al., 2017). Methodologically, this chapter has shown how historical reconstruction can help opening the 'knowledge value chain' in the world city network through which corporations understand and act upon this world. It is only a first example of how the enormous stock of 'old news' can actually help us to complement structural analysis of the world city network and illustrate agency. Our results vindicate criticism of the kind of expertise offered by APS in the instance of ABN AMRO (cf. Christophers, 2009): did management consultants really help to manage across borders, or did they help project a flat world that misguided senior management at the bank? It therefore also shows how consultants see a window of opportunity under financialized globalization to establish an aura of expertise that makes them obligatory passage points even for banks, which are traditionally considered APS themselves. The conditions that make this happen are structural: the growing importance of finance capital and financial markets, and eventually the corporate financialization of financial institutions. This indicates that there are power asymmetries within the APS complex, which pan out geographically (cf. van Meeteren and Bassens, 2016). Hiring management consultants connected ABN AMRO, a bank that was chasing the phantom of a global endgame from an increasingly semi-peripheral global city of Amsterdam, to an industry field of global highly leveraged banks. Ultimately, the expertise of flown-in consultants did not suffice to reorient the bank to operate under rapidly changing conditions of financialized globalization, even though global endgame diagnostics and remedies are still being peddled by global consultancy firms, such as AT Kearney, from their global city offices (Rothenbücher et al., 2013). The cautionary implication of the ABN story for global city makers – such as the Amsterdam financial centre growth coalition and its successors and counterparts in other second-tier global cities – is that, however attractive it appeared to be to buy into consultancy narratives for aspirational purposes, it ultimately only delayed the further un-making of Amsterdam as a global city in the realm of banking.

NOTES

1. We would like to warmly thank Ton de Graaf, company historian of ABN AMRO Kunst en Archief, for providing us access to and context for parts of ABN AMRO's internal archives.
2. Unfortunately ABN AMRO largely transferred its internal communication to a dynamic intranet in 2001; it is unknown to what extent this historical source is preserved.
3. Douglas (1986) argues that such naturalization is key to institutionalization as it makes discourse appear as an unquestioned truth.
4. See Claes (2008, pp. 94–95): 'Total Return to Shareholders (TRS) = Share price appreciation + dividend yield. Economic Value (EV) = Assigned Capital + Total Value Creation. Economic Profit (EP) = Net profit after tax -/- Capital Charge.'

REFERENCES

Aalbers, M.B., E. Engelen and A. Glasmacher (2011), '"Cognitive closure" in the Netherlands: Mortgage securitization in a hybrid European political economy', *Environment and Planning A*, **43** (8), 1779–1795.

Abraham, J.-P. and P. Van Dijcke (2002), *European Financial Cross-Border Consolidation: At the Crossroads in Europe? By Exception, Evolution or Revolution?*, Vienna: Société Universitaire Européenne de Recherches Financières (SUERF Studies, 22).

Bankers World (2000), 'Managing for value', *Bankers World*, **5** (5), 26–27.

Bankwereld (1996), 'In de bankwereld draait alles om ranking', *Bankwereld*, (4), 26–27.

Bankwereld (1998), 'ABN AMRO steeds nadrukkelijker aanwezig op de wereldkaart', *Bankwereld*, (63), 4–7.

Bankwereld (1999), '9 vragen aan drs. Tom de Swaan, Chief Financial Officer van onze bank', *Bankwereld*, (70), 4–5.

Bankwereld (2000), 'Interview met Rijkman Groenink', *Bankwereld*, (79), 4–5.

Bassens, D. and M. van Meeteren (2015), 'World cities under conditions of financialized globalization: Towards an augmented world city hypothesis', *Progress in Human Geography*, **39** (6), 752–775.

Beaverstock, J.V. (2007), 'World city networks "from below": International mobility and inter-city relations in the global investment banking industry', in P.J. Taylor, B. Derudder, P. Saey and F. Witlox (eds), *Cities in Globalization: Practices, Policies and Theories*, London: Routledge, pp. 52–71.

Berendsen, C. (1999), 'Global ambitions, ABN AMRO Bank 1990–1999', in J. de Vries, W. Vroom and T. de Graaf (eds), *Worldwide Banking, ABN AMRO Bank 1824–1999*, Amsterdam: ABN AMRO Bank, pp. 449–488.

Berger, P. and T. Luckmann (1966), *The Social Construction of Reality*, London: Penguin Books.

Boschma R.A. and M. Hartog (2014), 'Merger and acquisition activity as driver of spatial clustering: The spatial evolution of the Dutch banking industry, 1850–1993', *Economic Geography*, **90** (3), 247–266.

Broersen, E.N. and A.W.T.J. Verdonck (2002), 'Value based management en management control bij ABN AMRO', in E. de With, L. Traas, F.A. Roozen and H.B.A. Steens (eds), *Handboek Management Accounting*, Deventer: Kluwer, pp. D3005–1–D3005–32.

Chang, M. and E. Jones (2013), 'Belgium and the Netherlands: Impatient capital', in I. Hardie and D. Horwarth (eds), *Market-Based Banking and the International Financial Crisis*, Oxford: Oxford University Press, pp. 79–102.

Christophers, B. (2009), 'Complexity, finance, and progress in human geography', *Progress in Human Geography*, **33** (6), 807–824.

Claes, P.C.M. (2008), *Value-Based Management Control Systems: An Analysis of Design and Use*, PhD thesis, Vrije Universiteit, Amsterdam.

Cramb, G. (2000), 'Breaking the bank's European consensus: ABN Amro of the Netherlands is undergoing a fundamental reorganisation to change both its structure and culture', *Financial Times*, 27 July, p. 17.

Dankers J. and D. Arnoldus (2000), 'Management consultants in Dutch banks, 1950–1990', paper presented at the conference *External Experts in Organisations*, Reading, 19–20 May.

Deans, G.K., F. Kroeger and S. Zeisel (2003), *Winning the Merger Endgame: A Playbook for Profiting from Industry Consolidation*, New York: McGraw-Hill.

Denzin, N.K. (1970), *The Research Act: A Theoretical Introduction to Sociological Methods*, Chicago: Aldine Publishing Company.

DiMaggio, P. and W.W. Powell (1983), 'The iron cage revisited: Institutional isomorphism and collective rationality in organizational fields', *American Sociological Review*, **48** (2), 147–160.

Douglas, M. (1986), *How Institutions Think*, Syracuse, NY: Syracuse University Press.

Emirbayer, M. and A. Mische (1998), 'What is agency?', *American Journal of Sociology*, **103** (4), 962–1023.

Engelen, E. (2007), '"Amsterdamned"? The uncertain future of a financial centre', *Environment and Planning A*, **39** (6), 1306–1324.

Engelen, E. and M. Konings (2010), 'Financial capitalism resurgent: Comparative institutionalism and the challenges of financialization', in G. Morgan, J.L. Campbell, C. Crouch, O.K. Pedersen and R. Whitley (eds), *The Oxford Handbook of Comparative Institutional Analysis*, Oxford: Oxford University Press, pp. 601–624.

Engelen, E., M. Konings and R. Fernandez (2008), 'The rise of activist investors and patterns of political responses: Lessons on agency', *Socio-Economic Review*, **6** (4), 611–636.

Engelen, E., I. Ertürk, J. Froud, S. Johal, A. Leaver, M. Moran, A. Nilsson and K. Williams (2011), *After the Great Complacence: Financial Crisis and the Politics of Reform*, Oxford: Oxford University Press.

Faulconbridge, J.R., E. Engelen, M. Hoyler and J.V. Beaverstock (2007), 'Analysing the changing landscape of European financial centres: The role of financial products and the case of Amsterdam'; *Growth and Change*, **38** (2), 279–303.

Faulconbridge, J.R., D. Muzio and A. Cook, (2012), 'Institutional legacies in TNCs and their management through training academies: The case of transnational law firms in Italy', *Global Networks*, **12** (1), 48–70.

Fernandez, R. (2011), *Explaining the Decline of the Amsterdam Financial Centre: Globalizing Finance and the Rise of a Hierarchical Inter-City Network*, PhD thesis, University of Amsterdam.

Fligstein, N. (2002), *The Architecture of Markets: An Economic Sociology of Twenty-First-Century Capitalist Societies*, Princeton, NJ: Princeton University Press.

Froud J., C. Haslam, S. Johal and K. Williams (2000), 'Shareholder value and financialization: Consultancy promises, management moves', *Economy and Society*, **29** (1), 80–110.

Froud, J., S. Johal, A. Leaver and K. Williams (2006), *Financialization and Strategy: Narrative and Numbers*, Abingdon, UK and New York, USA: Routledge.

FSA (2011), *The Failure of the Royal Bank of Scotland*, London: Financial Services Authority.

Goffman, E. (1974), *Frame Analysis: An Essay on the Organization of Experience*, Boston: Northeastern University Press.

Hamoir, O., C. McCamish, M. Niederkorn, and C. Thiersch (2002), 'Europe's banks: Verging on merging', *McKinsey Quarterly*, (3), 116–125.

Hardie, I. and D. Howarth (eds) (2013), *Market-based Banking & the International Financial Crisis*, Oxford: Oxford University Press.

Het Financieele Dagblad (2007), 'ABN riep strijd over zich af', *Het Financieele Dagblad*, 11 October, p. 21.

James, M., L.T. Mendonca, J. Peters and G. Wilson (1997), 'Playing to the endgame in financial services', *McKinsey Quarterly*, (4), 170–185.

Jonker, J. (2008), 'Scale at any price: The rise and predictable demise of ABN AMRO, 1960–2006', Working Paper, Utrecht University.

Krijnen, M., D. Bassens and M. van Meeteren (2017), 'Manning circuits of value: Lebanese professionals and expatriate world-city formation in Beirut, *Environment and Planning A*, **49** (12), 2878–2896.

Larson, M.J., G. Schnyder, G. Westerhuis and J. Wilson (2011), 'Strategic responses to global challenges: The case of European banking, 1973–2000', *Business History*, **53** (1), 40–62.

Lee, R. (2002), '"Nice maps, shame about the theory?" Thinking geographically about the economic', *Progress in Human Geography*, **26** (3), 333–355.

Leyshon, A. and N.J. Thrift (1992), 'Liberalisation and consolidation: The Single European Market and the remaking of European financial capital', *Environment and Planning A*, **24** (1), 49–81.

McTaggart, J.M., P.W. Kontes and M.C. Mankins (1994), *The Value Imperative*, New York: The Free Press.

Nooteboom, B. (2008), 'Cognitive distance in and between communities of practice and firms: Where do exploitation and exploration take place, and how are they connected?', in A. Amin and J. Roberts (eds), *Community, Economic Creativity and Organization*, Oxford: Oxford University Press, pp. 123–147.

O'Neill, P. (2001), 'Financial narratives of the modern corporation', *Journal of Economic Geography*, **1** (2), 181–199.

Ortner, S.B. (2006), *Anthropology and Social Theory: Culture, Power, and the Acting Subject*, Durham, NC: Duke University Press.

Palan, R., R. Murphy and C. Chavagneux (2010), *Tax Havens: How Globalization Really Works*, Ithaca and London: Cornell University Press.

Rothenbücher, J., S. Niewiem and J. Schrottke (2013), 'The merger endgame revisited'. *AT Kearney Ideas and Insights*, accessed 1 March 2016 at https://www.atkearney.com/paper/-/asset_publisher/dVxv4Hz2h8bS/content/the-merger-endgame-revisited/10192.

Sayer, A. (1992), *Method in Social Science: A Realist Approach* (2nd edition), London: Routledge.

Schoenberger, E. (1997), *The Cultural Crisis of the Firm*, Cambridge, MA, USA and Oxford, UK: Blackwell Publishing.

Smit, J. (2008), *De Prooi*, Amsterdam: Prometheus.

Taylor, P.J. and B. Derudder (2016), *World City Network: A Global Urban Analysis* (2nd edition), London: Routledge.

Thrift, N.J. (2005), *Knowing Capitalism*, London: Sage.

Van den Brink, R.G.C. (2003), *Bankstrategie en Bankcultuur*, Amsterdam: Vossiuspers.

Van Meeteren, M. (2015), 'Learning by bumping: Pathways of Dutch SMEs to foreign direct investment in Asia', *Tijdschrift voor Economische en Sociale Geografie*, **106** (4), 471–485.

Van Meeteren, M. and D. Bassens (2016), 'World cities and the uneven geographies of financialization: Unveiling stratification and hierarchy in the world city archipelago', *International Journal of Urban and Regional Research*, **40** (1), 62–81.

Van Zanden, J.L. and R. Uittenbogaard (1999), 'Expansion, internationalisation and concentration, 1950–1990', in J. de Vries, W. Vroom and T. de Graaf (eds), *Worldwide Banking, ABN AMRO Bank 1824–1999*, Amsterdam: ABN AMRO Bank, pp. 335–391.

Watson, A. and J.V. Beaverstock (2014), 'World city network research at a theoretical impasse: On the need to re-establish qualitative approaches to understanding agency in world city networks', *Tijdschrift voor Economische en Sociale Geografie*, **105** (4), 412–426.
Westerhuis, G. (2008), *Conquering the American Market*, Meppel: Boom.
Wójcik, D. (2013), 'Where governance fails: Advanced business services and the offshore world', *Progress in Human Geography*, **37** (3), 330–347.
Yeung, H.W-C. (2003), 'Practicing new economic geographies: A methodological examination', *Annals of the Association of American Geographers*, **93** (2), 442–462.

Epilogue Placing politics and power within the making of global cities

Sarah Hall

As the chapters in this book clearly demonstrate, global cities do not come into the world economy pre-formed. Rather a considerable amount of work is undertaken by a range of actors, from individual economic agents, through advanced producer services (APS) firms to institutional actors in order to (re)produce the power of global cities within the contemporary world economy. Indeed, the sheer diversity of such actors and their concomitant spheres of influence is extremely well teased out in the chapters within this collection. This ranges from the individual financiers working in Tokyo's financial district in Yamamura's (2018) chapter to Hesse's (2018) exposition of the shipping companies shaping Hamburg's port development. Indeed, one of the many strengths of the chapters in this book is their breadth in terms of substantive area of economic activity (from finance, through management consultancy to real estate and infrastructure) to geographical location. In this respect, a much needed diversity of research sites beyond Western Europe is provided through work on elites in both Tokyo and Mumbai. This diversity of research approach is continued through the choice of methods that range from comparative quantitative work on London and New York to in-depth qualitative research with key informants whose daily working lives are vital in shaping the economic fabric of global cities.

However, for me, the most significant intervention made by the work contained in this book lies in its focus on agency and agents within global cities. In this respect, the diverse forms of analysis, methodological choices and geographical location all share a commitment to demonstrating how it is the interplay between actors and the institutional and regulatory landscapes within which they operate that are critical in shaping the trajectory of global city development. Indeed, a range of literatures are used to shed light on this intersection, from global production networks in the case of Jacobs (2018), to literature on financialization and the role of APS firms in the case of van Meeteren and Bassens (2018). In so doing, the chapters begin to signal how we must attend to questions of power and politics in the making of global cities and it is this area that I focus on in this short commentary. This area is important, because whilst practice and relational orientated approaches have done much to reveal the range of activities that go on in making global cities, particularly at the micro level, there remains a need to use this approach to address meso- and macro-level questions about the operation of global cities within the wider economy (Hall, 2011).

In this respect, Jacobs' (2018) chapter provides an important starting point. Drawing on work on relational and network thinking in general (on which see Yeung, 2005), and the important literature on global production networks in particular (Coe and Yeung, 2015), Jacobs argues that power within the global economy is not a fixed object that is held and deployed over others. Rather, power is a relational achievement which is always in a state of being reproduced through its deployment in a range of settings. Jacobs goes on to exemplify the theoretical and empirical insights that can be gained from such an approach through an insightful analysis of global commodity trading – a sector that Jacobs rightly notes has been overlooked by much of the work on APS firms in global cities and yet is central to the operations of manufacturing firms.

Global cities provide a particularly valuable vehicle with which to build on the practice-orientated perspectives developed in this book, through using this to explore the different spaces and scales through which power is exercised within the contemporary global economy (Hall, 2017). Indeed, the scale of the city is particularly instructive in this respect because when power has been discussed in the global economy, particularly in relation to finance where my own research interests lie, implicitly at least, the greatest attention has been paid to state power. For instance, in contrast to work that focuses on advanced producer services (APS) activities by geographers and other urbanists within the social sciences that takes cities as its starting point but has relatively little to say about power, there is an extensive tradition in international political economy (IPE) that focuses upon the power relations that underpin the global economy. In the case of money and finance, a considerable body of work has documented how one important dimension of state power stems from the power within the international financial system of any given country's currency. This is exemplified most clearly through work on the 'exorbitant privilege' of the US economy based on the hegemonic status of the US dollar from at least the post-war era onwards (Eichengreen, 2011). Indeed, the role and power of money in shaping transformational change in the global economy is shown in contemporary academic, public and political debate by questions surrounding the extent to which China will successfully challenge this hegemonic power of the US economy through the internationalization of its own currency, the renminbi (RMB) (Cohen, 2015). In what follows I use this case of China's currency internationalization to demonstrate why focusing on the space and scale of the global city, in ways that are developed in this book, is an important research endeavour if we are to better understand questions of power and politics within the global economy.

POWER RELATIONS AND THE MAKING OF GLOBAL CITIES: CHINESE CURRENCY INTERNATIONALIZATION AND TRANSFORMATIONS IN GLOBAL MONETARY ORDER

It is important to note that there remains considerable uncertainty surrounding the ability of China to successfully challenge US geo-economic and related forms of geo-political hegemony. These concerns stem in large part from uncertainties about the continued ability of China to experience significant economic growth as its domestic economy transitions from a manufacturing to services sector focus. However, and following the emphasis on practice, agents and relations set out in this collection, focusing on a potential end point regarding whether China's currency becomes globally hegemonic misses out on important details related to the practice and process through which China has become increasingly important within global financial networks. It is here that I suggest a focus on cities is important in developing a fuller understanding of questions of power and power relations within contemporary monetary transformation. Indeed, in many ways the case of Chinese currency internationalization clearly shows the limitations of focusing largely at the state level. At one level this stems from the fact that it is usually assumed that being associated with a rapidly internationalizing currency can lead to more power within the global economy. However, as the case of London's financial district shows, being associated with China's rapidly internationalizing economy offers opportunities but also risks, as London's continued role in RMB internationalization relies on policy decisions being made in Beijing over which London has only limited control (Hall, 2017).

Moreover, RMB internationalization has a distinctive geography that is led by a small network of international financial centres in global cities beyond mainland China including Singapore, Hong Kong and London (Töpfer and Hall, 2018). The use of these cities as offshore RMB centres clearly therefore raises a series of questions about how they are positioned within this process of monetary transformation, how they are identified as being potentially powerful within it and how their relative importance changes over time. By taking the global city as the analytical starting point, this unique geography can be better understood because it reveals how different forms of power and authority are exercised in different ways by a range of actors working at sub-national scales, but often with national and/ or international implications.

For example, it is clear that London's development as an offshore RMB centre has been driven by a range of quasi-state actors operating in an effort to reproduce London's position as a leading international financial centre. Of particular importance in this respect is the City of London authority that has developed close links with its counterpart in Hong Kong, the Hong Kong Monetary Authority. Through a series of annual bilateral meetings the City of London Corporation has sought to learn from the experience of Hong Kong, the largest and most mature offshore RMB centre, in order to facilitate London's development in this area. In so doing, it has been primarily concerned with economic development at the sub-national, city scale. This is in contrast to a reading of the development of offshore RMB markets in London as being developed at the state level that would emphasize the international power afforded to London through its role in the process. Clearly the close relationship between China and the UK partly explains London's power within RMB internationalization, but such a state-led focus only takes the analysis so far (see Lai, 2011 on the relationship between the UK and China in terms of banking in more detail). So in this instance, whilst the UK's nation state is involved in the (re)production of London as an offshore RMB centre, simply understanding this through the lens of growing state power misses the ways in which different actors, some of which form part of the British state such as the Bank of England and HM Treasury, work alongside other city-level institutions (notably the City of London authority) in order to facilitate London's relatively powerful position within RMB internationalization as compared with other international financial centres.

In addition to revealing the different actors involved in making and reproducing global cities, a focus on the city level also reveals the different arenas in which power is reproduced. In this respect, work on global cities, as exemplified by the chapters in this collection, reveals how global cities are key actors in the global economy in a number of different ways, ranging from shaping knowledge practices, the circulation of capital and goods, and changing regulatory environments. Whilst work that has examined questions of power in the global economy at the state level identifies these different elements of power, albeit often implicitly, a focus on the city scale is instructive in revealing through detailed empirical research how this works in practice. Turning again to the case of London's development as an offshore RMB centre, its power is exercised through a number of different registers. At one level, London is important because of the ways in which it is seen as a learning partner for the monetary authorities and regulators in Beijing as they seek to learn from London's experience as a leading international financial centre. This is particularly the case for Chinese state-owned banks that have very limited experience of operating outside their home market but are now increasing their overseas operations at a very rapid pace. Meanwhile, London is also powerful in terms of the market liquidity it can offer financial institutions seeking to develop their offshore RMB activities. Finally, London can also be understood as powerful in terms of how its labour markets afford Chinese financiers the opportunity to acquire the cultural capital of London before using this to develop their own careers by going on to work in rapidly growing city economies, particularly Beijing and Shanghai, within mainland China (Knowles, 2017).

THINKING THROUGH POWER AND THE FUTURE OF GLOBAL CITY MAKING

The value of attending to cities in terms of advancing understandings of power, politics and authority within the global economy from a practice and relational perspective is clearly revealed in a number of chapters in this collection. For example, the work of Lizieri and Mekic (2018) identifies the comparatively neglected role of real estate professionals in shaping the urban form of global cities, something that is particularly important in terms of how global cities are understood by competitors. This echoes important new research areas that are increasingly questioning the relationship between finance and city urban form, particularly in terms of domestic and commercial real estate as global cities face growing questions about the relative power of finance capital above their residents and workers (on which see Massey, 2007). Meanwhile, the chapters by Lambregts et al. (2018) and Yamamura (2018) in particular remind us to take seriously the geographies and power relations of our own knowledge production. In so doing, they speak to wider calls to question what counts as a global city, legitimate actors within them and the implications of this for our wider theoretical understandings of the global economy (on which see Robinson (2002, 2005)). It strikes me that foregrounding questions of power, power relations and challenges to this will form an important direction for future research concerned with the making of global cities and the agents involved with this, a research agenda that is clearly identified and developed in the chapters in this collection.

REFERENCES

Coe, N.M. and H.W-C. Yeung (2015), *Global Production Networks: Theorizing Economic Development in an Interconnected World*, Oxford: Oxford University Press.

Cohen, B.J. (2015), *Currency Power: Understanding Monetary Rivalry*, Princeton, NJ: Princeton University Press.

Eichengreen, B. (2011), *Exorbitant Privilege: The Rise and Fall of the Dollar*, Oxford: Oxford University Press.

Hall, S. (2011), 'Geographies of money and finance I: Cultural economy, politics and place', *Progress in Human Geography*, **35** (2), 234–245.

Hall, S. (2017), 'Rethinking international financial centres through the politics of territory: Renminbi internationalisation in London's financial district', *Transactions of the Institute of British Geographers*, **42** (4), 489–502.

Hesse, M. (2018), 'Focal firms, grand coalitions or global city makers? Globalization vs. new localism in Hamburg's maritime network', in M. Hoyler, C. Parnreiter and A. Watson (eds), *Global City Makers: Economic Actors and Practices in the World City Network*, Cheltenham, UK and Northampton, MA, USA: Edward Elgar Publishing, pp. 151–169.

Jacobs, W. (2018), 'Commodity traders as agents of globalization', in M. Hoyler, C. Parnreiter and A. Watson (eds), *Global City Makers: Economic Actors and Practices in the World City Network*, Cheltenham, UK and Northampton, MA, USA: Edward Elgar Publishing, pp. 41–59.

Knowles, C. (2017), 'Reframing sociologies of ethnicity and migration in encounters with Chinese London', *The British Journal of Sociology*, **68** (3), 454–473.

Lai, K.P.Y. (2011), 'Marketisation through contestation: Reconfiguring China's financial markets through knowledge networks', *Journal of Economic Geography*, **11** (1), 87–117.

Lambregts, B., J. Kleibert and N. Beerepoot (2018), 'The making of Mumbai as a global city: Investigating the role of the offshore services sector', in M. Hoyler, C. Parnreiter and A. Watson (eds), *Global City Makers: Economic Actors and Practices in the World City Network*, Cheltenham, UK and Northampton, MA, USA: Edward Elgar Publishing, pp. 124–150.

Lizieri, C. and D. Mekic (2018), 'Real estate and global capital networks: Drilling into the City of London', in M. Hoyler, C. Parnreiter and A. Watson (eds), *Global City Makers: Economic Actors and Practices in the World City Network*, Cheltenham, UK and Northampton, MA, USA: Edward Elgar Publishing, pp. 60–82.

Massey, D. (2007), *World City*, Bristol: Polity Press.

Robinson, J. (2002), 'Global and world cities: A view from off the map', *International Journal of Urban and Regional Research*, **26** (3), 531–554.

Robinson, J. (2005), 'Urban geography: World cities, or a world of cities', *Progress in Human Geography*, **29** (6), 757–765.

Töpfer, L.-M. and S. Hall (2018), 'London's rise as an offshore RMB financial centre: State-finance relations and selective institutional adaptation', *Regional Studies*, **52** (8), 1053–1064.

Van Meeteren, M. and D. Bassens (2018), 'Chasing the phantom of a "global endgame": the role of management consultancy in the narratives of pre-failure ABN AMRO', in M. Hoyler, C. Parnreiter and A. Watson (eds), *Global City Makers: Economic Actors and Practices in the World City Network*, Cheltenham, UK and Northampton, MA, USA: Edward Elgar Publishing, pp. 170–191.

Yamamura, S. (2018), 'The making of transnational urban space: financial profes-sionals in the global city Tokyo', in M. Hoyler, C. Parnreiter and A. Watson (eds), *Global City Makers: Economic Actors and Practices in the World City Network*, Cheltenham, UK and Northampton, MA, USA: Edward Elgar Publishing, pp. 106–123.
Yeung, H.W-C. (2005), 'Rethinking relational economic geography', *Transactions of the Institute of British Geographers*, **30** (1), 37–51.

Index